Behaviorism, Science, and Human Nature

Barry Schwartz

SWARTHMORE COLLEGE

Hugh Lacey

SWARTHMORE COLLEGE

W. W. Norton & Company

NEW YORK   LONDON

Library of Congress Cataloging in Publication Data
Schwartz, Barry, 1946–
    Behaviorism, science, and human nature.
    Bibliography: p.
    Includes index.
    1. Behaviorism (Psychology)   2. Conditioned
response.   3. Behavior modification.   I. Lacey,
Hugh.   II. Title.
BF199.S36   1982   150.19′43   81–18796
ISBN 0–393–95197–9   AACR2

BF
199
S 36
1982

ACKNOWLEDGMENTS

Cover photograph of Picasso sculpture by David Douglas Duncan. Copyright 1976 by David Douglas Duncan.

Figure 3–1 Schneiderman, N., Fuentes, I., & Gormezano, I. Science, 1962, 136, 650–652. Copyright 1962 by the American Association for the Advancement of Science.

Figure 4–2 Azzi, R., Fix, D.S.R., Keller, F.S., & Rocha e Silva, M.P. Journal of the Experimental Analysis of Behavior, 1964, 7, 159–162. Figure 1, p. 160. Copyright 1964 by the Society for the Experimental Analysis of Behavior, Inc.

Figure 5–4 Rachlin, H., & Green, L. Journal of the Experimental Analysis of Behavior, 1972, 17, 15–22. Figure 3, p. 20. Copyright 1972 by the Society for the Experimental Analysis of Behavior, Inc.

Figure 6–1 Jenkins, H.M., & Harrison, R.H. Journal of Experimental Psychology, 1960, 59, 246–253. Figure 2, p. 248. Copyright 1960 by the American Psychological Association. Reprinted by permission of the publisher and author.

Figure 6–5 Newman, F.L., & Baron, M.R. Journal of Comparative and Physiological Psychology, 1965, 60, 59–63. Figure 1, p. 61. Copyright 1965 by the American Psychological Association. Reprinted by permission of the publisher and author.

Figure 6–6 Jenkins, H.M., & Harrison, R.H. Journal of the Experimental Analysis of Behavior, 1962, 5, 435–441. Figure 2, p. 439. Copyright 1962 by the Society for the Experimental Analysis of Behavior, Inc.

Figure 6–9 Herrnstein, R.J., Loveland, D.H., & Cable C. Journal of Experimental Psychology: Animal Behavior Processes, 1976, vol. 2, 4, 285–302. Copyright 1976 by R.J. Herrnstein. Reprinted by permission of the American Psychological Association and the author.

Figure 6–10 Egger & Miller. Journal of Experimental Psychology, 1962, 64, 97–104. Copyright 1962 by the American Psychological Association. Reprinted by permission of the publisher and author.

Figure 7–2 Williams, D.R., & Williams, H. Journal of the Experimental Analysis of Behavior, 1969, 12, 511–520. Figure 2, p. 514. Copyright 1969 by the Society for the Experimental Analysis of Behavior, Inc.

Figure 7–4 Garcia, J., & Koelling, R.A., Psychonomic Science, 1966, 4, 123–124. Figure 1. Copyright 1966 by the Psychonomic Society. Reprinted by permission.

Chapter 7, excerpts. Breland, K., & Breland, M. American Psychologist, 1961, 16, 681–684. Pp. 682, 683. Copyright 1961 by the American Psychological Association. Reprinted by permission of the publisher and author.

W. W. Norton & Company, Inc. 500 Fifth Avenue, New York, N.Y. 10110
W. W. Norton & Company Ltd., 37 Great Russell Street, London WC1B 3NU

1 2 3 4 5 6 7 8 9 0

Contents

Preface

SINCE the seventeenth century, the growth of modern science has rapidly accelerated. New developments in physics, chemistry, and biology have brought about largely through experimental investigation, the discovery of empirical principles of ever-increasing sophistication and scope. In the light of these principles, many natural phenomena can now be explained and predicted. These principles have also resulted in technological applications that serve human ends. It is only in the present century that serious attempts have been made to focus the scientific lens directly on human affairs. Behaviorism represents one of the most sustained and important of those attempts. Behaviorism uses methods of science to predict and control human and animal behavior. It has established a rigorous and ongoing research program that is now more than sixty years old, and has met with some notable success.

There are two sides to behaviorism. On the one hand, there is a body of research done in well-controlled laboratory settings, primarily with animals as subjects, that has produced a set of well confirmed empirical principles. These principles have in turn been applied successfully in a number of well-controlled contexts with humans. The other side of behaviorism has been considerably broader in scope. This side—most clearly exemplified in the writings of B. F. Skinner—has argued that the methods of behaviorism can go far beyond the well-controlled laboratory or applied setting—that eventually, behaviorism can hope to offer a *complete* account of human behavior.[1] The grand designs of behaviorism are extremely controversial. Few would doubt that the behaviorist research program has yielded principles

1. Skinner, B. F. *Beyond freedom and Dignity*. New York: Alfred A. Knopf, 1971.

that will contribute to our understanding of human behavior, but many dispute that behaviorist principles can eventually constitute that understanding.

In this book, we explore both sides of behaviorism—the tradition of experimentation and application in narrowly circumscribed settings, and the attempts to extend behaviorist principles to all aspects of human life. In Chapters 1 and 2 we examine the behaviorist's assumptions about human nature, and about the methods appropriate for studying human nature. Then, in Chapters 3 through 6, we discuss the essential principles and phenomena of behaviorist research: Pavlovian and operant conditioning. In Chapter 7, we examine the evidence that these principles of conditioning might have only limited applicability in the natural environments of animals, and that in these environments, principles other than those recognized in the tradition of behaviorist research may be significant. In Chapter 8, we present and assess critically the applications of behaviorist principles in a number of different human environments. It is on the successes of the applications that behaviorism's more sweeping claims about human nature rest.

In Chapter 9, we present an argument that while the principles of behaviorism on which these successes are based do apply within some social contexts in the contemporary human world, there is good reason to believe that there is a well-defined limit to this applicability, a limit that is revealed not by the methods of experimental inquiry, but by the methods of historical inquiry. In short, the view that has guided us in writing this book is that it makes a difference, both to our judgments about further research and to our evaluation of the significance of the principles, to know whether the principles of behaviorism are general principles of human behavior, or whether they apply only in special circumstances. In this book, we introduce and discuss the positive achievements of behaviorism in a context that permits the reader to address the issues, and perhaps evaluate them.

Over an extended period that preceded the writing of this book, we have both gained significantly in our understanding of behaviorism, science, and human nature from our discussions and collaboration with Richard Schuldenfrei. Chapter 9 bears the most explicit mark of this collaboration, as it is largely derived from an earlier paper written by all three of us.[2] But Schuldenfrei's contribution to

2. Schwartz, B., Schuldenfrei, R. & Lacey, H. M. "Operant psychology as factory psychology." *Behaviorism*, 1978, 6, 229–254.

our thinking is also reflected throughout the book. In addition, we have learned from Paul Rozin of the University of Pennsylvania and John Staddon of Duke University, whose critical comments on earlier drafts of the book forced us to modify, and we hope, sharpen some of our ideas. We also wish to thank May D'Amoto of Brooklyn College, Mark Kristal of the State University of New York, at Buffalo, and Joseph Margolis of Temple University, for all of their comments on the manuscript. And Norton editor Don Fusting has helped us through all drafts of the book, greatly improving its clarity of organization and exposition. Finally, we are grateful to Didi Beebe, for typing, copying, cutting and pasting all of these drafts, always with good cheer and remarkable speed.

Lacey acknowledges the support of National Science Foundation Grant SOC 790 7600 and expresses thanks to Maria Ignes Lacey for first introducing him in a usefully critical way to the contributions and problems of behaviorism.

Schwartz has also had support from the National Science Foundation (Grant BNS78-15461) as well as the James McKeen Cattell Foundation, and the Swarthmore College Faculty Research Program, during preparation of parts of the manuscript, and for the conduct of some experiments that are described in it.

Barry Schwartz
Hugh Lacey
Swarthmore, Pa., 1981

Behaviorism, Science, and Human Nature

Chapter 1

Understanding Human Nature

ONE of our most distinctive qualities as human beings is our persistent effort to make sense of the world around us. Whether we are children or adults, farmers or professors, members of highly technological or of primitive cultures, a substantial part of our daily activity involves attempting to understand the events that affect our lives. The child strives to understand how to please its parents, how to balance a bicycle, where birds go in the winter, and why little stones sink in water while big boats float. The farmer seeks to understand the weather, how his tractor works, how to improve crop yield, what determines the market price of his product, and how to get his children interested in staying on the farm. The professor wants to know what caused the Second World War, the nature of genetic coding, the fundamental elements of matter, the meaning of Hamlet's crisis, and how to keep the students interested. The primitive hunter wants to know how to track animals, what may appease the gods, why the moon is not in the sky every night, and how to keep peace with the neighboring village.

The range of human concerns, of phenomena we seek to understand, is enormously varied, and differs from culture to culture, and from group to group. What people will accept in the way of an explanation is also quite varied. Explanations that satisfy a child may not satisfy an adult; those that satisfy an adult may mystify a child. The primitive hunter might listen to the professor explain the motion of heavenly bodies, and wonder how anyone could be so confused as to ignore the power of the gods, just as the professor might marvel at how anyone could believe that offerings to gods affect the weather. And the farmer might be puzzled at how a person could go to school for as many years as the professor did, and still learn nothing that was of any practical value to anyone.

Our quest for understanding is so regular a part of life that we may hardly notice it. We simply take it for granted that people seek understanding, and that seeking understanding needs no justification. We are curious, and there need be no limits to where our curiosity will lead us. But it is not just curiosity that motivates our search for understanding. Often, our desire to understand springs directly from our practical life. We attempt to understand certain phenomena because we wish to change them, or to prevent them from recurring, or to make them recur. Put more generally, we want to be able to intervene effectively in the course of events. We want to be able to control our environment. That is why the farmer seeks to understand the weather, agriculture and market economics. That is why the primitive hunter seeks to understand the gods. And that is why the young child seeks to understand bicycles and its parents.

How we understand an event can have a dramatic impact on what we do about it. Consider the different ways we might understand the energy crisis. We might understand it as an artificial crisis, created by oil-producing nations so that they can increase the price of their oil. If so, we might try to solve the problem by political and economic means, attempting to establish some leverage in the policy formation of these nations. Or we might understand it as a reflection of our careless and excessive use of fossil fuels. If so, we might impose substantial taxes on the fuels to influence people to use them more sparingly. Or we might understand it in terms of an inexorable depletion of these fossil fuels, so that ultimately, supply will never be able to keep up with demand. In this case, we might direct our efforts toward the development of alternate energy sources, like solar and nuclear power. The way we decide to understand this current event can have a dramatic impact on our future. And if we were to choose to pursue one of these courses of action exclusively, we would in essence be making a bet that our understanding of the problem was correct.

Understanding and Science

Because of this close relation between how we understand something and what we do about it, a particular orientation toward understanding has become increasingly dominant in the industrialized world over the last three centuries. It is the orientation reflected in the activities of natural science. Every aspect of life in our highly technological society testifies to the power of scientific modes of understanding to explain our world. Every time we turn on a light, or drive a car, or take a photograph, or turn on the television, or photocopy a letter, or compute our income tax with the aid of a calculator, we are presenting ourselves with evidence that science has delivered the goods. The kind of understanding that characterizes science is what has led to all of these technological innovations, and to the extent that they enable us to control our environment better than we could before, they are validating the scientific conception of the world.

This book addresses a particular application of that scientific conception. In the last century several scientific approaches to understanding human nature have developed within psychology. One of them, known as behaviorism or behavior theory, is an attempt to apply the experimental methods of natural science to the study of human nature. If it succeeds in discovering important generalizations about human nature, it will change the way we think about ourselves in significant ways. In this book, we will be presenting a picture of behavior theory—of its methods, its discoveries, its applications, and its general theoretical principles. We will also be evaluating whether or not it represents a successful application of the methods of science to the human domain.

But before discussing behavior theory itself, let us explore scientific understanding more generally. What is the scientific conception of the world? What does it mean to understand a phenomenon scientifically? While the specific features of scientific understanding will differ from one domain of science to another, there are certain characteristics which are shared by all the sciences.

Searching for Causal Laws

In attempting to understand a given phenomenon, the scientist searches for some other event or phenomenon that caused it. What does it mean to say that one event caused another? Though there is considerable controversy about what "cause" means precisely, we can identify some characteristics that most causal explanations share. Suppose we are interested in explaining the following phenomenon: You drop an expensive antique vase, and it falls to the floor and shatters into a hundred pieces. What caused the vase to fall and shatter?

Your response to this question might be "I dropped it." Let us examine some of the properties of this "causal" explanation. First, the cause you identified was an event that initiated a process that culminated in the phenomenon to be explained. Dropping the vase initiated the process of its falling, which culminated in its reaching the floor and shattering. Other conceivable causal accounts, such as for example, accounts that invoked the phases of the moon, would not obviously have this property. Second, the causal agent you identified was external to the phenomenon being caused. Dropping the vase is easily separable from the behavior of the vase itself. Other conceivable accounts, for instance, one that suggested it was the vase's destiny to fall and break, would not have this property. Third, the cause you identified was such that under the circumstances, had the cause not occurred, the phenomenon would not have occurred. Thus, if you had not dropped the vase, it would not have fallen and broken. What we might say is that dropping the vase was *necessary* for it to fall and break. But your cause was only necessary *under the given circumstances*. Had the circumstances been different (for example, an earthquake causing the floor and table on which the vase was standing to shake), the vase might have fallen without your intervention. Again, we could imagine other causal accounts (you were engaged in a heated argument with your friend and weren't paying attention) which do not obviously have this property. Fourth, under the circumstances, the cause you identified was all that was required to bring about the phenomenon. Thus, once you dropped the vase nothing else had to happen for it to fall and break. What we might say here is that dropping the vase was *sufficient* for it to fall and break. Again, notice that your cause was only sufficient under the circumstances. If you had dropped the vase while holding it over a mattress, it would still have fallen, but it would not have broken.

Thus we see that your causal explanation of the behavior of the vase identifies an agent external to the vase itself, whose action is necessary and sufficient to result in the vase's falling and breaking. Does this mean that "I dropped it" counts as an appropriately scientific explanation of the behavior of the vase? Not quite. For what is perhaps the most significant feature of scientific explanations is that they relate the specific phenomenon to be explained to other, similar phenomena. At the heart of scientific explanation is the search for *generalizations* or *laws*. While the fact of the matter is that this particular vase may have fallen and broken after you dropped it, we know that it would have fallen and broken no matter who dropped it. Indeed, we know that the fact that it was dropped is not essential to its falling and breaking. We know that no matter what is responsible for setting a vase in free fall, it will move toward the earth. Moreover, we know that the object needn't be a vase. Any object in free fall will move toward the earth, and any object composed of certain classes of materials will break when it contacts the hard ground. In addition, we even know the rate at which objects in free fall in a vacuum will approach the ground. They will accelerate at a rate of 32 feet per second each second they are in motion. Finally, we know that the cause of the behavior of the vase is the same as the cause of the motions of the planets. For when you say that the vase fell and broke because you dropped it, what lies beneath your explanation is a wealth of knowledge from physics about gravity and its effects on objects in free fall. It is this knowledge of physics that tells us to what general class of phenomena the behavior of the vase belongs. Without knowing this, we might still be able to say that the vase fell and broke because we dropped it. But we would not necessarily be able to use this knowledge to help us understand other phenomena, or perhaps predict or control events in the future.

Suppose for example, you think the vase fell because you dropped it, but you also think that this phenomenon belongs to the class of phenomena controlled by the gods, along with say, good harvests. With this understanding, you might pray to the gods in an effort to promote good harvests and prevent destroying precious objects. How you generalize a particular phenomenon has a lot to do with what you do about it in the future. Science is an attempt to discover which kinds of generalizations will provide the broadest and most powerful guidance about what to do in the future. When we said before that science has delivered the goods, what we meant was that the generalizations it has provided have enabled people to predict and control the world in which they live with unparalleled success. That is why the kind of understanding reflected by science's search for general, causal laws has become a model of what understanding should be in the technologically advanced world.

That scientific understanding involves generalizations, or laws, is significant for another reason. It is only because our claim that a caused b implies a claim about classes of events, A and B, to which a and b belong, that we are able to evaluate our causal judgments. Consider again the fallen vase. You believe the vase fell because you dropped it, and gravity took over. Someone else believes the vase fell because a demon in the center of the earth wanted it to. Still a third person believes the vase fell because you had done something to anger the gods. And a fourth person believes the vase fell because someone in China, with psychic power, whose ancestor made the vase, willed it to leave your hands and rush to the floor. Which explanation is the right one, and how do you know? In fact, any of these four explanations might suffice to account for the fact that this particular vase fell to this particular floor at this particular time. And so might dozens of other explanations. The way to begin selecting among explanations is to look for other supporting examples. Thus, you might drop other objects, and you might have other people drop objects, and you might drop objects at different times and places. In effect, you might perform experiments. If you did, you would discover that in every case, the object, once dropped, fell to the ground. This would give you confidence that your explanation, in terms of gravity, was the right one. But the important thing to notice is that the only reason to view these other phenomena as relevant to your fallen vase is your belief that an appropriate explanation of the vase's behavior will treat the vase, a, as a member of the class of all objects in free fall, A. Without this belief, there would be no reason to view these other phenomena as producing evidence relevant to the one you set out to explain.

What this discussion reveals about scientific understanding is that in pursuing causal laws, science tells us into what categories individual phenomena belong. And it is just this feature of scientific understanding that allows us to predict and control aspects of the future on the basis of what we understand of the past.

Thus, scientific understanding involves establishing causal laws, and it explains phenomena by revealing them as instances of these laws. The laws govern phenomena that occur or can be made to occur repeatedly and generally in nature. The search for such laws presupposes that the phenomena of nature or the processes underlying them are sufficiently orderly and repeatable that there are laws to be found. Without this belief in the orderliness of nature, it would not make sense to pursue such lawful regularities.

Science and Human Nature

How much of nature is orderly and repeatable in the way that the behavior of falling bodies is? Should science apply to all phenomena, or only to a subset of them? If only to a subset, what is that subset? The answers to these questions have changed over the years. The discoveries of Galileo and Newton, more than 300 years ago, ushered in the beginning of modern science. With these discoveries, people began to turn to the scientist for an explanation of the physical world. Physics provided us with the principles that governed the behavior of inanimate objects.

But it was believed that physics went only so far: Living things shared some special characteristics that inanimate things did not possess, and that principles of physics could not explain. The kind of understanding provided by physics could not appropriately be extended to living things. With the emergence of scientific biology in the eighteenth century, however, the explanatory domain of science was extended. At least some characteristics of all living things could be understood scientifically. Indeed, perhaps all characteristics of non-human living things were susceptible to a scientific analysis. But still, people were thought to be special. Scientific understanding had inherent limitations. While it might make comprehensible to us the physical stuff of which people were made, the human capacity for reason and the human soul placed human beings outside the bounds of physics or biology.

In the two hundred years or so since the beginning of modern biology, our attitude toward science has not changed very much. Our confidence in the kind of understanding provided by physics, chemistry and biology has grown, as each new technological change spawned by those disciplines has made its mark on our lives. But most of us still hold the view that the appropriateness of scientific understanding stops when we get to phenomena that are essentially human. In our everyday lives, we do not seek to understand our own behavior and that of our friends, loved ones, employees and political leaders in terms of causal laws. None of the features of our understanding of the fallen vase seem appropriate for understanding human action. Are human actions caused? Can we identify events external to the actor which under the circumstances are necessary and sufficient to set in motion a process that culminates in the action? Are human actions reliable and repeatable in the way that the "action" of the falling vase was?

An example might help illustrate how unaccustomed we are to explaining human action in the same way we explain other phenomena. Imagine reading a newspaper story about a teenage boy who enters a small radio store. After looking through the radios on display, the boy picks one up. But rather than going to the cashier to pay for the radio, the boy attempts to leave the store with it. The proprietor of the store reaches for a gun and yells at the boy to stop. He does not and the proprietor fires the gun. The bullet hits the boy in the head, and he dies.

If we were to read such a story, we might be sufficiently horrified by it to feel the need to understand what transpired. How would we attempt to understand this sequence of events? Let us pose some questions.

> *Why did the boy attempt to steal the radio?*
> *Why did the proprietor shoot the gun?*
> *Why did the bullet hit the boy?*
> *Why did the boy die?*

Many of us would answer the last two questions differently from the first two. For the last two questions, the kind of understanding provided by science is obviously appropriate. By identifying the angle of orientation of the gun, the position of the boy, the initial velocity of the bullet and the distance between the gun and the boy, we can use the laws of physics to understand why the bullet hit the boy in precisely the same way that we used them to explain the fallen vase. Similarly, by knowing where the bullet entered the boy's head, how far it went, and how long it took for help to arrive, we can use the biologist's understanding of brain function and its control of other biological functions to understand why the boy died. In both cases, we can specify an event external to the phenomena to be explained that was necessary and sufficient in the circumstances for the phenomenon to occur. And in both cases, we can relate the causal episode to more general causal laws.

But can we do the same for the first two questions? How would we explain why the boy attempted to steal the radio? In all probability, our explanation would involve some consideration of what the boy desired, that is, what his purpose or goal was. It would also involve consideration of what he believed the result of his action would be, that is, the degree to which we thought his action would achieve his goal. Finally, we might want to consider the deliberations the boy went through in deciding to engage in the particular action of stealing to achieve the goal of getting the radio. An explanation of this type is quite different from the way we explain the falling of the vase. Actions are oriented toward the future, toward their anticipated consequences. We can understand an action only when we understand the end to which it was directed. In contrast, our explanation of the fallen vase is oriented to the past—to the conditions that triggered the causal process. We do not consider the vase's anticipated ends in understanding its behavior. Explanations of actions in terms of their anticipated ends are often called *teleological* explanations.

Perhaps our teleological explanation of the boy's action is really no different from our causal explanation of the vase. Perhaps the different words we use obscure an underlying similarity. If this is true, we should be able to identify an event external to the boy that set in motion a process that was necessary and sufficient to result in the action. But what might that event be? Could it be that seeing the radio in the window caused the boy to enter the store and attempt to steal it? This is hardly persuasive. For without having the goal of getting the radio and the belief that it could be gotten by theft, the boy would not have acted as he did. But this goal and belief are not external to the action in the way that being released in free fall is external to the vase. In addition, we know that the boy could have gone into the store, intent on stealing the radio, and at the last minute changed his mind. He might have reassessed his chances of getting caught, and decided not to steal the radio. Alternatively, for all we know the boy could have entered the store intending to purchase the radio, and at the last minute decided to steal it because it appeared he could get away with it.

In general, when we are attempting to understand human action rather than the behavior of inanimate objects, notions of purpose, belief, expectation, and deliberation enter our reflections. We are comfortable with explanations of human action in these terms, and uncomfortable with explanations that have a scientific character. We assume that people have *reasons* for what they do, and our task in understanding is to discover those reasons. The reasons for a person's action seems to be simply of a different kind than the causes of a vase's behavior. For this reason, most people are convinced that the explanatory schemes offered by science are inappropriate for understanding human action.

This distinction between explanations based on reasons and explanations based on causes is reflected in many of our customary practices in dealing with people and in many of our cultural institutions. For example, we routinely hold people responsible for what they do. We praise or blame them when appropriate, or we send them to prison or elect them to high office. We would never consider holding the vase responsible for falling. This reflects our commitment to the belief that we can understand the vase in terms of forces external to it, while we can understand the person only in terms of forces that are internal to him or her. Thus, in our everyday understanding of human action or of human nature, we are content to bypass the explanatory power offered by the sciences.

Psychology and Human Nature

Although, in everyday discourse, we are satisfied to explain human action in the same general terms used 200 years ago, science has not stood still. Science began, in the nineteenth century, to extend itself to the domain of human conduct. The discipline of experimental psychology was founded by scholars who developed the view that many, if not all aspects of human nature could be studied scientifically. They believed that human nature could eventually be understood with concepts of the type developed in physics and biology. For the last century, experimental psychologists have been pursuing the natural laws that describe people. Sensation, perception, thinking, learning, memory, motivation, action, and social behavior are all being subjected to rigorous scientific analysis. While at present the existence of natural laws of human nature is more an article of faith than a reality, people are increasingly willing to put their faith in the scientific psychologist.

Fifty years ago people might have sought the advice of a priest if they were unhappy or in conflict. Now they seek the advice of the clinical psychologist. Fifty years ago parents would get guidance from their parents when faced with problems in raising their children. Now they go to family therapists. Fifty years ago people might have sought out their friends if they were having marital problems. Now they go to marriage counselors. Similarly, lawyers used to rely on their experience and intuition in selecting a jury. Now they also seek the advice of social psychologists. All around us, people are seeking the advice of experts—people whose expertise in various domains of human conduct is presumed to rest upon scientific understanding. What people who seek out these experts may not realize is that in the course of making such decisions, they are choosing to give up a piece of their everyday understanding of human nature, and replace it with a scientific one. Our confidence in the experts is a confidence in the scientific explanation of human nature. For though many psychologists who apply their expertise to real world problems do not aspire to discover general causal laws of human nature, it is the search for such laws in laboratories that lends authenticity to their applied activities.

Behavior Theory and Human Nature

Though all branches of psychology expect to find causal laws of human nature, that does not mean they are committed to the view that *all* of human nature is lawful. The psychologist who studies perception may believe that there are lawful regularities in the relation between light and vision, sound and hearing, and so on, but still explain human action in terms of reasons, purposes and beliefs. The psychologist who studies memory may believe there are lawful relations between the different ways we experience things, and our ability to recall them, but deny the lawfulness of human action. The psychologist who studies learning may believe there are regularities in our ability to profit from experience, but deny that those regularities extend to the entire range of human nature. In short, it is possible to pursue the understanding of some aspects of human nature scientifically without expecting that eventually all aspects of human nature will be so understood.

However, there is one branch of psychology where commitment to a complete and thoroughgoing scientific account of human nature is apparent. This branch of psychology is referred to as *behaviorism* or *behavior theory*. Behavior theory is explicitly committed to the view that human nature can be fully revealed and understood with the methods and principles of natural science. It has been at the heart of psychological activity for most of this century.

Assumptions of Behavior Theory

As we have seen, the goal of science is the discovery of lawful regularities in nature. The physicist studies the motion of a body in free fall, and relates that motion to the motion of all bodies, even the motion of the planets around the sun. He or she attempts to arrive at a general formulation which accurately describes all motion. The general formulation allows the physicist to predict the motions of bodies in other, different situations that have not yet been encountered. The physicist's activities are predicated on the view that certain central properties of the physical world are eternal, that phenomena or the processes that underlie them repeat themselves, that bodies will move in the same orderly way tomorrow as they do today. It is the physicist's view that, while many features of the physical world are always changing, it is just these general principles of physics that do not change.

When behavior theorists approach the study of human nature scientifically, they hold the same assumption about the nature of human action as physicists do about the motion of bodies. There are regularities to human action which are universal, which are a part of the essential nature of man. When these regularities are discovered and properly formulated, they will account for human action in the past and predict human action in the future. If significant features of human actions did not repeat themselves, if the conditions under which people behaved and the phenomena of behavior themselves continually changed from one period of time to the next, the pursuit of "laws" of behavior would be futile. We might come to an understanding of human action, perhaps in terms of people's goals, beliefs, and expectations, but we could not develop scientific laws. Thus, the assumption that significant aspects of behavior and its causal determinants repeat themselves reflects a commitment of the scientific study of human action.

There are obvious differences between people and inanimate objects that should make us pause to consider whether behavior theorists are justified in making the same assumptions about external regularities as physicists. People are reasoning, thoughtful, remembering creatures. They are changed as a result of their experiences in a way that falling vases, for example, are not. People carry experiences with them, and develop and learn and change in part as a result of those experiences. How can we seek something eternal in human nature when one of the obvious hallmarks of human nature is changeability?

It is just this characteristic of human nature—changeability or flexibility—which is the main concern of behavior theory. Experience certainly changes people. What behavior theory assumes, however, is that the very process of change is itself universal. Only certain kinds of experiences will change people, and these kinds of experiences will change people in lawful ways. The kinds of experiences which change people and influence action, and the nature of the change and the influence, are what behavior theory tries to find out. Behavior theorists are seeking the laws by which past experience influences future action.

This goal of behavior theory—to find the laws which relate past experience to future action—has two central features. First, the thing to be explained, according to behavior theory, is action, or behavior. People think, people feel, and people remember. At any moment, a multitude of interesting events is occurring within each of us. But science can gain only uncertain access to these internal events. Behavior, on the other hand, is objective. It is something which can be readily observed and measured. For this reason, behavior theorists by and large restrict their attention to behavior.

Second, behavior theory emphasizes that environmental events play the key role in determining human behavior. The source of action lies not inside the person, but in the environment. By developing a full understanding of how environmental events influence behavior, we will arrive at a complete understanding of behavior. It is this feature of behavior theory—its emphasis on environmental events as the determinants of human action—which most clearly sets it apart from other approaches to human nature. If it is true that human behavior is the reliable product of environmental events, then responsibility for behavior, whether noble or ignoble, rests not in the actor but in the environmental variables that give rise to the action. If behavior theory succeeds, our customary inclination to hold people responsible for their actions, and look inside them to their wishes, desires, goals, intentions, and so on, for explanations of their actions, will be replaced by an entirely different orientation. This new orientation is one in which responsibility for action is sought in environmental events. Such an orientation provides a view of the world that will leave no aspect of daily life untouched. If this orientation is valid, human nature will come to be understood in much the way that falling vases are.

While all scientific approaches to psychology hold that human behavior is lawful so that it occurs under the control of antecedent variables, it is an assumption specific to behavior theory that the key controlling variables are environmental rather than internal events. Other approaches, cognitive psychology, for example, emphasize the controlling role played by internal states of the organism. These approaches may seem to fit better with the assumption of our ordinary language that actions can be explained in terms of factors like reasons and goals. These approaches share with behavior theory the view that behavior may be given causal explanation, even though they search for causes that are internal to the organism. They do not contradict our earlier claim that causes are external to their effects. For example, a clock's movements are clearly subject to causal explanation, yet those causes are internal to the clock. A clock is a complex object that undergoes change as a consequence of events involving its parts. It may stop because a spring breaks. If so, the cause is not the action of an object external to the clock. But the spring breaks because the movement of the clock's wheels caused too much tension in it. The change in the spring is caused by action external to it from other parts of the clock. In turn, the breaking of the spring causes the movements of the hands of the clock to stop. Again there is external causality, and the stopping of the clock is the same event as the stopping of the movements of its hands. There is nothing to explain about the functioning of the clock over and above the functioning of its parts.

Similarly, it might be argued that the proper way to explain human behavior is causal, but in terms of the functioning of the internal parts of a human being. Cognitive psychology, which makes this argument, actually compares the internal states of a human being with the internal states of a computer. Whether such explanations can eventually be reconciled with the ordinary language explanations of human action still remains to be determined. But in contrast to cognitive psychology, behavior theory is content to dispense with our ordinary language explanations altogether. It presumes that its methods are sufficient to produce a complete account of behavior. This means that in principle, its methods could produce a set of laws relating behavior to environmental events such that almost any given behavior could be explained in terms of one or another of these laws.

Behavior Theory as a World View

Behavior theorists claim that the causes of behavior lie not within the actor but in the environment. The claim that action is influenced by events in the environment is so obviously true that any account of human action must recognize and incorporate it. When we say that the boy attempted to steal the radio because he wanted it, we are certainly acknowledging the contribution of environmental influences to his behavior. What distinguishes behavior theory is not the thesis that actions are influenced by environmental events, but that an analysis of how environmental events affect behavior will tell us all we need to know about the determinants of action. Thus, an analysis of environmental events will provide a complete account of human action. More specifically, behavior theorists expect that the major burden of explaining human action will be carried by a small set of environmental events, events which we typically call rewards and punishments. The central thesis of behavior theory is that virtually all significant voluntary human actions can be understood in terms of their past relations to rewards and punishments. What controls voluntary action is its past history of association with rewarding or punishing environmental events.

From the perspective of behavior theory, the acts for which we credit or blame people are not acts for which rewards or punishments are absent. They are acts the rewards and punishments for which are subtle and as yet unnoticed. Behavior theorists believe that all behavior of consequence is controlled by rewards and punishments. Sometimes the controlling environmental contingencies may be obvious (as when we slow down on the highway upon spotting a police car), and sometimes they may be subtle, but always they are responsible for what we do. In the words of one of the major figures of behavior theory, B.F. Skinner (1904–):

> An experimental analysis shifts the determination of behavior from autonomous man to the environment—an environment responsible for . . . the repertoire acquired by each member [of the species]. . . . Is man then "abolished"? Certainly not as a species or as an individual achiever. It is autonomous inner man who is abolished, and that is a step forward.[1]

It is hard to imagine a view of human nature more opposed to our ordinary conception of ourselves than this one. We have all grown accustomed to thinking of ourselves as the controllers of our own lives. Society holds us responsible for our actions, and we readily accept that responsibility. We place an extraordinary value on our freedom of choice, and we resent and resist any efforts at coercion. We formulate our own goals, and feel we act on the basis of our own preferences and desires, and not in keeping with external pressures. All of these features of our conception of ourselves are built into our

1. Skinner, 1971, pp. 14–15.

everyday understanding of human action in terms of goals and purposes.

Behavior theory challenges this conception of ourselves. If you want to know why someone did something, do not ask. Analyze the person's immediate environment until you find the reward. If you want to change someone's actions, do not reason or persuade. Find the reward and eliminate it. The idea that people are autonomous and possess within them the power and the reasons for making decisions has no place in behavior theory.

The thesis about human nature on which behavior theory rests is one which many people find repugnant and degrading. Nevertheless, behavior theory is becoming an increasingly influential part of our culture. The reason for its influence is that it has yielded a set of empirical principles which has been applied with some success in social settings as diverse as mental hospitals, schools, factories, and prisons. One may ignore the physicist when he limits his domain to laboratory experiments and abstract theory. However, when his domain is extended in application to automobiles, airplanes, atomic energy, and so on, he can no longer be ignored. Similarly, when behavior theory is extended in application to areas which touch our daily lives, it also cannot be ignored.

Chapter 2

Methods of Behavior Theory

THE goal of behavior theory is the discovery of a comprehensive set of scientific laws with which to explain behavior. As we indicated in the last chapter, it is thought that these laws, once identified, will replace our everyday explanations of human behavior. Having set out to explain behavior scientifically, how does one actually discover the laws of which an explanation will consist? What methods of inquiry does one use? And how does one know that these methods are actually succeeding in revealing laws? In this chapter, we will address these issues. We will describe the historical origins of the basic methods of behavior theory, and show how these origins are reflected in modern research. We will also discuss some of the assumptions that underlie these methods, and some of the criteria behavior theorists use to judge whether their inquiries are revealing significant laws of human nature.

Experimentation: The Tool of Behavior Theory

It is often said that the hallmark of science is its devotion to the facts. Other modes of inquiry may involve speculation, opinion, inter-pretation, and argument. In science, however, one is committed to finding out facts about the universe. But this view is naive, for two reasons. First, science is not unique in its insistence that explanations of the world around us square with the facts. Any explanatory scheme, to be taken at all seriously, must take into account the facts of human experience. Thus, respect for the facts does not distinguish science from other forms of inquiry. Second, this view seems to imply that it is obvious what is or is not a fact—that facts are out there in the world, in plain view, waiting to be collected by anyone. It also suggests that any fact whatsoever is worth noting. These suggestions are simply false. One of the major burdens of a scientific explanation is to tell us what facts are, why they are worth knowing, and where they are to be found. It is a fact that the authors of this book have offices in a building located ten miles southwest of the center of Philadelphia. It is a fact that one of us had a poached egg for breakfast this morning. It is hard to see how collecting facts of this sort will advance our understanding of human nature very far. A science must be able to distinguish facts like these, which are trivial, from other facts, which are important.

A fact is important if it helps us formulate a generalization, or test a generalization that has already been formulated. For example, if someone had proposed the generalization that for successful collaboration in writing, authors must interact continually, then the fact that our offices are in the same building might become important, though their location with respect to Philadelphia would not. Often, it is only after some explanatory claim or generalization has been proposed that we even know what facts to look for in order to evaluate that proposal. While initial attempts to explain no doubt arise from some facts, they also set the stage for the discovery of others. For this reason, it is a mistake to view science as the mere collection of facts about nature.

Once we have some tentative explanation or generalization in hand, where do we go to collect the facts that might help us evaluate the generalization? We could just decide to observe nature carefully, hoping that relevant facts will appear. The problem with such a strategy is that we might have to observe for a long time before a relevant fact appeared. And even when one finally did appear, the circumstances of its occurrence might be sufficiently complex that it would be difficult to interpret. Modern science has as its hallmark methods of obtaining relevant facts which are much more intrusive and aggressive than careful observation. Modern science creates situations designed to make the relevant facts appear, and appear with special clarity. We call such created situations experiments.

Consider the possible generalization that cigarette smoking causes lung cancer. How might we attempt to evaluate this claim? To begin with, we can simply observe and collect facts (though notice, the generalization itself makes it clear that only some facts are worth collecting). We can keep track of how often people who do not smoke get lung cancer and how often people who do smoke get lung cancer. These facts might lead us to believe that people who smoke are more likely to get lung cancer than people who do not. From this, we might be willing to conclude that the generalization is true—that smoking causes lung cancer. But this would be a mistake. Consider the counter claim that excess tension causes cigarette smoking *and* lung cancer. If this claim were true, we would expect people who are tense but do not smoke to be high risks for lung cancer also. We could evaluate this claim by observing people who are tense and those who are not and keeping track of how often they get cancer. But now our observational method has run into trouble. How do we know that a person is tense? We cannot tell just by looking. Moreover, even if we could eliminate this particular counterproposal by observation, many others could surely be constructed to take its place. The complexity of everyday life is such that there is no shortage of possible generalizations regarding possible causes of lung cancer.

The way out of this problem is to do experiments. We might keep people in simple, well-controlled environments that are identical in every way except that some people inhale cigarette smoke while others do not. If the smokers are more likely to get lung cancer than the non-smokers, we may now conclude with some confidence that cigarette smoking causes lung cancer. We might state that "all other things being equal, a person who smokes is more likely to get lung cancer than one who does not." We will be confident of the validity of this claim because in our experiment, we have made "all other things equal." And we have done this explicitly so that if there is a relation between smoking and cancer, it will appear clearly and unambiguously.

Research of this type on smoking and cancer has of course been done, though obviously not with people. Rats or rabbits are raised in identical environments except for the presence or absence of smoke in the lungs. It is this *experimental* evidence for the relation between smoking and cancer that makes us confident that our natural observation of the incidence of cancer in smokers is in fact the result of a causal relation between the two. But notice, the experimental work with animals depends upon the tacit assumption that what is true for rats and rabbits is also true for people. It is presumed that the harmful effects of smoke in the lungs are not peculiar to people. Thus we might end up with the generalization that smoking causes lung cancer in all creatures that breathe with lungs.

The role of experiment in this example is crucial. It shunts to the background, or keeps constant, factors thought to be unimportant. It highlights factors thought to be critical. The experiment gives us access to facts we might never notice in years of careful observation. Experiment is the central tool of most modern science. It is certainly the essence of inquiry in behavior theory. This experimental mode of inquiry certainly distinguishes it from philosophy, literature, or history. However, being experimental does not distinguish behavior theory from other branches of psychology, or from say, biology. What distinguishes behavior theory from these disciplines is the kinds of experiments behavior theorists do. And what dictates the kinds of experiments behavior theorists do is a commitment about the factors that are likely to be essential to an explanation of behavior. This commitment can be traced to the origins of behavior theory, and it has been reflected in the research methods used by behavior theorists from the beginning. Thus, we can best understand the kinds of experiments that modern behavior theorists do by looking at how behavior theory began.

Pavlov and Conditioned Reflexes

The beginning of modern behavior theory may be found in the work of Ivan P. Pavlov (1849–1936). Pavlov was a Nobel Prize winning Russian physiologist who had devoted most of his career to the study of digestion in dogs. Pavlov knew that dogs would reliably salivate when food was placed in their mouths, and he was studying the role of the "salivary reflex" in digestion. In the course of his research, Pavlov made an observation that changed his career. He noticed that sometimes, dogs that had been under study for some time would salivate even before food was placed in their mouths. They would salivate at the sight of a familiar laboratory assistant, or at the sound of the door to the laboratory opening. Salivation when food was placed in the mouth was no mystery. It was simply a part of the dog's physiology. But what about salivation to laboratory assistants and opening doors? Clearly, these reflexes could not have been a part of the dog's physiological equipment.

Pavlov realized that the dogs were salivating at the occurrence of these other events because these events had repeatedly and reliably

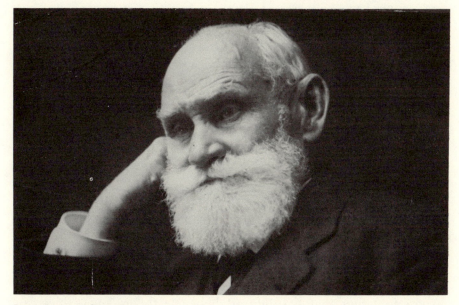

Ivan Petrovich Pavlov.
(*Courtesy of Sovfoto*)

preceded the delivery of food to the mouth in the past. The dog was associating the sight of the assistant, or the sound of the door with food. Once this association was made, the dog would respond to these stimuli in just the way it responded to food placed in the mouth. Pavlov termed the salivation he observed to stimuli other than food a "psychic reflex." Its occurrence was *conditional* upon the animal learning to associate stimuli like laboratory assistants with food. Because this psychic salivation was conditional upon certain experiences, reflexes like it have come to be called *conditioned reflexes*. The development of these reflexes has come to be called *Pavlovian conditioning*, or *classical conditioning*.[1]

Why was Pavlov so excited about his discovery? He saw it immediately as a window to the laws of the mind. It was clear to Pavlov that while inborn reflexes formed a significant part of the behavior of all organisms, an even more significant portion of behavior could not be inborn. That people respond to a flame applied to a finger is almost surely inborn. But that people also respond when hearing someone

1. Pavlov, 1927.

scream, "Fire!" is not. The word "fire" must somehow be associated with actual flame so that either the flame or the word will produce the appropriate reflex. Salivation at the sight of a lab assistant had to be an instance of the association of inborn responses with new stimuli.

Thus, for Pavlov, the study of conditioned reflexes was the study of the laws of learning by association. Organisms began with a set of simple reflexes, and experience in the world both broadened the range of events which would produce the reflex and combined simple reflexes into complex reflex sequences. All of knowledge and action could be understood in terms of the elaboration through experience of simple, inborn reflexes.

Pavlov spent the rest of his life doing experiments to determine the laws of conditioning. Through the study of conditioned salivation in dogs, he attempted to uncover the situations in which conditioning would occur, how fast it would occur, how strong it would be, and so on. Aside from actually making discoveries that have stood the test of generations of further research, Pavlov also established a model for experimentation that has infused behavior theory ever since. By studying conditioned salivation in dogs as a route to laws of all learning, Pavlov was assuming that fundamental learning processes were almost universal, that is, not peculiar to individual animal species, and that the seemingly complex examples of learning that occur under natural conditions could be understood in terms of the action of the simple principles he was discovering experimentally. As we will see, virtually all research in behavior theory shares these assumptions.

Pavlovian Conditioning: The Research Paradigm

Pavlov's discovery was that environmental events that previously had no relation to a given reflex could come, through experience, to trigger the reflex. Prior to experience, organisms possessed a number of reflexes that were built into the nervous system. Because these reflexes were built-in, that is, not conditional upon experience, Pavlov called them *unconditioned reflexes*. An unconditioned reflex has two components. There is first the environmental event, or stimulus, that triggers it, as food in the mouth triggers salivation. This environmental trigger is called the *unconditioned stimulus*, or US. Second, there is the reflex response itself, for example, salivation. This is called the *unconditioned response,* or *UR.* The relation between the US and the UR is typically schematized in this way:

$$US \text{ (Food)} \rightarrow UR \text{ (Salivation)}$$

The phenomenon of Pavlovian conditioning occurs when some other stimulus, called the *conditioned stimulus,* or *CS,* comes to produce the reflex response. Thus, in Pavlov's initial discoveries, the sight of the lab assistant, or the sound of the door, was a CS, a stimulus that prior to the animal's learning experience, had no relation to the salivation UR.

In a Pavlovian conditioning experiment, the CS (for example, a tone) is presented, and followed closely in time by presentation of the US (food in the mouth); each of these pairings is a "trial." After a number of pairings of the tone and food (CS and US), the dog begins salivating reliably when the tone comes on, in advance of the presentation of food. This salivation is the conditioned response (CR). The procedure typically employed to produce Pavlovian conditioning is depicted in Figure 2–1.

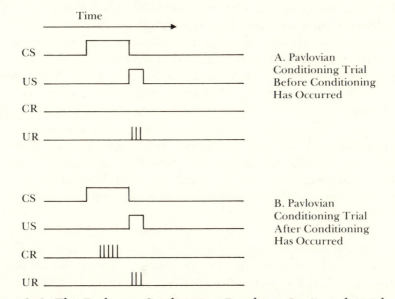

Figure 2–1. The Pavlovian Conditioning Paradigm. *In A, early trials are depicted. The CS is presented and followed by the US. URs occur to the US (vertical lines) but there are no CRs. In B, after conditioning has occurred, CRs (vertical lines) occur to the CS and before the US.*

Since Pavlov's initial investigations, the methods used for the study of Pavlovian conditioning have broadened significantly in scope. Many reflexes aside from salivation in many organisms aside from dogs have been studied. Because of technical problems involved in measuring salivation, much research on Pavlovian conditioning is now done with the eyeblink reflex in rabbits, cats and often humans, among other species. Also, heart rate, electrical skin resistance and blood pressure have been frequently studied in a variety of species. As we will see in Chapter 3, in virtually all cases, researchers have observed the same phenomena that Pavlov observed in studying the salivary reflex in dogs. Though the particular conditioned responses may differ from one situation to the next, the events which seem critical to producing them are the same.

Thorndike and the Law of Effect

Pavlovian conditioning is a powerful and general phenomenon, but can it really be the key ingredient of all learning? Pavlovian conditioning requires a triggering stimulus (US), a reflex response (UR), and a conditioned stimulus (CS). If we think about our own everyday activity, or the activity of our household pets, can we find all the necessary triggering stimuli and reflex responses? Is walking to the library a reflex response? If so, what is its triggering stimulus? Is rolling over a reflex in dogs? If so, what triggers it? Almost from the outset of research in behavior theory, it was clear that Pavlov's hope that conditioned reflexes were the building block of all learning was a little too grandiose. When the conditioned reflex concept was applied to moderately complex situations, in which the experimenter did not provide the triggering stimuli, substantial problems arose. We can best see this with an example, one extensively studied by E. L. Thorndike (1874–1949).[2]

Imagine a cat in a cage, the door of which is held fast by a simple latch. Just outside the cage is a piece of salmon in a dish. The cat moves around the cage, sniffing its corners. Suddenly, it sees the salmon, moves to the part of the cage closest to it and begins extending its paws through the bars toward the fish, which it cannot reach. The cat reaches more and more vigorously and begins scratching at the

2. Thorndike, 1898.

Edward L. Thorndike. (*Courtesy of the
Granger Collection, New York*)

bars. After a while, the cat stops this activity and starts moving actively
about the cage. A few minutes later, it bangs against the latch and
frees it. The door opens and the cat scampers out and eats the fish.
The cat is placed again in the cage and a new piece of fish is placed in
the dish. The cat goes through the same sequence of activities as
before and eventually opens the latch, seemingly inadvertently. This
is repeated again and again. Gradually, the cat stops extending its
paws through the bars and spends more and more of its time near the
latch. Next, the cat begins directing its activity almost exclusively at
the latch, now no longer inadvertently. Ultimately, the cat develops
a quick and efficient pattern of movements which enable it to open
the latch and free itself almost immediately.

This situation, while still enormously simpler than those occurring
in the natural environment, is considerably more complicated than
one in which only reflexes triggered by the experimenter are studied.
How can we use conditioned reflexes to explain the behavior of the
cat? The immediate task is to enumerate the reflexes involved. There

might be a sniffing reflex, a looking reflex, a reaching reflex, a jumping reflex, a running reflex, and so on, but could there be a latch opening reflex? No, but presumably latch opening reflects the development of a complex combination of reflexes. The next task is to identify the stimuli which trigger the reflexes. This is more difficult. What are the odors that trigger sniffing? What triggers agitation? The salmon presumably triggers reaching, but, if so, why does the cat stop reaching? The latch might trigger some set of paw movements, but, if so, why didn't they occur when the cat was first in the cage? And doesn't the salmon have something to do with the latch opening response? Finally, there is the task of explaining the changes in the cat's behavior in the cage over time.

It is clear that either much work would be required for the conditioned reflex concept to provide a satisfactory account of the actions of the cat, or an alternative to the reflex concept would have to be provided. Thorndike offered the latter.

Thorndike argued that most behavior could not be triggered automatically and blindly in the way the salivation could be. Instead, behavior seemed to be goal-directed and intelligent. The cat seemed to want the salmon, and to try a number of different means to get it, eventually discovering one that worked and then persisting in it. The particular behavior that ended up dominating the cat's activity became dominant precisely because it worked, because it produced the desired effect. There were no reflexes, conditioned or unconditioned, involved. There seemed to be a significant class of behavior, even in cats, that was influenced by its anticipated consequences rather than its triggering stimuli.

In acknowledging this seemingly goal-directed feature of behavior, Thorndike also proposed a principle to explain it: the *law of effect*. According to Thorndike, some behavior occurs in a random, trial and error fashion, varying in form from moment to moment. The law of effect tells us that if some of these variations happen to be followed closely in time by pleasurable consequences or rewards (for example, getting salmon), they are strengthened or stamped in and become more likely in the future. Other variations may not be followed by pleasurable consequences, or may even be followed by noxious or unpleasant consequences or punishers. If they are, they get weakened and become less likely in the future. In this way only those activities that produce rewards get selected from an organism's full range of activity, and continue to occur in the future. The adult organism seems to behave intelligently. But this "intelligence" is just the result of the action of the law of effect, selectively strengthening only those actions that work.

Thorndike's discovery of the law of effect greatly expanded the research domain of behavior theory. It identified a process, in addition to Pavlov's, which had to be understood for the laws of behavior to be fully formulated. Moreover, since so much human behavior seemed non-reflexive and goal directed, it seemed clear at the outset that any explanation of human behavior would depend heavily on the process Thorndike had discovered. As a result, the bulk of the research done in behavior theory over the years has focussed on the law of effect. The changes in behavior produced by the law of effect are typically referred to as *operant* or *instrumental conditioning*.

Operant Conditioning: Research Paradigms

The development of Thorndike's initial findings into a full-fledged research program was accomplished by others, most notably, B. F. Skinner. Skinner took up the study of rewards and punishments in the 1930's, and he developed a set of methods and a terminology that have characterized much of behavior theory ever since.[3]

Skinner called the kind of behavior change produced by the law of effect *operant conditioning*. He called it operant conditioning because behavior operated on, or had an effect on, the environment. The crucial elements of operant conditioning are the response, or operant, and the consequence. The consequence may be positive, in which case it is called a *reward*, or a *positive reinforcer*, or it may be negative, in which case it is called a *punisher*, or a *negative reinforcer*. The relations between operant responses and their consequences may be schematized in this way:

response → positive reinforcer: increase in future likelihood of the operant;

response → negative reinforcer: decrease in future likelihood of the operant.

Skinner took great pains to distinguish operant conditioning from Pavlovian conditioning. We can examine the differences between them in Figure 2–2.

3. Skinner, 1935, 1938.

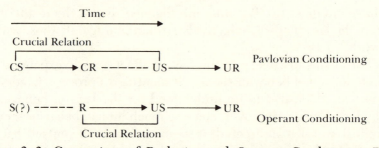

Figure 2–2. Comparison of Pavlovian and Operant Conditioning Procedures. *In both procedures, the sequence of events is the same. However, the crucial components of the sequence are different. In Pavlovian conditioning, it is the relation between CS and US which is responsible for the CR. After conditioning, the CS causes the CR (arrow). In operant conditioning, it is the relation between the response (R) and the US which is crucial (arrow).*

In this diagram, there are two types of connecting lines—dashed lines and solid lines with arrows. They are intended to signify two different kinds of relations. The dashes merely indicate that one event follows another. The arrows, on the other hand, are meant to indicate that one thing is caused by or produced by another. Thus, in the case of Pavlovian conditioning, the US causes the UR and the CS causes the CR, but the CR has no effect. It merely precedes the US. Food is placed in the dog's mouth whether or not it salivates. The situation is quite different in the case of operant conditioning. Though there are presumably some stimuli around in the situation (S?), they do not cause the response. On the other hand, R produces the US. The dog must do something (R) to get food (US). Once the food is in its mouth, presumably a UR (salivation) occurs. But the UR is usually not of interest, and thus not measured in operant conditioning experiments.

When the two conditioning paradigms are placed side by side in this way, they appear remarkably similar. They both begin with neutral stimuli, then conditioned responses, then unconditioned stimuli and unconditioned responses. However, the location of the causal arrows makes all the difference. In Pavlovian conditioning experiments, it is the relation between two stimuli, CS and US, which produces the conditioned response. In operant conditioning experiments, it is the relation between response and a stimulus (R and US) which produces conditioning. Note also that in Pavlovian conditioning, the CR and UR are intimately related; both are reflexes. In contrast, in operant conditioning, the operant response could be anything. We could

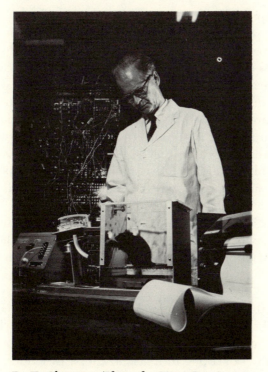

B. F. Skinner. (*Photo by Nina Leen—*
Life Magazine, © *Time, Inc.*)

require a dog to press a lever, sit on its haunches, turn in a circle, or
dozens of other things. Any response will do as long as the animal can
make it.

Consider a simple human example of the difference between
operant and Pavlovian responses. There are many ways a person can
arrange to have a sirloin steak. One could buy a steak at a butcher
shop, bring it home and cook it; one could walk to a restaurant; one
could go to a neighbor's backyard barbecue, and so on. Each of these
acts is an operant response or a series of them. On the other hand,
when the sizzling steak is actually placed on the table, no matter how
it got there, the Pavlovian response will be salivation. This distinction
may be stated in a more general and technical way. There need be
no intrinsic or built-in connection between the operant response and
the US. On the other hand, the Pavlovian CR *is* intrinsically related
to the US. The form of the CR is powerfully influenced by the nature
of the US.

The Unconditional Stimulus (US) or Reward

Let us now consider the US as it is used in the two types of conditioning paradigms. In the examples discussed thus far, the US was the same—food. In general, stimuli which are USs in Pavlovian conditioning experiments can be (and have been) USs in operant conditioning experiments. Typically USs used in operant conditioning experiments are not called USs: They are called rewards or punishers. All that is required for a stimulus to be a reward or a punisher is that it be biologically important, that is, that the stimulus produce a strong and permanent unconditioned response. The set of possible USs is rather small, and the set which is commonly used is smaller still. Food, water, and electric shock are the most common USs in experimental settings. Though the set of USs is small, we will see in Chapter 6 that behavior theory has provided an account of how previously insignificant stimuli may come to function as rewards or punishers.

Discrimination

Let us return now to Figure 2–2. What can be said of the peculiar component of the operant conditioning paradigm which is identified as "S(?)"? Any environment, no matter how simple, contains a multitude of stimuli. For a dog in its cage, there are odors, there are the bars of the cage, there is the latch of the cage, there are lights, there is some kind of material underfoot, there is air temperature. The list could go on. What role do these stimuli play in influencing the occurrence of operant behavior? They do not trigger it, in the way that CSs trigger conditioned reflexes. As we have seen, the critical determinant of operant behavior is that it has been followed in the past by reward. Nevertheless, these stimuli do influence the occurrence of operant behavior. Suppose that we train a dog to push a lever by following lever pushes with bits of food. After the dog has learned to push the lever, two shapes, a square and a circle, are sometimes placed in the cage. If the dog pushes the lever when the square is present, it gets food, but when the circle is present, pushes on the lever do nothing.

When the dog is first exposed to these new conditions, its behavior continues as before. After some experience, though, the dog stops pushing the lever when the circle is present and continues as before when the square is present. The dog has learned a *discrimination*. It has learned not that squares and circles are different (which presumably it already knew) but that squares and circles provide different information about the potential consequences of lever pushing.

Circles mean stop—don't bother; squares mean go. These two stimuli are now exerting control over the dog's lever-pushing behavior. We can take the question mark away from the S in Figure 2–2. However, though circles and squares now influence lever-pushing, they are not CSs. They do not trigger lever pushing; they merely set the occasion for it by signaling when it will be followed by food and when it will not be. Just as it would be a mistake to claim that red lights elicit a "step on the brake" reflex and green lights a "step on the gas" reflex, so also it would be a mistake to characterize lever-pushing as a reflex. To emphasize the difference between these stimuli and CSs, they are called by a different name. Stimuli which set the occasion for the emission of an operant response are called *discriminative stimuli.* In the example just given, the square would be termed an S^+ since it signals a positive relation between the behavior and the reward. The circle is termed an S^-. The role of discriminative stimuli in the control of behavior will be taken up in Chapter 6.

Measuring the Operant Response

When we do an operant conditioning experiment, what features of the behavior should we measure? What should we focus on as an index of the effects of reward or punishment? Skinner has suggested that perhaps the best measure of operant conditioning would be one that allowed an estimate of the likelihood of occurrence of the response (its probability) at any moment. There are difficulties in judging the probability of a response directly, but some idea of its probability can be inferred from its frequency. It is reasonable to assume that the more often one does something in general, the more likely one is to do it at any particular time. Thus, Skinner argued that operant conditioning experiments should measure the frequency or rate of occurrence of the particular response.[4] With this aim, it would be desirable to measure a response which occurs rapidly and with little effort. Furthermore, the experimental situation should allow the animal to make the response repeatedly, without intervention. In this way, one could develop very fine measurements of conditioning as it occurred. The response would perhaps occur initially only a few times in an hour as the organism explored its environment. As the response was followed by reward, its frequency would increase, ultimately perhaps to 75 or 100 times per minute. If such a response could be found, one could

4. Skinner, 1950.

measure the strength of conditioning (in responses per minute) with ease and precision.

The Conditioning Chamber

Having developed this strategy, Skinner set out to develop the experimental situation in which to execute it. The product was an apparatus like the one in Figure 2–3. To eliminate potentially distracting stimuli from intruding, the control panel and the rat are enclosed in a soundproof, opaque chamber. The experimenter can observe the animal's behavior through a little peephole. The lever,

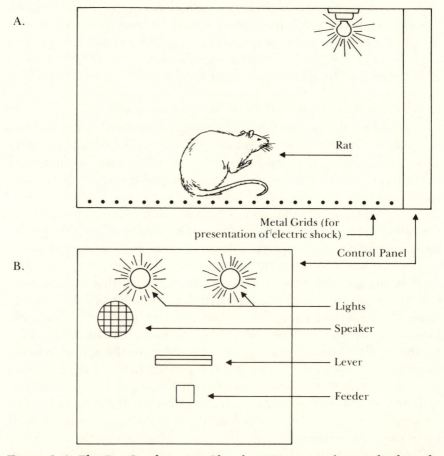

Figure 2–3. The Rat-Conditioning Chamber. *Diagram of a standard conditioning chamber for rats* (A) *and a rat's-eye view of the control panel housed in the chamber* (B).

feeder, lights and tone are electrically connected to automated equipment outside the chamber. The response to be measured is the lever press. Each time the rat presses the lever a switch is closed. This switch closure may be arranged to produce food and at the same time automatically count the responses on a recording device.

The second commonly used apparatus is shown in Figure 2–4. All of its constituents are essentially equivalent to those in the rat chamber, but it accommodates a different animal—the pigeon. There is only one major difference between this apparatus and the previous one. Rather than pressing a lever, the pigeons are required to peck at one of the round disks or keys which are mounted above the feeder. This difference between the rat and the pigeon chambers is only apparent. From the experimenter's point of view, the responses are identical. They are, in both cases, the closure of a switch which sends

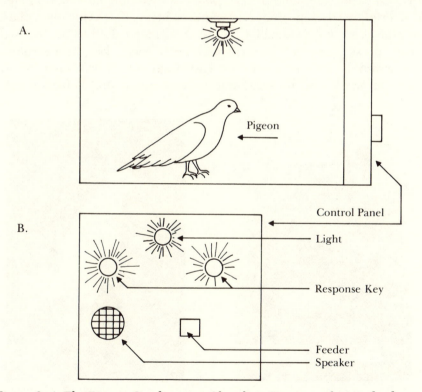

Figure 2–4. The Pigeon-Conditioning Chamber. *Diagram of a standard conditioning chamber for pigeons* (A), *and a bird's-eye view of the control panel housed in the chamber* (B).

an electric signal each time the key is pecked or the lever is pressed. The specific behavior which causes the switch to close is of little interest. The rat may "peck" the lever (press it with its nose) and the pigeon may "press the key" (hit it with its wings) and it will still be treated as the same response. Indeed rats and pigeons may make the response in a different way each time. As long as (and only when) the switch is closed, it is a lever press (key peck). This research strategy indicates something very important about operant conditioning. What is conditioned in operant conditioning experiments is not a single response but a whole class of responses. The operant is actually a response class. And the individual members of this class need have only one thing in common—that they close the switch.

Thus, in the most commonly used methods for studying operant conditioning, rats press a lever for food or pigeons peck a key for food. In both cases, the measured response is ideal for the experimenter. It is brief, easily repeated, and requires little effort. However, these responses are not as ideal for the rat and pigeon. Left alone, rats will rarely press a lever and pigeons will rarely peck a key. This creates a minor problem. In order for the law of effect to work—for behavior to be strengthened by satisfying consequences—the behavior must

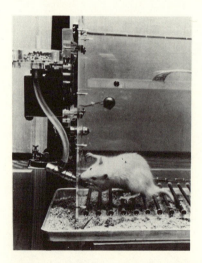 

A rat trained to press a lever for food reinforcement, (*Courtesy of Pfizer Inc.*) and a pigeon pecking a lit key for food reinforcement. (*Photo by W. Rapport, courtesy of B. F. Skinner*)

occur at least once so that the satisfying consequence may be produced. The way to solve this problem is to help the rat or pigeon along a bit by means of a procedure called *shaping by successive approximation.* In this procedure the experimenter might observe the rat, and rather than waiting for a lever press to occur, the experimenter waits for some movement toward the lever, then delivers food. This makes movements toward the lever a bit more likely. The experimenter now waits until the rat moves closer to the lever before presenting food. Each food delivery requires a response which is closer to a lever press than the one before it. Eventually, the animal will press the lever and soon thereafter, the lever press response will be firmly established. In effect, the experimenter "shapes" the behavior of the animal.

While shaping of behavior by successive approximation seems to be a formal experimental procedure, it is actually commonplace in the natural environment, so much so that we hardly notice it. When we teach children to swim, or to dress themselves, or to write the alphabet, we start with simple, easily executed components, reward them, and gradually shape the desired response. If we waited for the desired response to occur full-blown before we rewarded it, few children would ever swim or write.

Assumptions Underlying the Methods of Behavior Theory

Why should behavior theory have settled on the research methods just described, rather than dozens of other possible methods? There is nothing obvious about these methods. Having learned of the initial discoveries of Pavlov with dogs, and Thorndike with cats, one could have attempted to study the behavior of animals in very complex situations. Alternatively, one could have moved to the study of more complex animals, or to the study of children learning in school, in an effort to ascertain whether rats, dogs, monkeys, and children learn in similar ways. Finally, one could have decided to study organisms in their natural habitat, to see whether Pavlovian and operant conditioning work in nature the way they work in a laboratory. Each of these alternatives represents an effort to decrease the gap between the situation one studies and the objective one is primarily interested in— the explanation of human behavior. One could have chosen to explore any or all of these methods.

Instead, for the most part, behavior theory moved in exactly the opposite direction. It sought the simplest possible situation. It developed that situation to be as unlike the natural environment as possible. It chose to study organisms very far removed in complexity from humans.[5] What provided a justification for using so simple and artificial a situation to attempt to develop the laws of human behavior? Are there assumptions about what the laws of behavior will look like that are implicit in the methods used to discover them? To answer these questions, we must consider a few different issues.

Learning about People by Studying Animals

Almost from its inception behavior theory has focused primarily on the study of animals. The best prospects for laws of behavior—even human behavior—were all developed through the study of animal behavior. That animals have been the subjects of study reflects some of the assumptions which have guided behavior theory. Central among them is the view that complex behavior can be understood in terms of the operation of simple principles—principles which will have their influence even in the barest of environments with the simplest of organisms. Though rats, dogs, and pigeons display none of the richness and complexity of humans, their behavior can be understood in terms of principles like the law of effect. Once the law of effect has been fully understood as it applies to the behavior of nonhumans, it should be a reasonably straightforward matter to apply it to complex, human behavior. Behavior theorists assume that the difference in complexity between human and nonhuman is only quantitative, not qualitative.

Moreover, there is much to be gained by studying animals. Using animal subjects allows one to maximize experimental control. One can construct very simple environments in which animal behavior may be studied. One can control the past experience of animal subjects, and expose them to conditions of pleasure, severe stress, and deprivation. The same, obviously, cannot always be done effectively or ethically with humans. In short, an experimenter can create a wholly artificial world in which animals are born, raised, and studied. Potentially significant environmental conditions can be created singly or in combination. With human subjects, one can only approximate this

---

5. Not all research in behavior theory has followed this strategy. There is, for example, a great deal of research done on the control of human behavior in applied settings (see Chapter 8). But even here, the central principles of behavior theory have been derived from simple settings like these.

degree of experimental control. While all conditions can be determined for a few hours by the experimenter, the human subject comes into the laboratory with a rich history of previous experience that the experimenter cannot control. To what extent do these uncontrollable natural experiences influence the effects of the laboratory experience? There is no way to know. Thus, there is much to be gained by studying animals rather than humans. To believe that nothing significant is lost by this strategy depends upon accepting the assumption we have already discussed.

Behavior as Subject to External Influences

When we discussed the purpose of establishing experimental environments at the beginning of this chapter, we indicated that experiments allow one to create situations in which the critical determinants of a phenomenon emerge with clarity. They accomplish this by keeping out a host of factors in the natural environment that might confuse things, and by keeping in only those factors presumed to be essential. Suppose, for example, we are interested in determining the effects of gravity on bodies in free fall. We might go into our living room, stand on a table, and drop from the same height an iron ball and a slip of paper. Presumably the iron ball will land first. Then we drop them again. Will the ball land the same amount of time ahead of the paper or not? Perhaps, but perhaps not, for how the slip of paper falls may well depend upon its orientation at the time of release. Perhaps a gust of wind will enter from an open window and change its rate of fall. Or perhaps someone is playing tricks—an air-blower is turned onto the paper from above, and a large magnet is hidden in the ceiling, so that the paper may even land first. In daily life an enormous multiplicity of factors can act with respect to any phenomenon, so much so that it is very difficult to obtain precise empirical generalizations from daily experience. In an experiment we simplify the environment and thus prevent some of the factors from exerting an influence. Ideally, we separate out all factors so that only one is operative. With the falling bodies, for example, we want to design an experiment to study the isolated effect of gravitational force. So we construct an environment which renders other forces inoperative. We drop the bodies in a vacuum to eliminate resistance and other mechanical forces; we insure that there are no magnets in the vicinity. Under these conditions it will turn out that every time we drop objects simultaneously from the same height they will land simultaneously.

It is the very same logic of experimentation as simplification that led to the experimental methods of behavior theory. But in designing experimental methods of this type, one must have a pretty good idea about which factors to leave in and which to keep out. One needs strong hunches about gravity and other forces *before* one drops objects in a vacuum. What the experiment does is confirm or refute hunches that are already present. Similarly, one must have strong hunches about what the key influences on behavior are before designing the experimental methods of behavior theory. Without them, one would face the real danger that the methods designed kept out important influences and left in trivial ones. What are the hunches about what is important that underlie the methods of behavior theory?

First, it is clear that behavior theory focuses on influences from the environment rather than influences internal to the organism. If organisms were autonomous initiators of their behavior, or if a complex series of internal processes mediated between the occurrence of environmental events and an organism's behavior, the use of pigeons and rats to discover laws that govern people would be a questionable research strategy. For it is surely implausible that the internal processes of the pigeon are enough like those of the person that one can make inferences about the latter by studying the former. The belief that such internal processes as these are relatively unimportant is what justifies using pigeons or rats to find out about all organisms. If internal processes are unimportant, there is no need to attempt to study them and to devise experiments to test speculations about how they operate. Behavior theory asserts that there is no need to construct theories about internal processes, and this is perhaps its most distinctive methodological assumption. It contrasts sharply, for example, with cognitive psychology, whose primary concern is to develop and test hypotheses about the cognitive abilities and internal processes that underlie human behavior. Behavior theory's view of the unimportance of internal processes and its methodological rejection of hypotheses about internal processes are grounded in an important argument. Skinner presented this argument succinctly:

> The objection to inner states is not that they do not exist, but that they are not relevant in a functional analysis. We cannot account for the behavior of any system while staying wholly inside it; eventually we must turn to forces operating upon the organism from without. Unless there is a weak spot in our causal chain so that the second link is not lawfully determined by the first, or the third by the second, then the

first and third links must be lawfully related. If we must always go back beyond the second link for prediction and control, we may avoid many tiresome and exhausting digressions by examining the third link as a function of the first. Valid information about the second link may throw light upon this relationship but can in no way alter it.[6]

Few will doubt that environmental events set the context and provide the occasion for human behavior. What may be doubted is whether the inner events which occur between occurrences of the environmental events and behavior are simply causal consequences of the external, environmental events. Cognitive psychologists would maintain that they are the joint product of environmental events and the current internal state of the person. If so, then failure to consider internal processes will result in an inevitable incompleteness of causal analysis. The methodology of behavior theory rests on the assumption that internal processes are merely mediators between the action of the environment and the subsequent occurrence of behavior. Only if this assumption is correct can the focus on the environment rather than on internal processes hope to produce a complete account of behavior.[7]

Given that behavior theory focuses on environmental influence, the next question is what kind of environmental influence? A quick review of the methods of behavior theory makes the hunches that are operative here apparent. The critical environmental events are rewards and punishments. Both Pavlovian and operant methods have in common the presence of biologically significant stimuli, like food, water, or pain-inducing electric shock. In the domain of Pavlovian conditioning, the expectation is that associations are formed when insignificant stimuli (tones, lab assistants, and so on) precede significant ones. In the domain of operant conditioning, the expectation is that voluntary behavior is controlled by its biologically significant consequences. Indeed, it is the central thesis of behavior theory that virtually all significant voluntary human behaviors can be understood in terms of the relations of similar past behaviors to rewards and punishments. What controls voluntary behavior is its past history of association with rewarding or punishing environmental events.

We all acknowledge that some behavior is controlled by rewards and punishments, that to understand what causes people to act as

6. Skinner, 1953, p. 35.
7. For an assessment of this assumption, see Lacey, 1979.

they do, it is necessary to take rewards and punishments into account. Rewards and punishments are a palpable part of each of our lives. Yet, we would argue, there is more to human beings than that. While rewards and punishments are always an influence on human action, they are perhaps the least distinctly human influence. What we most care about, if we are to understand human action, is what people do despite the presence of obvious bribes or threats.

Thus, our everyday conception of ourselves acknowledges that reward and punishment play a role in influencing what we do, but gives greater value to other kinds of influences. If there are these other kinds of influences, the methods of behavior theory are designed to exclude them from experimental settings. Therefore, the view that behavior theory will yield a relatively complete explanation of human behavior must assume that such an explanation can be based almost entirely on the influence of rewards and punishments. This assumption is not so much *evaluated* by means of the experimental methods of behavior theory as it is *presupposed* by them.

We have identified two distinctive methodological features of behavior theory: its commitment to explaining behavior in terms of factors external to the organism, and its emphasis specifically on the set of external factors we call rewards and punishments. Though each of these features is of central importance to understanding behavior theory, our focus throughout this book will be on the latter. That is because the emphasis on rewards and punishments has immediate practical consequences when behavior theory principles are applied, as we shall see in Chapters 8 and 9.

Prediction and Control as Goals of Behavior Theory

We have briefly described the experimental methods of behavior theory, and some of the general hunches that underlie them. These methods have been devised in order eventually to produce a complete science of behavior. Remember, if a complete science of behavior is to be possible, all behaviors must occur under the control of some antecedent influences, and if behavior theory is correct, those influences will be predominantly environmental events. Presumably, a complete behavior theory will specify these influences, and in so doing, all the laws that are involved in the control of behavior. Thus a completed behavior theory must explain behaviors that occur not only in experimental, but also in ordinary social settings.

In the ordinary social settings within which most human behavior occurs, the situations and interactions are so complex, with so many variables operative at the same time, that it is impossible to discover laws simply by observing these settings. Thus we perform experiments in which we create simplified settings in order to isolate key influences, and find the laws which describe a particular influence upon behavior. And to the extent that an experiment is successful it does demonstrate that certain variables can influence behavior in a certain way. We know these variables *can* influence behavior because they *do* influence it within the experimental setting. How does this knowledge gleaned from experiments fit into the hoped for completed science of behavior? What does the demonstration that certain variables control behavior in experimental settings tell us about the variables that control behavior in ordinary, noncontrived social settings? There are no obvious answers. Yet, it is widely taken for granted that experimental results do give us knowledge about the variables that control behaviors in nonexperimental settings. Why is this so?

Behavior theory offers us two criteria for determining the general adequacy of its results: First, we will know that we have discovered important principles of behavior if we can use them to *predict* what organisms will do. If the law of effect is an important principle, then we should be able to predict that if some behavior is followed by a rewarding event, its likelihood of occurrence will increase in the future. To be able to make such predictions, we must know both important general principles, and the circumstances in which they apply. It is commonplace in science generally to take successful prediction as an indication that we have knowledge of natural laws.

Second, according to behavior theory, if we have knowledge of important general principles, we should be able to use them to *control* what organisms do. Again, if the law of effect is an important principle, we should be able to manipulate the availability of reward so as to get pigeons to peck at lit keys, or rats to press levers. Being able to control phenomena is not so commonplace a criterion of knowledge as being able to predict. In astronomy, for example, we may be able to predict planetary motion perfectly without ever being able to exert any control over it.

The reason for the appeal to control as a criterion of knowledge in behavior theory depends not just on the belief that principles of behavior can be discovered, but also on beliefs about what these principles will involve. As we just saw, behavior theory has the hunch that the major influences on behavior are environmental events.

Moreoever, they are environmental events—rewards and punishments—that are relatively easy to manipulate. If these events do in fact control behavior, and if we, in turn, can control these events, it follows that we should be able to control behavior.

Do these criteria of prediction and control succeed in giving good reason to believe that the laws discovered in the behavior theorist's experiments are the laws that explain significant behaviors in ordinary social settings? Certainly there are settings intermediate between the experimental and natural settings in which we do use the laws to obtain prediction and control of behavior. These intermediate settings are those in which principles discovered in experiments are applied in the natural environment. Thus, we might take principles discovered in the laboratory and use them in a classroom or a mental hospital to control behavior. If we are successful, our confidence that these principles are operative all the time would grow. If we can use the law of effect to control the behavior of school children or mental patients, we have reason to believe that the law applies to more than pigeons and rats in sterile boxes.

Or do we? Is it not possible that when we apply our laboratory derived principles in natural settings, all we are doing is turning these natural settings into extensions of the laboratory? When we bring the law of effect into the classroom, we are intentionally applying principles discovered in the laboratory. But unless there is a supercontroller who is secretly shaping our lives, not all social settings are intentionally applied settings of this kind. So, what ground is there for believing that experimental results give knowledge of the controlling variables of behavior in the everyday human environment?

This question clearly applies in all the sciences. How, for example, in physics, do we move from knowledge of generalizations in experimental settings to claims to know the laws of the physical universe? What has the knowledge of generalizations about motions of balls rolling on inclined planes, falling bodies, and simple pendula to do with the laws of all motions in the universe? Again, it is not enough to point out that these generalizations are also exemplified in a wide variety of machines of great utility and significance in practical life, for these machines were made because they exemplified the generalizations. The accepted answer of the scientific tradition has two aspects. First, it argues, as we have, that in experiments it can be demonstrated that certain influences upon events exist. Second, it claims that experimentally discovered generalizations are dramatically exemplified by certain phenomena that are clearly not human creations. Newton, for example, showed that the laws of motion are exemplified not only by balls rolling down inclined planes but by the motions of the planets. This is perhaps the paradigmatic instance of the capacity of experiments to generate knowledge of natural phenomena. Given such demonstrable success, it has become the scientific tradition to attempt to explain any physical phenomenon in the light of principles drawn from experimental studies.

Returning to behavior theory, one might look in a similar manner to experiments to isolate the variety of influences upon human behavior, and then use these results to construct plausible hypotheses to explain behaviors in complex, social settings. The seriousness of this endeavor must be justified as it is in natural science, by demonstrating that the experimental principles are actually exemplified in some nonapplied settings. That is, one must find a behavioral equivalent of the laws of the planetary motions. Without such a demonstration, there is no way to know whether experimentally-derived generalizations are just that—experimentally-derived generalizations exemplified in limited circumstances—rather than the laws which govern behavior in general. Put another way, is it possible that behavior theory discovers only generalizations about settings in which explicit human controls (experimenter's, teacher's, therapist's) are dominant, rather than the laws in accordance with which behavior in general occurs? One's evaluation of a program of experimental research in behavior theory will depend on the answer to this question.

Prediction and control, then, are criteria for determining that we have discovered laws. But they are not criteria for determining the completeness of the set of laws we have discovered or that our methods could discover. The methods, we have seen, rest upon certain hunches concerning what the influences upon behavior are. More formally, we can say that these methods rest upon an underlying general conception of human nature, that is, a set of proposals about what kind of explanation is appropriate for human behavior, and what kinds of variables can influence human behavior. In large part, especially if one fails to find a behavioral equivalent of the planetary motions— the plausibility of the claim that the generalizations obtained under experimental conditions give us access to the controlling variables of behavior in general is sustained by a commitment to this conception of human nature. We saw in Chapter 1 that behavior theory rests upon the proposal that human behavior is lawful, and that this proposal rests uneasily with the common-sense view that we do things that we believe will contribute toward the fulfillment of our goals. We also saw that behavior theory assumes that the significant behavioral laws will involve events and influences external to the organism. Given such a view, it clearly makes sense that prediction and control would be research goals of first importance, and that the laws tested by these criteria would be regarded as significant laws of noncontrived social environments as well. Suppose that in contrast to the views of behavior theory, behavior is lawful, but that it is ordinarily causally related to internal events (for example, mental states as cognitive psychology claims) which we cannot manipulate. If this were true, then we might eventually be able to predict behavior, but not always be able to control it. And this would be true even if there were some circumstances (for example, experimental ones) in which we *could* control behavior by manipulating external events. Or suppose that human actions were under "autonomous control." Then there may not even be laws, much less prediction and control, of certain behaviors. Thus, the fact that prediction and control of behavior are primary goals of inquiry stems from the conception of human nature that underlies behavior theory.

We thus see that this view of human nature profoundly influences the character of research in behavior theory: It sets as the object of behavior theory the discovery of laws relating behavior to antecedent environmental variables, and it legitimizes as the test of success the prediction and control of behavior. In other words, it is an appeal to a particular conception of human nature that bridges the gap between phenomena observed in experimental situations and human behavior in the social environment in which it usually occurs.

Chapter 3

Pavlovian Conditioning

As you walk past the bakeshop and smell the fresh bread, your stomach starts to grumble and saliva forms in your mouth.

As the national anthem comes to an end your excitement grows in anticipation of the start of the football game.

Your heart pounds when you hear the screech of brakes down the street.

Your pulse quickens as you spot the flashing lights of an approaching patrol car through your rear-view mirror.

THESE little vignettes are all examples of Pavlovian conditioning. The smell of food has reliably preceded the ingestion of food in your past; the sound of the national anthem has reliably preceded the beginnings of athletic events; screeching brakes reliably precede collisions, and looming patrol cars reliably precede traffic tickets. Each example includes one event or stimulus (CS) which is of no special significance. The music and the screeching brakes are just sounds; the flashing light is just a light. This nonsignificant, or neutral stimulus becomes associated with another stimulus (US), that is significant. Food and the stimuli that comprise a traffic accident are probably inherently significant, that is, we might respond to them as significant stimuli even if we had virtually no previous experience with them. Football games and traffic tickets depend for their significance upon our experience. In either case, because the CS has reliably preceded the US in the past, we come to respond to the CS in a way that is different from the way we used to. In the first two examples, the USs are pleasurable. The conditioned responses that develop to the CSs are *appetitive.* In the last two examples, the USs are aversive. The conditioned responses that develop to the CSs are *defensive.*

45

These four examples have a number of features in common. First, they are mundane. Everyone can identify countless experiences like these in the ordinary course of living. This suggests that the phenomenon of Pavlovian conditioning, which unites these examples, is a pervasive and important one in human experience. Second, none of these examples is an instance of intelligent, goal-directed action. The conditioned responses are all involuntary, and all affective or emotional. Third, each of these examples represents an association between two stimuli, the conditioned stimulus (CS) and the unconditioned stimulus (US).

We will see in the course of this chapter that the phenomena of Pavlovian conditioning make a very significant contribution to the shape of human activity. Their effects extend far beyond the domain of involuntary or reflexive behavior. Pavlovian conditioning can have an effect on the entire range of seemingly intelligent, voluntary behavior.

Pavlovian Experimental Procedures

In doing a Pavlovian conditioning experiment, one begins by choosing a CS and a US. The CS can be almost anything, as long as it is detectable by the animal being studied. The US must be a stimulus that produces unconditioned responses, as food (US) produces salivation (UR), and shock (US) produces heart rate and blood pressure changes (UR), often referred to as fear responses. The choice of a US is especially important, since the type of US used will affect the type of conditioned responses one observes. One may produce conditioned salivation if food is the US, but conditioned fear (heart rate changes) if shock is the US.

Once the CS and US have been selected, the experiment proper can begin. Usually, one starts out by giving the animal periodic, brief presentations of the CS without the US, to make sure the CS by itself does not produce the conditioned responses one will be measuring. Thus, if one is planning to use a tone as a CS and food as the US, one first presents the tone several times (each time say five seconds long), and checks to make sure that the animal does not salivate to the tone. Once the tone is established as a neutral stimulus, we are ready for the next step. We now present the tone, but this time each tone presentation is followed by the delivery of food. The animal, of course, will salivate when food is in its mouth. But at some point, the animal will salivate to the tone, before food has even been presented: Conditioning has taken place.

There are a number of different ways to measure Pavlovian conditioning. First, one can measure the *magnitude* of the conditioned response. How many drops of saliva occur when the tone is sounded? Second, one can measure the *latency* of the conditioned response. How long after the tone is sounded does salivation begin? Finally, one can measure the *probability* of the conditioned response. On what proportion of tone presentations does salivation occur? One reliably finds that as conditioning proceeds, conditioned response magnitude and probability increase and conditioned response latency decreases.

Figure 3–1 depicts the course of learning in a typical Pavlovian

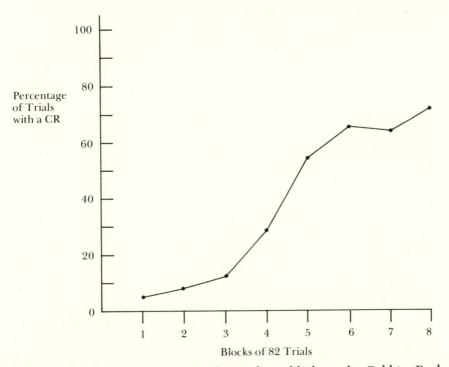

Figure 3–1. Development of Conditioned Eyeblink in the Rabbit. *Each point represents the proportion of trials out of 82 in which an eye-blink occurred to the CS. Very little responding occurred in the first three blocks. In the fourth block, the rabbit responded in 28 percent of the trials. By the sixth block, responding occurred in 65 percent of the trials. (After Schneiderman, Fuentes, & Gormezano, 1962.)*

conditioning experiment. The subjects were rabbits and the US was a puff of air delivered to the cornea. Air puffs produce eye blinks and the conditioned response measured was an eyeblink following the CS. Plotted in Figure 3–1 is the proportion of trials in each session in which a conditioned eyeblink occurred. The figure indicates that the likelihood of conditioned responses increased gradually over the course of training until a leveling off point, or asymptote was reached. If, after the conditioned response was occurring reliably, the CS were repeatedly presented without the US, the conditioned response would gradually disappear. This elimination of Pavlovian CRs is known as *extinction*. Thus, repeated pairing of CS and US produces conditioning, after which presentation of the CS alone produces extinction.

Second-Order Conditioning

Significantly, once Pavlovian conditioning has occurred through CS–US pairings, the CS can be used as a US to produce further conditioning. Suppose we pair a tone with shock repeatedly, until the tone reliably produces conditioned fear responses. Now, we start pairing a light with the tone. Although the light is never itself paired with shock, as a result of pairings with the tone, it comes to produce conditioned fear responses. This phenomenon is known as *second-order conditioning*, because the US is a stimulus which is itself a CS in association with another stimulus. The fact that opening kick-offs in football games and traffic tickets may function as USs reflects the possibility that they were CSs at one time in the individual's past experience. For example, the loud roar of a crowd may be a US producing a UR of arousal. Opening kick-offs, having been paired with roaring crowds, may be first-order CSs. And the national anthem, having been paired with opening kick-offs, may be a second-order CS. The fact that second-order conditioning can occur further extends the potential scope of Pavlovian conditioning processes as an influence on our lives.[1]

Faced with these clear-cut, reliable, pervasive demonstrations of Pavlovian conditioning, researchers have focused on one major issue: What events are necessary for Pavlovian conditioning to occur?

1. See Rescorla, 1980, for a thorough discussion of second-order conditioning.

What Produces Conditioning?

For many years, researchers thought that for Pavlovian conditioning to occur, all that was required was that CS and US occur repeatedly in close temporal proximity. Thus, if tone presentations were followed a few seconds later by shock presentations, conditioned fear would develop. If, on the other hand, an animal received both tones and shocks in an experiment, but always separated by a period of say five minutes, a fear response to the tone would not develop. This view of conditioning is often referred to as the *contiguity* view. Whatever else may be going on in an experimental setting, as long as (and only if) CSs and USs occur in close temporal contiguity, Pavlovian conditioning will occur.

In the last fifteen years, our understanding of Pavlovian conditioning has undergone a substantial revision that has fundamentally changed our conception of the conditioning process: We now know that conditioning involves more than simple temporal contiguity. Animals seem to evaluate the *information* conveyed by various stimuli, and selectively to associate the most informative stimuli with USs. For conditioning to occur, a potential CS must tell the animal something about the US which it would not otherwise know.

This new understanding of conditioning was initiated in 1967, when Robert Rescorla suggested that contiguity of CS and US, while perhaps necessary for conditioning to occur, was not sufficient. What was necessary was that there be in addition a differential *contingency* between CS and US.[2]

What is the difference between contiguity and contingency? Let us consider a commonplace example. Imagine a person who habitually listens to the forecast of the next day's weather. Sometimes the weather report predicts rain, and the next day, it rains. Sometimes the weather report predicts warmth and sunshine and the next day it is warm and sunny. There are, therefore, numerous instances in which the forecast is paired with the actual weather, that is, the forecast is accurate. One might expect that the forecast would influence this person's behavior. We can describe such a situation formally, using the mathematical language of probability theory, in this way:

1. the probability that it will rain given that the forecast is rain is 1.0, that is, every time the forecast is rain, it will rain.

2. Rescorla, 1967.

2. the probability that it will not rain given that the forecast is no rain is 1.0, that is, every time the forecast is no rain, it will not rain.

3. the probability that it will rain given that the forecast is no rain is 0.0.

4. the probability that it will not rain given that the forecast is rain is 0.0.

In describing the relation between weather forecasts and the weather, we would say that a differential contingency existed between forecast and weather such that the forecast provided *information* about the weather. If weather forecasting were this good, one could choose the next day's clothing each night with complete assurance that it would be appropriate for the next day's weather.

But let us be more realistic. Suppose that it rained every time the weather forecast said it would, but that it also rained about once in every ten times that the forecast said it would not. To describe this situation formally, statements (2) and (3) above must be modified. Now, the chances that it won't rain if the forecast is for no rain are 0.9 (nine chances in ten), while the chances that it will rain if the forecast is for no rain are 0.1 (one in ten). In this case, the weather reports are no longer perfect. However, they are still quite helpful and it is still sensible to pay attention to them.

But now consider still different conditions. Suppose that, no matter what, it rains about one day in five, and that rain is no more likely when the weather report calls for it than when it does not. Whether it rains and whether the forecast predicts rain are independent of each other.

If this were the state of meterology, it would make no sense to listen to weather forecasts. Notice, though, that there will still be occasions in which the forecast of rain is paired with the outcome rain. Thus, this last situation represents a case in which contiguity continues to exist between CS and US but a *differential contingency* between CS and US is absent.

Let us return now to the Pavlovian conditioning experiment. Imagine a standard procedure in which a tone is paired with shock. We would describe such a procedure as follows:

5. the probability of shock given that a tone has sounded is 1.0.
6. the probability of shock given that no tone has sounded is 0.0.

If we added some extra tones so that only half the tones were followed by shock, we would have to modify statement (5) to indicate that the chances of shock given that a tone has sounded are only 50–50. However, the chances of a shock in the absence of a tone would remain 0.0. Thus these conditions still represent a case in which a differential contingency between CS and US exists. The tone is not as informative as it was before (there are frequent false alarms), but it still provides valuable information: Shock will *never* come unless a tone has come first.

But now suppose we added some extra shocks as well—shocks that occurred in the absence of the CS. Indeed suppose we added enough shocks so that shock was just as likely to come in the absence of the tone as in its presence. As in the case of the weather report, in this case the tone would provide no useful information about the shock. Tone and shock would continue to be paired as they were at the start of the experiment, that is, they would sometimes be contiguous. However, the extra tones and extra shocks would eliminate the differential contingency between tone and shock that was present at the start of the experiment.

What Rescorla proposed was that if a subject were exposed to this last procedure, in which tones and shocks were occasionally paired, but each also occurred without the other, conditioning would not occur, despite the presence of CS–US pairings. To confirm this he exposed dogs to a variety of Pavlovian fear conditioning procedures. One group of dogs (A) received standard CS–US pairings. A second group (B) received the same number of CSs and USs, but they were neither paired nor unpaired; they were independent. That is, the occurrence of the CS provided no information about the occurrence of the US, though pairings occasionally occurred by chance. Here, the contingency view would predict no conditioning to the CS. A third group (C) also received independent presentations of CS and US with one important exception: If the US was scheduled to be delivered more than 30 seconds after the last CS, it was automatically cancelled. Thus, while the number of accidental CS–US pairings for these last two groups would be the same, the groups would differ in that for the last group, the chances of shock in the presence of the tone would be greater than the chances of shock in its absence, since some shocks scheduled in the absence of the tone would not actually be delivered. Thus, the contingency view would predict conditioned

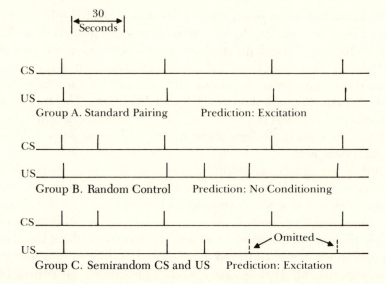

Figure 3–2. Diagram of Procedures Used to Test the Contingency Theory of Conditioning. *Group A receives only pairings of CS and US. The expectation is that this "standard" pairing procedure will produce excitatory conditioning. Groups B and C receive the same number of CS–US pairings. They differ only in that, for Group C, USs scheduled to come more than 30 seconds after the last CS are omitted (broken lines). According to contiguity theory, the groups should not differ. However, according to contingency theory, the CS should be informative for Group C and not for Group B so that only Group C should show excitatory conditioning.*

fear in this last group. These three procedures and the expected results are depicted in Figure 3–2.

The results of the experiment confirmed Rescorla's analysis. The tone CS produced conditioned fear responses for groups A and C, but not for group B. Thus, it is clear that in Pavlovian conditioning experiments, the subject is sensitive to the degree to which one stimulus provides *information* about the other.

Overshadowing and Blocking

The importance of the informativeness of stimuli to conditioning is revealed in other ways as well. Suppose an animal is exposed to a procedure in which two stimuli, for example, a light and a tone, precede shock. What will the animal learn about the two stimuli? The answer is that it depends on the stimuli. As Pavlov himself discovered, if the light is very dim, and the tone is very loud, the tone will completely *overshadow* the light. The animal will come to make conditioned responses to the tone, but respond to the light as if it had never been paired with shock.[3] This is true even though if the tone were absent, the animal would quickly come to make conditioned responses to the light. On the other hand, if the two CSs are equally noticeable, or salient, conditioning will occur to both of them.

It has recently been shown that overshadowing can also occur as a result of an animal's previous experience with the stimuli in the experiment. This kind of overshadowing, known as *blocking*, highlights the importance of informativeness to conditioning.[4] The basic experiment illustrating blocking involved the following procedures, depicted in Figure 3–3A. Rats were exposed to 16 trials in which a tone was followed by shock. Then, they received 8 trials in which a compound stimulus of the tone together with a light were followed by shock. Finally, they were given a presentation of the light alone to see whether it produced any conditioned responses. What might we expect the result of such an experiment to be? The tone alone provides information that shock is coming, and the rats presumably learn this in the first 16 trials. Then light and tone together are followed by shock. What does the light tell the animal? As far as one can tell, everything to be known in this situation can be learned from the tone. The light is a redundant, noninformative addition to the situation. Thus, despite pairing of light and shock, from the perspective of informativeness, we would predict that the light will not produce conditioned responses. And it doesn't. That this effect is due to the experience the rats have had with the tone alone is clear from another procedure (Figure 3–3B). If light and tone are presented as a compound from the beginning, and then light is tested by itself, it produces strong conditioned responses.

Many variants on this basic procedure have now been performed, and they reliably yield results consistent with the importance of information. Suppose rats receive 16 trials of tone-shock followed by 8 trials where light and tone are given together (Figure 3–3C). On these

3. Overshadowing was initially reported by Pavlov (1927). For more recent discussions, see Kamin (1969) and Mackintosh (1975).
    4. Kamin, 1969.

54 PAVLOVIAN CONDITIONING

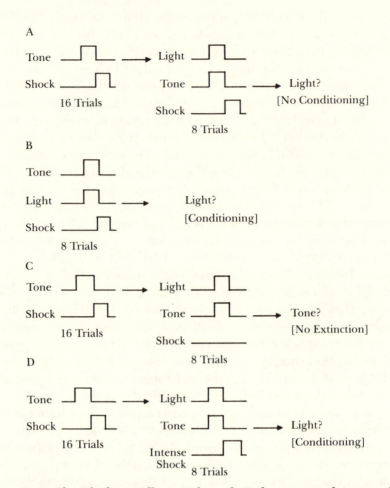

Figure 3–3. The Blocking Effect. *A through D depict procedures in which the redundancy of the light as a CS is varied. In A, the light is redundant (the animal has already learned all there is to be learned from the tone), and no conditioning occurs. In B,C, and D the light is not redundant, and it has measurable effects on the animal's behavior. In B, since the animal has not learned anything yet, either about the tone or the light, neither stimulus blocks the other. In D, since the shock has been made more intense when the light was introduced, the light is not redundant; it signals this increased intensity. In C, the appearance of the light is coupled with the absence of shock. The animal associates the light with the absence of shock so that the tone is protected from extinction.*

last 8 trials, however, there is no shock. Is the light still redundant? In this case, because the light is telling the animal that shock is not coming, the light is not redundant. On the contrary, the light becomes an extinction stimulus. After 8 of these trials, the tone is again presented alone. Although 8 extinction trials would usually be sufficient to reduce substantially the amount of conditioned responding obtained, one discovers that on this procedure, the tone has undergone virtually no extinction. It is the light that has been associated with no shock while the tone has been blocked or protected from extinction. Consider what this phenomenon requires the animal to do. The animal first notices the light, a new stimulus. Then the animal fails to receive a shock, a new event. If there had been no new stimulus, extinction to the tone would have begun. Instead, the animal seems to associate the change in the US with the change in the CS.

In a similar experiment (Figure 6–3D) tone-shock pairings were followed by tone plus light-shock pairings. With the compound, however, the shock was more intense. When the light was tested alone, a substantial amount of conditioning was revealed. Here again, the introduction of the light was correlated with an important change in the US, an increase in the intensity of the shock. As a result, the light was not a redundant stimulus. Hence, these results are consistent with the concepts of informativeness and redundancy.

The Adaptive Nature of Pavlovian Conditioning

In discussing what conditions produce conditioning, we reached the conclusion that conditioning depends upon the existence of a relation between CS and US whereby the CS provides information about the imminent occurrence of the US. The question before us now is what does the organism *do* with that information? How does the capacity for conditioning give organisms that possess it an adaptive advantage over organisms that do not? That is, how does Pavlovian conditioning improve an organism's chances for survival? To answer these questions, we must focus on the nature of conditioned responses.

Pavlov's view of the conditioning process was that the CS becomes a literal substitute for the US. Whatever responses the US triggers are also triggered by the CS once conditioning has occurred. Thus, if food triggers salivation, licking of the lips, and general agitation, an effective CS comes to trigger salivation, licking of the lips and general agitation. If a puff of air triggers tensing of facial muscles and an eyeblink, a CS will trigger tensing of facial muscles and an eyeblink. This account of conditioning is typically referred to as the *stimulus substitution* view. The value of conditioned responses like these for an organism's survival may often be that anticipatory responses prepare the organism for the US and allow the organism to cope more effectively with it when it occurs.

There is now, however, substantial evidence against the view that CRs invariably mimic URs. While they sometimes mimic URs, they are sometimes unrelated to URs and sometimes even the direct opposite of URs. What all CRs seem to have in common is that they are adaptive—they enhance the animal's chances for survival in its natural environment.

An example of the adaptiveness of the CR comes from studies where electric shock is a US. We have been describing the UR produced by electric shock as fear. In fact, shock produces a variety of skeletal and autonomic responses which can be separately measured. The most dramatic UR to shock seems to be general mobilization of the sympathetic nervous system: Heart rate and blood pressure increase when shock is presented. What would be the adaptive value of an anticipatory increase in heart rate to a CS for shock? Such a CR would seem to be maladaptive. It would serve to increase the strain on a cardiovascular system which is already being strained by the shock. A much more adaptive CR would be a *decrease* in heart rate, in direct opposition to the unconditioned response. Such a CR would indicate the ability of the body to anticipate cardiovascular strain and compensate for it in advance. It turns out that with extended training, cardiac *deceleration* is the most common result of Pavlovian fear conditioning experiments. In the well-trained animal, the CS decreases heart rate and the US increases heart rate.[5]

Consider another particularly dramatic example of the adaptiveness of the CR. Rats were given injections of insulin every other day. The effect of insulin is to reduce the amount of glucose in the blood, to produce hypoglycemia. Hypoglycemia is a very dangerous condition which can sometimes put organisms into a severe state of shock. The diabetic coma results from hypoglycemia. Now the question is this: If the injection procedure itself becomes a CS, and insulin is a US, and hypoglycemia is the UR, what will the CR be? Nothing could be less

5. See Obrist, Sutterer and Howard, 1972.

adaptive than a CR which was the same as the UR. When rats were injected with salt water to test for the CR produced by the injection itself, it turned out that the injection produced an *increase* in the level of blood sugar, not a decrease. The conditioning process worked to compensate for the potentially lethal effects of the US.[6]

In recent years, evidence has emerged to suggest that in general, when pharmacological agents are used as USs, the conditioned response to the injection itself is the opposite of the response to the drug. If the US is glucose, which increases blood sugar, the CR to the injection is a decrease in blood sugar.[7] If the US is morphine, which reduces pain sensitivity, the CR to the injection is heightened pain sensitivity.[8] Indeed, it has recently been suggested that the general phenomenon of *drug tolerance* (with repeated administration of some drugs, larger and larger doses must be used to produce the same effect) is the result of CRs to the injection which are opposite in direction to URs to the drug. Before conditioning occurs, morphine only has to dull ordinary pain sensitivity. After repeated injections of morphine, the drug must overcome a supersenstivity to pain that has been conditioned to the injection. Thus smaller doses can be successful early in treatment but not late in treatment.[9] Moreover, there is now good evidence that tolerance to a drug can be conditioned not just to the injection procedure, but to external, environmental stimuli like lights and sounds as well.[10]

Fear and Anxiety

There is another respect in which Pavlovian conditioning is adaptive. In the case of aversive or fear-provoking stimuli a Pavlovian CS gives organisms a signal that something unpleasant is coming. The organism shows fear to the signal. But in the absence of the signal, the organism can be relaxed and free from fear: The absence of the signal is itself a signal for safety.

In the literature of psychopathology, a distinction has long been maintained between fear and anxiety. Fear is said to be objective; it

6. Siegel, 1972.
7. Deutsch, 1974.
8. Siegel, 1975.
9. Siegel, 1977.
10. Hinson, Krank and Siegel, 1978.

is focused on particular objects or situations. It is usually "rational." Anxiety, on the other hand, is subjective; it is unfocused or diffuse. It is difficult or impossible to specify the source of the anxiety, and thus, difficult or impossible to prevent it from occurring. Anxiety, rather than fear, is thought to be the main component of many types of psychopathology. People occasionally find themselves emotionally paralyzed without being able to identify the source of the paralysis. This leaves them withdrawn, unable to act and miserable.

There is much to be said about fear from the perspective of Pavlovian conditioning. Procedures using shocks as USs and tones or lights as CSs reliably produce fear in reaction to the light or tone. Is there also something to be said about anxiety from a Pavlovian point of view? In the last few years, research in Pavlovian conditioning has produced some important insights into the nature and origins of anxiety. To discuss these insights, it is best to begin by providing an example.

Suppose a rat has been pressing a lever for food. Lever pressing occurs at a high and steady rate. Now, a tone is occasionally sounded, and followed by a painful electric shock. These tone-shock pairings produce Pavlovian conditioned fear, and the fear is indicated by a change in the rate at which the rat presses the lever. During the tone, lever pressing is substantially, sometimes entirely, suppressed. Notice that lever pressing has nothing to do with the shock, and that the failure to press the lever costs the (hungry) animal food. Despite this, suppression of lever pressing occurs reliably. This phenomenon is called conditioned suppression or conditioned emotional response (CER).[11]

From what we know about Pavlovian conditioning, what should one expect to happen if instead of being paired, tone and shock occur independently of each other? The occurrence of tone would then provide no information about the occurrence of shock. Since we know that Pavlovian conditioning depends upon an informative relation between CS and US, we would expect that this procedure would not produce conditioning. But what does that mean with respect to lever pressing? Does it mean that lever pressing will continue at the same steady rate as before the shock was introduced?

Indeed, such a procedure does not produce conditioned fear. Rats behave no differently in the presence of the tone than in its

11. Estes and Skinner, 1941.

absence. What they do is suppress lever pressing at all times. Again, although lever pressing has nothing to do with shock, and although failure to press costs the rats food, they stop pressing the lever altogether. In addition, the rats do not simply stop pressing the lever, they also huddle in a corner of the chamber, frozen with terror. Even more dramatic is the fact that when these rats are examined after the experiment, stomach dissection reveals a substantial number of ulcers—ulcers not produced by the shock itself (since animals exposed to the tone-shock pairings fail to develop ulcers) but produced by the *unpredictability* of the shock.[12]

In the situation in which tone is paired with shock, the animal becomes afraid of the tone, but when the tone is gone, the animal is safe. It can relax. The tone provides valuable information, and when it is absent, the source of the animal's fear is absent. The fear is objective and while it is certainly debilitating, it ends when the objective stimulus ends. On the other hand, in the situation in which shock is unpredictable, there is no stimulus which might prepare the animal for the shock. Shock may come at any time, without warning. Thus, the animal is afraid all the time. It is afraid of the situation in which both food and shock are occurring. The result is akin to what clinicians call anxiety: an emotional state which is generally and profounding debilitating and which completely suppresses effective action. It may be that exposure to unpredictable aversive events is what produces anxiety—in humans as well as rats.

Compare two imaginary college courses, both of which include frequent quizzes during the semester. In one course, the quizzes are always announced the class before. In the second class, quizzes are never announced. A student in the first course might be afraid during each interval between the announcement of a quiz and its occurrence. But on all other occasions, the student would be relaxed. In contrast, a student in the second course might be afraid all the time.

Or imagine a child in a doctor's office. The doctor's style with children is honesty. When something is going to hurt, the doctor says so; when there is no likelihood of pain, the doctor also says so. We would expect the behavior which results to bear an interesting resemblance to the behavior of rats that receive tone-shock pairings. Children should be deathly afraid when the doctor warns them about impending pain and otherwise, relaxed and cooperative. Now imagine

12. Seligman, 1968, 1969, 1975 (Chapter 6).

a different doctor. This one, in order to avoid having to deal with wrought-up children, always tells patients that procedures will involve no pain. Then, before they can resist, the doctor catches them by surprise with the injection or whatever else must be done. At first, this second doctor will have less trouble than the first. Ultimately, however, the doctor's patients will become generally frightened and resistent to treatment of any kind. While there are no danger signals to produce crying and tensing, there are also no *safety signals* to produce relaxation.

We have come therefore to another view of the phenomena of Pavlovian conditioning. If stimuli predict significant future events, their absence predicts the absence of these important events. And such stimuli are important both because of what they predict, and because of what their absence predicts. Pavlovian conditioning is important not only because CSs signal USs and produce adaptive conditioned responses, but because the absence of these CSs provides important information which allows relaxation. Conditioned fear implies conditioned relaxation. Both are probably critical to the emotional well-being of organisms.

One final point should be made about the phenomena of conditioned fear and anxiety as they are reflected in the lever pressing of rats. In these situations, Pavlovian conditioning (or its absence) affects not just reflexive responses like salivation and heart rate, but intelligent, voluntary, goal-directed responses—the stuff of which most human action is composed. The conditioned emotional response is an important example of how stimuli can have important effects on ongoing, goal-directed, operant behavior. But this is just one example among many. The role of stimuli in influencing the occurrence of operant responses is pervasive. The role played by Pavlovian conditioning in influencing operant responses is also pervasive. We will examine some of these influences in greater detail in Chapter 6. But before doing so let us examine operant behavior—the subject of the next two chapters.

Chapter 4

Operant Behavior

The lecturer looks nervously about the room as she speaks. Her gaze rests for a moment on a student who responds with a comprehending, attentive nod. On her next sweep of the room, her eyes find this student more quickly. Again, there is comprehending nod. By the end of the lecture, the lecturer spends most of her time staring at the attentive student.

Until his last speeding ticket, he typically drove at 70 miles per hour on the highway. Now, he never exceeds 55.

Your history course is uninformative and uninteresting; so you drop it.

The radio weather report indicates a hot, humid day; so you stay in your air-conditioned house.

THESE examples have a number of things in common. First, they are all mundane. We can recognize these events, or events very much like them, as daily occurrences in all of our lives. Second, they are examples of intelligent action of a particular sort. In each case, there is a relation between actions and subsequent environmental events. In the first two examples actions *produce* certain environmental events: A glance in the direction of a particular student produces an attentive nod, and speeding produces traffic tickets. In the third example, the action eliminates an environmental event (the history course) that is already present. In the last example, the action avoids an event (heat and humidity). A central thesis of the study of behavior theory is that most human action can be profitably analyzed and understood in terms of effects like these on the environment. More specifically, the claim of behavior theory is that the likelihood of occurrence of actions like the ones in the examples is controlled by their past consequences. By studying the effects past consequences of actions have on their future occurrence, one can develop a set of powerful principles capable of predicting and controlling most human behavior. This thesis is really a restatement of Thorndike's law of effect (see Chapter 2, pp. 24–27): Voluntary behavior that produces positive consequences continues to occur, while voluntary behavior that produces negative consequences does not.

Each of the four examples has the same two key ingredients. First, there is some action, some response. Staring at a student, driving seventy miles an hour, dropping a course, and staying in air conditioning are all responses. Second, in each example, the response has some significant consequence. Some consequences, like attentive nods or cool, dehumidified air, are positive or pleasurable. Others, like speeding tickets, are negative. We call the first class of events *rewards* or *positive reinforcers;* we call the second class *punishers* or *negative reinforcers.* The study of operant behavior is the study of how behavior is affected by the occurrence of positive or negative reinforcers. It is the study of the relation between responses and consequences—of how these consequences influence the future occurrence of the response.

Types of Response-Outcome Relations

While the examples that began the chapter have much in common, they were chosen because each one represents an instance of a different class of response-outcome relation. The different types of response-outcome relation have different effects on behavior.

In the first example, the consequence of the response of looking at a particular student is an attentive nod. This consequence is a positive one, and the response produces it. This response-outcome relation typifies a class of relations known as *positive reinforcement.* The effect of a relation like this is that the future likelihood of the response is increased. Examples of this type of relation are everywhere: the salesman who earns commissions for sales, the child who gets to go to the movies for doing homework, the homemaker who receives lavish praise for a good meal, and so on.

In the second example, the consequence of the response of speeding is a traffic ticket. This consequence is a negative one, and the response produces it. This type of response-outcome relation is known as *punishment.* The effect of a relation like this is that the future likelihood of the response is decreased. As with positive reinforcement, examples of punishment are so commonplace in the natural environment that they hardly need mentioning: The child is sent to its room for misbehaving; the college student fails a course for not turning in required work; the businessman is fined for cheating on his taxes.

In the third example, the consequence of the response of dropping the course is that the student no longer has to sit through tedious lectures. The tedious lectures are negative or aversive, and the response eliminates them. This type of response-outcome relation is known as *escape*. An escape relation results in an increase in the future likelihood of the escape response. Thus, we escape heat and humidity by going into air-conditioned buildings, we escape bad television shows by changing channels or turning off the set, and we escape unpleasant bosses by quitting our jobs.

In the final example, the consequence of the response of staying in the house is that you avoid having to suffer heat and humidity. The heat and humidity are aversive, and your response prevents them from impinging on you. This type of response-outcome relation is known as *avoidance*. An avoidance relation, like an escape relation, also results in an increase in the future likelihood of the response. We avoid bad television shows by not turning on the set, we avoid unpleasant bosses by not taking jobs under them, and we avoid boring courses by not signing up for them.

However, these various examples can each be construed as involving more than one of these four basic response-outcome relations. Speeding is punished, with a fine. Refraining from speeding is reinforced—as an avoidance response. Staring at the attentive student is reinforced, by a nod. Failing to stare at the student is punished, by the vacant stares of other students. Dropping bad history courses is reinforced—an escape response. Signing up for these courses is punished. It is generally true that a given situation can be construed in different ways, as including one or another of these basic relations. The relations are not, indeed, so easily distinguished from one another. Separating them as we have is a theoretical move, designed to help us organize the effects various response-outcome relations have on subsequent responses. The study of operant behavior is in effect the study of how these four types of relations affect the future actions of organisms.

Some Methodological Issues

That the phenomena of reinforcement, punishment, escape and avoidance seem so pervasive in human life offers both promise and problems to behavior theory. Since behavior theory seeks a relatively complete explanation of human behavior, it is promising that the phenomena it studies are so commonplace in human experience. If they were not, behavior theorists would either have to broaden the scope of their inquiry substantially or abandon their goal of a complete explanation. The pervasiveness of these phenomena makes it at least plausible that by understanding how reward, punishment, escape and avoidance work, we can understand a lot about what makes people act as they do.

But this very pervasiveness raises a problem. How does one study these phenomena? Which of the myriad possible examples of reward and punishment does one analyze? How does one know that by analyzing one example, one can generalize to all the others? If reinforcement, punishment, escape and avoidance affect the entire, vast range of voluntary activities, which of these activities should be considered typical of them all? In establishing experimental situations, care must be taken to ensure that the results one gets from those situations will be representative of all situations involving voluntary behavior and its consequences. The behavior theorist's effort to solve this methodological problem involves making decisions about what is to count as behavior, and decisions about what criteria to use in setting up representative experimental settings. We will discuss each of these issues in turn.

What Is Operant Behavior?

If human behavior is lawful, there must be true generalizations about behavior. For there to be such generalizations, behavior must fall into categories such that many different particular instances of behavior belong to the same category. If each instance of behavior is unique, we cannot make generalizations about it. The generalization that "speeding is punished" depends upon the legitimacy of treating different instances of speeding as members of the same class. But is that legitimate? The muscle movements involved in speeding will differ, depending upon what kind of car you drive, how your body is positioned relative to the gas pedal, what the speed limit is, and who you are. What is the justification for ignoring all these differences between individual instances of speeding, and treating them as members of the same class? Stated more generally, how are we to decide what counts as a unit of operant behavior?

To begin with, if we want behavior theory to be an empirical science, we must be able to classify instances of operant behavior on the basis of observation. But on the basis of observation, any item of behavior may be described in numerous ways. Consider an example. We observe a child walking down a hallway, and may so describe its behavior. We may also describe the child as walking to the kitchen, or walking into the house, or leaving footprints on the carpet. Descriptions like these are of two kinds: Either the movement of the child is classified as a certain kind of movement (walking, as distinct from running), and related to objects in the immediate environment (kitchen, door, hallway); or the movement of the child is classified on the basis of its effect (footprints on the carpet). Typically, in studies of operant behavior, individual behaviors are classified on the basis of their effects. Thus, when a rat presses a lever, the individual muscle movements involved are irrelevant. What unites all lever presses is their common effect on the environment—depressing a lever and closing a switch. Similarly, the pigeon's key pecks are united by their environmental effect—also a switch closure. Since the effect of the lever press and the key peck are the same, they in turn can be treated as essentially interchangeable examples of operant behavior. That rats usually close switches with their paws, and pigeons with their beaks, is of little consequence.

When we characterize behaviors in these ways, it is clear that they are events involving the whole organism: The organism moves relative to an environment; the organism produces certain effects in the environment. Of course, while engaging in behavior, parts of the organism's body move, and it will often be the case that the behavior is what it is because of the characteristic movements of parts of the body. It is clear, however, that just knowing how an organism's body parts are moving will not tell us all we want to know about its behavior. The fact that two behaviors consist of the same bodily movements is neither sufficient nor necessary for classifying the two behaviors together. It is not sufficient because the same bodily movements may be involved in behaviors we will want to treat as belonging to different classes. For example we will want to treat the slap you deliver to a friend's face when you are insulted as belonging to a different class from the slap you deliver when you spot a tarantula on his cheek, even though the two slaps are comprised of the same movements. It is not necessary, because the same behavior, for example, getting back at your friend, for insulting you may be performed with different bodily movements—a slap in the face or a kick in the shins. What unites all examples of operant behavior is that they are activities of the whole organism that have effects on the environment; and the central thesis of behavior theory is that it is these environmental effects that control the occurrence of the activities.

Which Operant Behaviors Should Be Studied?

Now that we know what will count as behavior, we still have the problem of deciding which of the myriad examples of operant behavior we should use for detailed investigation. What characteristics do we want our typical experimental settings to possess? To answer this question we must consider again the goals of behavior theory. Behavior theory is seeking *general* laws of behavior. Can we obtain such general laws by studying pigeons pecking at lit keys? On the face of it, the answer seems to be no. We may find out about pecking, but people don't peck. Even rats don't peck. Why should we believe that the laws of pecking will be the laws of all operant behavior?

The behavior theorist's answer to this question is that while pecking may be an operant that is peculiar to pigeons and other birds, the relation between it and the environmental events that control it is not. Pecking may produce food or prevent its delivery, produce shock or prevent its delivery. If the occurrence of pecking is governed by whether previous pecks have produced or prevented reinforcement or punishment, we say that pecking is under operant control. To the extent that pecking *is* controlled by its consequences, the behavior theorist would argue that it is representative of other behaviors of other organisms that are under operant control. Thus, one might just as well study hopping on a foot treadle, turning in circles, or strutting, as operants. One might study the delivery of food, water, electric shocks or blasts of hot air as consequences. And one might study pigeons, rats, monkeys or people as subjects. Which particular behavior-outcome pair, and which species one chooses are arbitrary, so long as it is true that the behavior in the pair is controlled by the consequence. Thus, what is critical to any behavior-outcome pair is that it preserves the operant relation of control over behavior by outcome.

The need to be sure that the behavior one is studying is controlled by its consequences before it can be judged as an example of operant behavior dictates certain methodological principles that make some pairs better suited for studying than others. Suppose, for example, we decided to reinforce salivation in dogs with food. The consequence of salivation (food) might well have some control over its occurrence. Nevertheless, salivation would be a poor choice of behavior to study. This is because, as we saw in Chapters 2 and 3, salivation is *also* controlled by Pavlovian factors. Thus, we would have a hard time distinguishing the Pavlovian influence from the operant influence. In general, we try to choose behavior-outcome pairs to study that are not susceptible to these Pavlovian influences.

And Pavlovian influence is just one kind of non-operant influence on behavior—one we know something about. There might well be other non-operant influences that we do not know much about, and these must also be prevented from intruding into our experimental settings. To do this, we choose behavior-outcome pairs which we are reasonably sure the animal has not had experience with prior to our experiment. Indeed, we choose behaviors that occur sufficiently *infrequently* prior to our experiments that it is unlikely that they have been influenced by anything before we impose our contingencies. If we choose our behavior-outcome pairs with these methodological principles in mind, we can be confident that when we introduce the operant relation between behavior and outcome, the changes in behavior we observe are due to its relation to the outcome. We can be confident of this because any relation at all between the behavior and the outcome is just a contrivance of the experimental design.

Choosing behavior-outcome pairs in this way is important for two reasons. First, if there is no non-operant influence on the particular response-outcome pair we study, we can have some confidence that what we discover about this pair will be true of all operant, response-outcome pairs. The one we study is just one representative example out of many we might have chosen. Second, it is the assumption of behavior theory that in general, human behavior has this operant relation to its outcomes. We stay in the house to avoid heat and humidity. But we could also move to a different climate, or go to an air-conditioned movie, or countless other things. A parent takes a child to a movie for doing her homework. The parent could also give the child a quarter, or an ice-cream sundae. Speeding is punished with a ticket. It could also be punished by a lecture from a policeman, a complaint from a passenger, or an accident. For behavior theory, the hallmark of human operant behavior is that behavior and outcome, or means and ends, bear no intrinsic relation to each other. The relation they have is the result of contingencies between them established by characteristics of the environment that could, in principle, be different.

With this view that as long as relations between behaviors and outcomes are operant, what we find with one behavior and outcome will be true of all behavior-outcome pairs, the methods of behavior theory have been created to insure that pure operant control occurs. It is this presumption about the general nature of the operant-outcome relation in the environment that justifies using the intensive study of just a few behavior-outcome pairs to produce generalizations about all such pairs. We will critically evaluate this presupposition later in the book. For now, our task is to describe the research program to which it has led.

Fundamental Research Issues

The study of operant behavior is the study of how contingencies between behavior and positive or negative reinforcement influence the future occurrence of the behavior. This general research concern can be divided into two major categories. First, researchers are concerned with identifying the role of reinforcement in the acquisition of new responses in learning. Second, they are concerned with how reinforcement influences the occurrence of responses after they have been very well learned—the issue emphasized in the examples which began the chapter. Little learning of new responses occurred in these examples. Instead, the future likelihood of already learned behavior was modified by its consequences. In a sense, of course, this also represents learning—learning when to do certain things and when to refrain from doing them. Thus, the distinction we are making between the acquisition of new responses and the conditions which influence the occurrence of old ones is not a clear and sharp one. Nevertheless, it is a distinction which proves useful in organizing the research on operant behavior.

A second important distinction may be made within the domain of research on acquisition of new responses. One might ask: How does reinforcement contribute to response acquisition? Alternatively, one might ask how reinforcement *can* contribute to response acquisition. The first question assumes that reinforcement is important and seeks the laws that describe its effect on learning. The second is an engineering question. It acknowledges that reinforcement need not be so important for learning, as things stand, but seeks to discover how it may be used to make learning more effective, more rapid, and more efficient (see Chapter 8 for a discussion of attempts at behavioral engineering). This distinction is a very important one. In attempting to discover the way in which reinforcement affects learning, one is assuming that some necessary relation between learning and reinforcement processes is a fundamental feature of organisms. In contrast, when one is evaluating how reinforcement *can* affect learning, one is only looking for effective procedures—procedures which may bear no relation to the way learning occurs ordinarily. Thus, the first orientation is one that leads investigators to expect to find laws of human nature; the second is not.

One can see this distinction clearly in other domains. The human body has a variety of endogenous defenses against invading disease-producing organisms. One might be interested in discovering the laws that govern the workings of these defenses. However, if one is a pharmacologist whose job is to synthesize disease-fighting drugs, it is not the point to produce drugs that mimic the body's natural defenses. The point is to produce drugs that will successfully fight disease, whether or not they do it in the same way the body does. Thus, that a particular drug can eliminate a disease has no necessary implications for how the body ordinarily accomplishes this result. Similarly, that reinforcement can produce learning has no necessary implications that it is responsible for all natural examples of learning.

There is a final distinction to be made which is related to the distinction between studies of how responses are acquired and studies of maintenance of already acquired responses. Reinforcers have at least two distinguishable characteristics, and thus far we have discussed only one of them. Reinforcers have hedonic value: Positive reinforcers are pleasurable and negative reinforcers are aversive. Virtually all research on operant behavior assumes that this hedonic property is the relevant one in determining the outcome of experiments. In addition, reinforcers are informative: They tell an organism whether it is on the right track or not. Consider as an example, a student learning to play the piano. The student plays an exercise and as the playing proceeds, the teacher occasionally comments "good" or "bad." The comment "good" may be a reinforcer; it may give the student pleasure. However, quite apart from its hedonic character, the comment gives the student information. It tells the student that the piece is being played properly.

When one is concerned with response acquisition, either the informative or the hedonic properties of a reinforcer, or both, may contribute to its effect on behavior. When one is concerned with maintenance of already acquired behavior, the informative properties of the reinforcer are probably not very significant.

This distinction between informative and hedonic properties of reinforcers is not often made in research on operant behavior. The reason, in part, is that most research is done with animals in situations in which the hedonic properties of the consequences of responses are clearly relevant. It is hard to imagine why a rat would press a lever or a pigeon peck a key except if the consequence of these responses is pleasurable. In the case of humans, this is less clear. One might want to learn to play the piano or to swing a golf club properly. The reinforcers for these responses might be a well-played piece of music or a well-hit golf shot. The teacher's "good" in this case would be hedonically irrelevant, as would a piece of candy or a quarter. The relevant function of all of these consequences would be the information they provided about progress toward the goal. This distinction between hedonic and informative aspects of reinforcers is one that should be kept in mind as we discuss the experimental study of operant behavior, and especially as we attempt to apply principles of operant behavior outside the laboratory.[1]

Conditioning and Extinction

Consider a rat which is about to be trained to press a lever for food reinforcement. While in its cage, the rat has engaged in a variety of different activities: It has eaten, licked from a water spout, groomed,

1. What makes this distinction between hedonic and informative properties of reinforcers significant is that at present, there exists no general account of what makes something a reinforcer. See Schick (1971) for a discussion of the problem, and Premack (1965) for an attempted, but incomplete solution.

sniffed about the cage, poked its nose through the openings in the cage, reared on its hind legs, and so on. It has never done anything like lever pressing. Then, the rat is placed in the experimental chamber. After an initial fear reaction to being handled, and to being in a novel environment, the rat begins to do the same kinds of things it did in its cage: It sniffs, rears, explores, and grooms. The feeder operates and the rat approaches it hesitantly, picks up the food pellet, and chews it. The feeder operates a few more times until the rat shows no hesitancy in approaching it and in ingesting the food. Now the rat spends most of its time around the feeder—sniffing at it, poking its nose at it, rearing on its hind legs near it and so on. At this point, the experimenter is ready to train the rat to press the lever. No more "free" food is delivered. Instead, food delivery is made dependent upon an appropriate response from the rat. But what is an appropriate response? The experimenter could wait until the rat actually presses the lever, either by accident or in the course of exploring its novel environment. But more typically, one shapes the response by the method of successive approximation (Chapter 2, pp. 34–35). One waits for the rat to move in the direction of the lever, then presents food. This makes movements toward the lever more likely. One now waits until the rat moves even closer to the lever before presenting food. Once this has occurred, one requires the rat actually to contact the lever, and so on.

If we watch the rat carefully during the period of lever-press shaping, we might observe a learning pattern like this: After hovering around the feeder for a while without getting food, the rat leaves the feeder area and explores other parts of the experimental chamber. Eventually it rears right near the lever, and when it comes down, its front paws brush against the lever and depress it. The feeder operates and the rat scurries over to get the food pellet. It returns to the area around the lever, and sniffs around. This time, while sniffing at the lever, the rat's nose inadvertently depresses it. Again the feeder operates. Now the rat returns to the lever and begins exploring it with its paws. Again the lever is depressed and again the feeder operates. At this point, the rat's behavior is extremely inefficient. Most of its activity around the lever—its pawing and sniffing and rearing—does not depress the lever. Occasionally the lever is pressed, however, and the feeder operates. The rat comes to spend all of its time around the lever. It has clearly learned something. But what has it learned?

Careful observation would reveal that the rat has not learned to do anything new and different. It has learned to do the same things it has been doing for months in its cage, but to do them in a particular place. With continued experience, the rat's behavior changes. It learns that rearing is unnecessary to produce food; only landing on the lever is necessary. It learns that sniffing at the corners of the lever is unnecessary to produce food; only depressing the lever with the nose is necessary. The rat seems to identify the single feature shared by each of its different activities with respect to the lever, and that is the downward deflection of the lever. Once this information is acquired, the efficiency of the rat's behavior increases dramatically. The rat may end up lying down with its mouth poised at the feeder, reaching one paw over to the lever to depress it smoothly and economically.

Once could tell a similar story about pigeons learning to peck keys. Adult pigeons do not have to learn to peck. What they have to learn is to peck at a particular place. Early in training, the pigeon's behavior is erratic; it bobs up and down, stretches its neck, pecks around the lit key and so on. Later in training, the pigeon has eliminated virtually all of the unnecessary behavior and it stands by the key, striking it efficiently and accurately again and again. If one plotted the frequency with which the lever press (or key peck) occurred over the course of a series of experimental sessions, one might observe a curve like the one in the left part of Figure 4–1. Over the course of training, the response occurs with increasing frequency until it reaches a leveling off point or asymptote. At this point, training is complete. The organism has acquired a response.

Suppose that after a number of sessions of lever-press training, reinforcement is discontinued. The rat may continue to press the lever as before, but lever presses no longer produce food. The result of such a procedure is depicted in the center of Figure 4–1: The frequency of lever pressing declines precipitously, until the rat stops pressing the lever entirely. This procedure is known as *extinction*. It is through extinction that we can eliminate behavior that has already been acquired and occurs with substantial frequency. If one identifies the reinforcer that has been operative in a situation, and discontinues it, the response will eventually stop occurring.

What exactly does an extinction procedure do to responding? It does not undo conditioning. The rat after session 32 in Figure 4–1 is not the same as it was before session 1. One way to see this is to reintroduce reinforcement for lever pressing. After only a few rein-

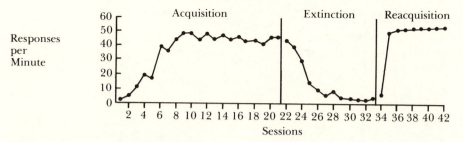

Figure 4–1. Acquisition, Extinction, and Reacquisition of Lever Pressing. *This hypothetical curve depicts the growth in the frequency of lever pressing over the course of a number of experimental sessions, followed by its extinction when reinforcement is discontinued. When reinforcement is reintroduced, lever pressing is reestablished much more rapidly than it was at first.*

forcements, the rat's lever pressing will be just as frequent and efficient as it was at the peak of training. Thus shaping seems to create new units of activity in animals. Extinction keeps these units from occurring—it suppresses them—but it does not destroy them.

On the surface, the extinction procedure can be viewed as a punishment procedure. If we withhold dessert from a child for misbehavior, are we punishing the behavior or extinguishing it? If we withhold food from a rat when it presses the lever, are we punishing the behavior or extinguishing it? The crucial distinction between punishment of this type and extinction is this: In punishment, when we withhold the reinforcer, we do so contingent upon the response we are punishing. If the child does not misbehave, it gets dessert. In contrast, in extinction, we simply discontinue the reinforcer, no matter what the organism does. Food is not withheld *because* the rat is pressing the lever; food is simply withheld.

What Produces Conditioning?

What aspect of the relation between the reinforcer and the response is crucial for conditioning to occur? Historically, as we saw in the case of Pavlovian conditioning, accounts of how reinforcement works have emphasized temporal relations. When a reinforcer is delivered, whatever response has just preceded it will be strengthened or increased in frequency. Thus temporal *continguity* of response and reinforcer has been viewed as the critical characteristic of the operant conditioning process.

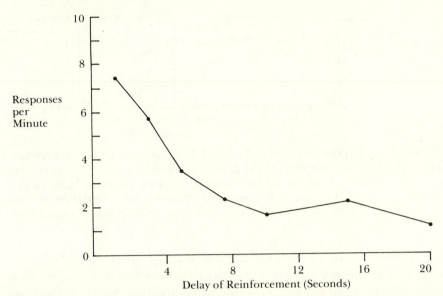

Figure 4–2. Effects of Delay of Reinforcement on the Rate of an Operant Response. *As delay of reinforcement increases, responses per minute maintained by reinforcement decreases. The subjects were rats, and the operant response was a lever press. (After Azzi, Fix, Keller, & Rocha e Silva, 1964, Figure 1.)*

Evidence for the importance of response-reinforcer contiguity comes from experiments in which the delivery of reinforcement is delayed: The response occurs, and only some seconds later, the reinforcer is presented. If one plots the frequency of responses maintained by reinforcement that is delayed, as in Figure 4–2, one finds that the greater the delay of reinforcement is, the lower response rate is.[2]

However, there is evidence that temporal contiguity of response and outcome is not all that is needed for conditioning to occur. In an experiment that is conceptually very similar to the one done by Rescorla on contingency and Pavlovian conditioning (see Chapter 3, p. 51), rats were trained to press a lever for food. The experimenter varied the likelihood that any given lever press would be followed by food. He also varied the likelihood that food would come in the absence of a lever press. He found that although there were frequent occasions in which lever pressing and food delivery were temporally

2. Azzi, Fix, Keller, and Rocha e Silva, 1964.

contiguous, if food was just as likely in the absence of a lever press as it was when a press occurred, the rats did not persist in pressing the lever. Thus, temporal contiguity between response and food is not sufficient to sustain reliable responding.[3] There is further evidence that temporal contiguity of response and outcome is not all that is needed for operant conditioning to occur. In at least some situations, when organisms are exposed to procedures in which important events (like food or electric shock) are presented as independent of their behavior, they learn precisely that—that events are beyond their control. They generalize this learning to new situations, with the result that the development of effective responses in these new situations is retarded—even sometimes prevented altogether. This phenomenon, known as *learned helplessness,* has been demonstrated in a variety of species, including humans. It should be noted that in a learned helplessness procedure, responses do occur, and they are occasionally followed by important events. But again, this temporal contiguity is not sufficient to sustain the responses.[4]

Operant Conditioning and the Process of Induction

The process of operant conditioning we just described has much in common with traditional views about how people acquire knowledge generally. Indeed, the acquisition of an operant has important similarities to a central part of scientific inquiry, the part of scientific inquiry known as *induction.*

Scientific understanding is built upon the discovery of generalizations. But where do the generalizations come from? How are regularities discovered? It is generally agreed that generalizations are the result of empirical investigation. Science involves a form of investigation in which the legitimacy of generalizations and theories is evaluated against their relations to empirical data, or observed facts. Our knowledge of the general is tested against our knowledge of particulars. When we first investigate a domain, we come to know about its particulars, that is, we observe individual phenomena. This observation later becomes the touchstone of our knowledge of the general. But how do we go from observations of the particular to knowledge

3. Hammond, 1980.
4. See Maier, 1970; Maier and Seligman, 1976; Seligman, 1975.

of the general? One way is by a process of induction. But what is induction?

Suppose we observe a pigeon moving about in an enclosed space. At a particular moment, the pigeon approaches a small, brightly illuminated disk (a pecking key), and strikes it with its beak. As soon as the disk is struck, a bit of grain is delivered into the enclosed space, and the pigeon eats the grain. After it eats the grain, the pigeon immediately pecks at the disk again, and more grain is delivered. This process continues, and the pigeon pecks at the disk with increasing frequency as the pecks continue to be followed by the delivery of grain. Let us identify the fact that the pigeon's peck is followed by food, and its increased subsequent frequency, as the central events in this example. To be able to extract something general from the example, we must decide what general classes these events belong to. This decision is not straightforward, for while the pigeon is pecking, it is doing many other things (for example, shuffling its feet, puffing up its chest, turning its head about). While the food is delivered, other things are happening (the device used to deliver the food makes a clicking noise). And while the pigeon's frequency of pecking increases, other things are happening (it is getting more active, its digestive system is working on the previously eaten grain). We could, in short, revise "The pigeon's peck, being followed by food, results in the pigeon's pecking more frequently," to "The pigeon's shuffling, being followed by a clicking noise, is followed by the pigeon's shuffling its feet nearer to the source of the clicking noise."

The point of this example is that any particular event can be grouped with many different classes of events on the basis of countless observable characteristics. This is no less true in physics than it is in psychology. When we say, "Two balls dropped simultaneously from the same place above the ground hit the ground at the same time," we might say instead, "When a red and a yellow ball are dropped to the ground, the yellow one makes more noise on impact." Both of these statements, and both of the statements about the pigeon's behavior, as well as countless others, might be consistent with the particular observation we make.

But suppose that we observe pigeons pecking on a variety of occasions, and we observe that events of the class "pecks being followed by food" are always, without exception, followed by events of the class "pigeon's pecking increasing in frequency." From this, we *induce* the generalization that "if a pigeon's key peck is followed by food, the pigeon increases its rate of pecking." Induction is the procedure by which we come to some general claim about classes of events based upon our particular observation of particular members of these classes. We might want to make the classes even more general, and from our observation of pigeons pecking keys for food form the generalization that "if an organism's operant behavior is followed by a reinforcer, the organism increases the rate of that behavior."

Now consider the pigeon. It wanders about the chamber, doing one thing or another when suddenly, food appears. To "understand" this event poses the same problem for the pigeon as it does for the experimenter. How should the event be characterized? How should the animal's behavior be characterized? What are the appropriate classes? The pigeon's "answer" to these questions will determine what it does next to get food. Will it flap its wings and peck, preen and peck, preen and flap and peck? Only the correct generalization will result in the pigeon's making efficient pecks at the key and abandoning its other activities. We saw in our discussion of response shaping that such a process often occurs early in training. An animal will engage in a great deal of activity that includes much that is unnecessary, but happens also to include the crucial ingredient (key peck or lever press). With experience, the unnecessary activity drops out. Does this indicate that the animal is refining its generalizations just as the scientist might? While the process by which the pigeon or rat refines its inductions from the past to the future is surely not conscious, and thus importantly different from the behavior of the scientist, we can see that the two kinds of activities have a great deal in common.

Obviously, inductive inference is fallible, for at least two reasons. First, suppose we observe 100 separate occasions in which (a) pigeons' pecks are followed by food, and (b) the rate of pecking increases in frequency. Moreover, suppose we observe no cases in which (a) is not followed by (b). From this it does not follow that in our very next observation (a) will be followed by (b). Thus, it does not follow that all (a)s are followed by (b)s. Perhaps there was some special factor, unknown to us, which was present in the first 100 cases we observed, and will not be present in the next. Second, induction is fallible because we may identify *a* and *b* as members of the wrong classes. We might, for example, classify the falling balls by their color. The way to minimize both of these sources of fallibility of our inductions is to make observations of many instances in a wide variety of different circumstances. As the circumstances vary, it becomes increasingly unlikely that some crucial factor, unknown to us, is common to all of them, or that we will continue to classify events inappropriately.

Again, the same is true of the pigeon. Even though for 100 days, pecks have produced food, they may not on the 101st. The experimenter may disconnect the feeder. Or perhaps the pigeon has been using the wrong categories. Perhaps it is not just pecks that are required, but pecks preceded by wing flaps. The pigeon may eventually develop the correct categories because when it is using the wrong ones, responses do not always produce food. Thus, what is shaped in operant training is the correct kind of induction.[5]

While both scientists and pigeons may perform inductions, scientists, at least, have other means for making inferences as well. These other kinds of inferences are called *deductions*. Suppose we assert that all occasions of pigeons' key pecks followed by food result in increases in the rate of key pecks. Moreover, we observe that a pigeon's key peck has just been followed by food. From this, we can infer that its rate will increase. Stated more generally, the following deductive inference is valid:

> All A's are followed by B's
> An A is occurring
> Therefore, a B will occur.

These types of inferences are important, for they make apparent the fallibility of inductively-derived generalizations, and exhibit the logic by which such generalizations may be challenged. For if it is observed that an *A* is occurring and then it is observed that a *B* does not occur, the validity of the deductive schema above requires the conclusion that the generalization is false. This feature of scientific inference allows that a single observed counter-instance suffices to invalidate a generalization. The falsity of an empirical generalization may therefore be deduced from observations. In contrast, the truth of an empirical generalization may only be induced. Even if a thousand cases of *A*'s are followed by *B*'s it does not prove, unequivocally, that "all *A*'s are followed by *B*'s." As a result, empirical generalizations are often said

---

5. This account of how scientific inferences should be made is a controversial one. One of its strongest proponents is B.F. Skinner (1950). It is interesting that Skinner's views about conditioning—about how organisms do form generalizations—is matched by his views about science—about how people should form generalizations.

to be falsifiable.[6] If just once, we observe that a pigeon's key pecks have been followed by food, yet not increased in frequency, we know that the generalization that "every time key pecks are followed by food they increase in frequency" is false.

We have sketched this parallel between the process by which an animal may come to produce only those responses necessary for reinforcement and the process by which a scientist may come to state a true generalization not in order to suggest that the two processes are identical. Rather, it is to show that the process of operant conditioning reflects a familiar aspect of human activity.

Punishment

From the point of view of behavior theory, the control of behavior by environmental events is a fact. Behavior theory is not an effort to invent techniques of control so much as an effort to understand and describe behavior control as an existing characteristic of the natural environment. Behavior theorists argue that individuals routinely manipulate the behavior of others using the same techniques (though perhaps unsystematically and inefficiently) that behavior theory has elucidated.

In some aspects of human life this claim can hardly be denied; the use of punishment and the threat of punishment are salient characteristics of everyone's upbringing; they are the main constituents of most legal and penal systems; they are significant components of most educational programs. There is no one whose behavior has not been influenced by anticipated aversive or unpleasant consequences. While one may deny having studied hard in order to get good grades, or having worked hard in order to receive a promotion, one cannot deny having eased off the accelerator as a police car came into view to avoid a traffic ticket, or having cleaned up one's room to avoid a parental lecture. In short, there seems to be an asymmetry in people's willingness to acknowledge the sources of control of their behavior. Control of behavior by aversive consequences is readily acknowledged while control of behavior by positive consequences is not. With punishment such an obvious part of everyone's life, let us examine what behavior theory has to tell us about it.

6. Popper, 1959.

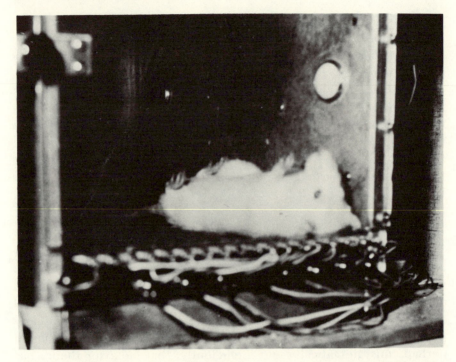

A way to solve the problem of punishment. *This rat's lever-presses produce both food pellets and shock through the grid floor. The rat lies on its back so that its fur insulates it against the shock, and presses the lever with its hind foot to produce food. (Courtesy of Nathan H. Azrin, Nova University)*

Suppose an animal is engaged in some operant response for food, responding at a moderate, steady rate. Suppose that after responding is stable, the procedure is changed so that each response also produces a brief, painful electric shock. Responses are now being punished with shock while at the same time being reinforced with food. The result of this punishment contingency is that rate of responding is substantially suppressed. As the intensity of the punishing stimulus increases, the degree of suppression increases. If very intense shock is used, suppression may often be virtually complete. What other factors influence the effectiveness of punishment, and just how effective is it as a tool of behavior control?

Factors Influencing the Effectiveness of Punishment

We saw earlier (see Figure 4–2) that if reinforcement is delayed, its ability to increase response rate is diminished, in proportion to the amount of delay. Delay reduces the effectiveness of punishment in the same way. As the interval between response and punishment increases, the amount of suppression produced by the punishing stimulus decreases.[7]

If we ask ourselves why it is that an organism responds at all when its responses are punished, we can deduce another factor which is likely to influence the effectiveness of punishment. Organisms respond because responses produce food as well as shock, and because they are food deprived. If an alternative means of obtaining food were provided, the effectiveness of the shock ought to be greatly enhanced. And indeed it is. A number of experiments have shown that punishment suppresses responding much more when an alternative route to reinforcement exists than when it does not. In one such study, human subjects were engaged in a button-pushing task for reinforcement. When there was only one button to push, the subjects pushed the button 500 times in only a few minutes. When each button-push produced a loud, annoying buzz (the punishing stimulus), the rate of button-pushing was moderately suppressed; subjects still pushed the button 500 times, but now in a period of about 18 minutes. Finally, when each button-push produced the buzz, but another button was present on which responses produced reinforcement but no buzz, there was virtually immediate and complete suppression of pushing on the first button.[8]

Punishment in the Natural Environment

There are few aspects of child rearing and education which arouse as much controversy as the use of punishment. For generations, punishment was the major tool of both parent and teacher. In the last few decades, influenced in part by conclusions drawn (sometimes erroneously) from laboratory research, punishment has been losing favor. Some argue against the use of punishment on ethical grounds; others argue that punishment simply does not work. Still others are concerned that it works all too well. Finally, some express concern that it has harmful side effects. We will take up some of these concerns now, and see what the laboratory can tell us about the effectiveness and the drawbacks of punishment as a technique of behavior control.

7. Camp, Raymond and Church, 1967; Church, 1969.
8. Herman and Azrin, 1964.

Does Punishment Work?

In light of all the evidence just discussed, it seems odd that one should ask this question at all. If the experiments we have been discussing show anything at all, surely it must be that punishment works. Yet the question continues to be asked. This is due in part to early research on punishment which seemed to show that while punishment did suppress behavior, its effects were temporary and its effects were hardly more pronounced than the effects of the same aversive stimuli delivered independently of the animal's behavior.[9] This research seemed to suggest that aversive stimuli produced a temporary suppression of operant responses, whether or not they actually depended upon those responses. The effect of punishment, that is, of an explicit relation between responses and aversive stimuli, over and above the effect of the aversive stimuli themselves, seemed negligible. Also, if punishment did actually work, its effect might be temporary. We might be inclined to say that punishment did not work, or at least did not work very well, if it turned out that behavior was suppressed only as long as the punishment contingency remained operative.

Thus, the question, "Does punishment work?" is not as easily answered as it might appear. A more relevant question might be: Does a *dependency* between responses and aversive stimuli result in greater suppression of those responses than occurs when the aversive stimuli are merely presented independently of responses? Years of research which have revealed techniques that increase the effectiveness of punishment make the answer to this question clear. There is no doubt that punishment can suppress responding more effectively than non-contingent presentation of aversive stimuli. Thus we must ask a second question: Under what conditions does punishment work?

Maximizing the Effects of Punishment

The reader may be able to guess from the preceding discussion what some of the operations are that can maximize the effectiveness of punishment. We have already seen that the effectiveness of punishment is a function of the intensity of the punishing stimulus and of the delay between response and punishment. It follows from those experiments that to maximize the effectiveness of punishment:

9. Estes, 1944.

1. The punishing stimulus should be as intense as possible.

2. The delay between response and punishment should be as short as possible.

3. It is also true that punishment should be certain. When responses are only punished occasionally, the effectiveness of the punishment procedure is reduced.[10]

What else can be done to maximize the effectiveness of punishment? Since the behavior to be punished is presumably occurring because it is producing reinforcement, any operation which weakens the relation between response and reinforcement at the same time that punishment is being delivered should enhance the effectiveness of the punishment. A variety of such operations can be identified:

1. Have the delivery of punishment serve as a signal that reinforcement is not available for the punished response. If this is not possible, then

2. Decrease the frequency with which the reinforcer is available as a consequence of the response, or

3. Arrange a dependency between the reinforcer and an alternative response. Establish alternative routes to the goal which are not undesirable. Complete suppression of a response with only mild punishment is possible if an alternative response which produces the same reinforcement is available. If one's child continues to steal pennies in the face of intense punishment, then establishing a set of little jobs for earning pennies may successfully eliminate stealing. Even intense punishment may not be effective at permanently suppressing behavior, so that the punishment contingency can be removed, unless an alternative route to the goal has been established.

This last observation also suggests certain conditions in which punishment is distinctly inappropriate. If one is attempting to build appropriate responses into a person's behavioral repertoire, punishment is not likely to be helpful. For example, if one is teaching arithmetic, punishing errors on arithmetic problems is unlikely to improve performance. If the appropriate responses are not available to the

10. See Azrin, 1956; Azrin, Holz and Hake, 1963.

child, that is, if the child does not possess the skills required for successful arithmetic work, punishment will not put them there.[11]

The ineffectiveness of punishment in building a behavioral repertoire has been discussed on numerous occasions by B.F. Skinner. Skinner argues that punishment makes an essentially negative contribution to the behavioral repertoire. It eliminates behavior which, for one reason or another, is undesirable; it does not substitute a response which provides an acceptable means to the reinforcer. If one's aim in using principles of behavior theory in the long run is to establish reasonably complete and effective behavioral repertoires, punishment does little in the service of this goal. Skinner's proposed alternative is the reinforcement of some other response which is both acceptable and effective. Indeed, as we have seen, such a strategy substantially enhances the effectiveness of punishment in suppressing a target response. But if reinforcement of an alternative response, coupled with extinction of the undesirable response, is an effective way to alter the behavioral repertoire, why bother with punishment at all? The answer is that unlike extinction coupled with reinforcement of another response, punishment works almost immediately. A single presentation of a punishing stimulus may be sufficient to completely suppress the target response. Some situations require rapid effects, and there is no substitute for punishment.

A particularly dramatic example comes from research on schizophrenic children. One of the more striking symptoms often displayed by some schizophrenic children is self-destructive behavior. Such children will repeatedly claw at themselves until they bleed, punch themselves in the head, or hit their heads against the wall. To prevent serious injury, such children must often be kept restrained and sedated. In dealing with a problem of this sort, speed is of the essence. For this reason, painful electric shocks are often administered. In the case of one boy who would hit his head up to 2000 times in an hour if unrestrained, twelve shocks contingent upon this self-mutilation were sufficient to eliminate the behavior. While most of these children's problems cannot be solved with punishment, a necessary first step to more complete therapy is the elimination of self-mutilation.[12]

11. However, it might have an indirect effect, even in this case. If a child lacks appropriate arithmetic skills for lack of trying, then punishment of arithmetic errors might induce the child to try harder.
12. Bucher and Lovaas, 1968; Lovaas and Simmons, 1969.

This concludes our discussion of punishment phenomena. It seems as though the mere presentation of an aversive stimulus suppresses responding. A punishment contingency works primarily to suppress responding selectively. When properly arranged, punishment can suppress responding rapidly and relatively permanently.

Avoidance

Two of the examples presented at the beginning of this chapter—dropping a course because the lecturer is boring and staying indoors because it is hot and humid—illustrate other types of relations between responses and consequences—relations we called escape and avoidance. Escape procedures have effects which bear a striking resemblance to the effects of positive reinforcement. When responses are reinforced by escape, they increase in frequency. When the magnitude of the negative reinforcer is varied (for example, the amount of time free from shock as a consequence of an escape response), the frequency of escape responses varies directly with reinforcement magnitude. This phenomenon has a direct parallel when food reinforcement is used to maintain responding. Because of the parallels between escape and positive reinforcement, little needs to be said about escape behavior. Instead, we turn our attention to avoidance learning.

There are many different procedures used for studying avoidance. In one type of avoidance procedure, animals are exposed to discrete trials. Periodically, a stimulus (say a tone) is presented. If the animal makes the required response while the tone is on, it prevents shock from occurring at the end of the tone. If the animal does not make the required response, then when the tone goes off, it is followed by prolonged electric shock. If the animal now makes the required response, it turns off, that is, escapes, the shock. Thus, avoidance procedures of this type are actually escape-avoidance procedures. Figure 4–3 presents a schematic diagram of the standard escape-avoidance procedure.

In one of the more common types of avoidance experiment, animals are placed in a chamber which is divided in half by a barrier. The animal is placed on one side of the chamber, or *shuttle box,* and is required to jump over the barrier to the other side of the box to escape or avoid shock. Dogs exposed to such a procedure will learn

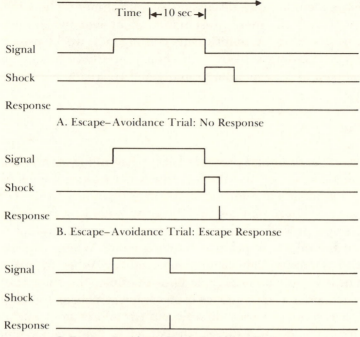

Figure 4–3. Schematic Diagram of the Standard Escape–Avoidance Procedure. *Depicted are a trial in which no response occurs (A), a trial in which an escape response occurs (B), and a trial in which an avoidance response occurs (C). A response is indicated by a vertical line.*

to avoid shock in 20 trials or so.[13] Rats exposed to the same procedure will learn to avoid shock in 40 or 50 trials.[14]

The development of avoidance responses often follows a reliable pattern. Early in training, animals do not avoid shock at all; when the shock comes on, they suffer through it for a while, jumping about in the box, and eventually jump over the hurdle. In other words, they escape the shock but do not avoid it. As trials proceed, animals continue to escape shock and not avoid it but the latency of their escape responses grows shorter and shorter. There comes a point at which they escape the shock virtually at the moment it begins. When finally they begin to avoid the shock, the avoidance responses come at the

13. Solomon and Wynne, 1953.
14. Kamin, 1956.

onset of the stimulus which signals shock; the animals do not wait until just before the shock is due to arrive. Since the earliest avoidance responses come near the beginning of a trial, it appears that the onset of avoidance reflects a change in the animal's sensitivity to the contingencies which are operative in the situation.

Theories of Avoidance

If one were to describe the phenomenon of avoidance to an individual who knew nothing about behavior theory, that individual would probably have no trouble providing an explanation. It seems obvious intuitively that if an animal knows that the only way to avoid pain is by making the response, it will surely learn to make it.

Let us attempt to make this intuitive explanation a bit more rigorous. What it means to "know" about an avoidance contingency is being aware that a response leads to no shock and no response leads to shock. This knowledge, coupled with the reasonable assumption that an animal will prefer no shock to shock seems enough to explain avoidance.

Despite the simplicity and appeal of our intuitive explanation, avoidance learning has posed substantial theoretical difficulty for behavior theory. The feature of our intuitive account which makes it problematic for the behavior theorist is the nature of the reinforcing event. What event maintains avoidance? Our intuitive account suggests that the absence of shock is the crucial event. But how can the absence of something be an event? When does it start? How long does it last? An organism that has never received a shock will not press a lever to avoid shock. What an account of avoidance must provide is some event other than the absence of shock that can be said to maintain the response.

Consider a discrete-trial, escape-avoidance procedure. A tone is presented and followed by shock. The animal learns to escape the shock. But while the animal is escaping shock, something else is occurring. On each trial, the tone is being paired with shock. This pairing is a perfect example of the conditions that produce Pavlovian conditioning (see Chapter 3). But what is the conditioned response that pairings of tone and shock produces? The argument is that the pairings produce conditioned fear; the animal learns to be afraid of the tone just as it is afraid of the shock. After a number of tone-shock pairings, the animal will respond to escape the fear-provoking tone, even before the shock has occurred. But escape from the tone is avoidance of the shock. Thus the two-factor theory of avoidance suggests that avoidance is not really avoidance at all. It is escape from a stimulus which, through pairing with shock, has become fear-provoking. Notice how elegantly two-factor theory solves the problem mentioned earlier of having a nonevent (the absence of shock) maintain avoidance; it is not the absence of shock at all, but the elimination of the tone, the CS, which maintains avoidance. Similarly, since escape is crucial to successful avoidance behavior, the theory maintains that both Pavlovian and operant factors influence and maintain avoidance.[15]

Two-factor theory seems a sensible and straight-forward account of avoidance learning. What evidence is required to support the two-factor theory of avoidance? To begin with, it is clear that when avoidance is being learned, the signal should be fear-evoking. There is no doubt that it is. There are a number of experiments which are variants on the following procedure: Animals are first trained to escape and avoid shock. After they have learned to avoid shock, they are put in a new situation, in the presence of the signal for shock. Now, if they learn to make a response which is completely different from the previous avoidance response, they can escape the signal. Shock never occurs in this new situation. Animals reliably learn to make the response which escapes the signal. What could possibly be maintaining the response if the signal is not fear-evoking?[16]

Despite the plausibility of the two-factor theory of avoidance, there are problems with it which suggest that it can not tell the whole story. First, if an animal's avoidance response is actually an escape from fear there should be signs that the animal continues to be afraid of the CS. Many experiments have been done in which little or no sign of fear is found in well-trained animals though they continue to make avoidance responses.[17] Second, a close look at avoidance procedures indicates that if avoidance responding is the result of fear of the CS, it should not persist. Every time the animal responds to the

15. Two-factor theory probably began with a classic paper by O.H. Mowrer, 1947. Early contributors to the development of two-factor theory include N.E. Miller, 1948. More recently, two-factor theory has been developed largely by R.L. Solomon and his collaborators (e.g. Rescorla and Solomon, 1967).

16. See Miller, 1948; McAllister and McAllister, 1962.

17. See Rescorla and Solomon, 1967; Solomon and Wynne, 1954; Kamin, Brimer and Black, 1963.

tone and prevents the shock, it is experiencing a CS followed by no US. When discussing extinction (p. 72), we saw that when lever presses stop producing food, they stop occurring. And recall that extinction occurs in Pavlovian conditioning also (Chapter 3, p. 48). After CS–US pairings have established a conditioned response, presentations of CS alone will extinguish that response. Thus avoidance responses are also Pavlovian extinction trials. Fear should be eliminated and avoidance responses should stop. They do not. Whereas complete extinction of fear in a Pavlovian conditioning setting may occur within 12 trials if the shock is mild and within 50 if the shock is intense, no sign of extinction of avoidance responding may be seen even after several hundred trials.[18]

It might be argued that avoidance situations are sufficiently traumatic that once responding develops, it can never be extinguished; responses once learned are irreversible. As it turns out, there are at least two methods one can use to produce very rapid extinction. The first method is to simply have the shock occur whether or not the avoidance response occurs. This sort of procedure, in which the response has no reinforcing consequence, is more analogous to extinction of appetitive responding than is turning off the shocker. When shock is delivered whether or not the animal jumps over the hurdle or presses the lever, extinction is rapid.[19]

The second method for producing rapid extinction is known as *response blocking.* To take a typical example, an animal that has been trained to jump across a barrier from one side of a box to the other to avoid shock is placed on the side in which the trials normally begin. The CS is presented. When the animal attempts to make the avoidance response, it encounters a floor-to-ceiling obstruction which makes it impossible to get to the other side of the box. The animal is thus forced to remain in the presence of the CS. Shock is not delivered. When the avoidance response is blocked in this way, avoidance responding is rapidly extinguished.[20]

Results like these have led theorists to formulate an alternative to two-factor theory which is largely a precise statement of the intuitive theory with which we began this discussion. Animals learn to expect shock if they don't respond and no shock if they do respond, and since

18. Annau and Kamin, 1961; Solomon and Wynne, 1954.
19. Davenport and Olson, 1968.
20. Baum, 1970.

they prefer the latter to the former, they respond.[21] Whether this account of avoidance bears the weight of future research remains to be seen. But the importance of two-factor theory extends beyond the domain of avoidance learning. It shows us that there is more to understanding behavior than the principles of operant conditioning. At the very least, Pavlovian conditioning relations can be present and influential in situations in which operant relations are also present. We will see later in Chapter 6, that Pavlovian influence on operant behavior is pervasive.

21. Seligman and Johnston, 1973. See Herrnstein, 1969, for other problems with two-factor theory.

Chapter 5

The Maintenance of Behavior:
Intermittent Reinforcement,
Choice and Economics

THE last chapter was concerned primarily with specifying the different kinds of contingencies that can exist between operant behavior and environmental events, and with indicating the effects of those different contingencies on behavior. The emphasis was on learning—on the modification of operant behavior by its consequences, and particularly on the acquisition of new classes of operant behavior. Certainly, any serious attempt to explain human behavior would have to offer some account of how behavior is modified.

But there is another aspect of behavior that also requires attention. By the time most people have reached adulthood, the learning of most of the different kinds of activities they will engage in for the rest of their lives has already been acquired. People know how to speak and read, they know as much mathematics as they ever will, they know whatever is needed to perform their jobs, they know how to drive, they know how to play certain kinds of games, how to cook, and so on. But once a relatively complete repertoire of operant behavior has been established, what sustains it? What keeps already acquired operants occurring? In short, what environmental conditions are responsible for *maintaining* operants once they have been established?

Not surprisingly, behavior theory has sought to explain the maintenance of behavior in terms of the same behavior-outcome relations used to explain its acquisition. Operant behavior is maintained by just those contingencies of reward, punishment, escape and avoidance that originally established it.

91

At first blush, this may seem implausible. Any of us, after a casual inspection of just the last few days of our lives, can produce a long list of activities we engaged in without reinforcement of any sort. Doing our jobs does not result in reinforcement hour after hour and day after day. Neither does studying. Even recreational activities are not always reinforced. Why then do we continue to engage in these activities?

The answer, for behavior theory, is that even if an operant is not reinforced each time it occurs, it still may be true that the operant is maintained by reinforcement. It is possible that reinforcement if only occasional or intermittent can still effectively control behavior. When we are acquiring an operant, it may be reinforced on each occurrence. But once it is acquired, such regular reinforcement may not be required to sustain it. If intermittent reinforcement can maintain behavior, is it plausible that our daily activities can be understood solely in terms of their reinforcing environmental consequences? Consider a rat in a conditioning chamber, pressing a lever for food. Only some of its lever presses are reinforced. The rat presses the lever steadily, perhaps as often as 60 times per minute. This kind of situation captures the intermittency of reinforcement in the natural environment, but clearly, something is still missing. The rat must simply "decide" whether or not to press the lever at any given moment. The conditioning chamber really offers little else to do, and no reinforcement other than food. It is not surprising that under these circumstances, a rat (or a person) will produce the operant repeatedly. But our lives are not that simple. The ubiquitous feature of human life is choice. The issue for us is not whether or not to engage in some operant for intermittent reinforcement. Rather, we must decide which operant and which reinforcement. Should we study, and presumably obtain reinforcements like knowledge and good grades, or should we pass the evening chatting with friends? Should we order strawberry shortcake for dessert, and be reinforced by the pleasant taste, or grapefruit, and be reinforced by our slender shape? Should we practice law, or practice plumbing? Should we go north for Christmas to ski, or south to lie on the beach? Virtually every kind of human activity is the result of a choice among possible operants and possible reinforcers.

While it is true that even the rat pressing the lever has a choice available (pressing or not pressing), this is surely a degenerate form of choice. It is degenerate largely because it is hard to imagine what could possibly induce the rat not to press the lever in the typical, impoverished experimental setting. Thus, to study choice, one must give organisms real choices. One must establish situations in which different kinds of activities produce different kinds of outcomes, and find out what influences an organism's decision to allocate time and energy to one activity rather than another.

For choices to be significant ones, it must be the case that choosing between A and B means you can't have both. You can't be a lawyer and a plumber, you can't ski and soak up the sun, you can't study and socialize. If we could do all the things among which we are choosing, then choice would largely involve deciding what to do first. Sometimes choice is like this. But often, choosing one alternative precludes others. One way of looking at choices of this type is that people have limited resources of time, energy, money, or all three, and choosing involves making decisions about how those limited resources should be allocated. Viewed in this light, the study of choice overlaps with the discipline of economics. Economics is primarily concerned with specifying the factors that influence the allocation of limited resources, both at the level of individual people and at the level of entire societies or economic systems. Thus, behavior theory and economics share common concerns. Both disciplines view organisms as making choices about the allocation of their resources. For economics, the coin of the realm is money, while for behavior theory, it is operant behavior. But these differences in currency are not necessarily an obstacle to using the principles from one domain to explain the phenomena observed in the other. And we shall see that behavior theory has come in recent years to depend upon central economic concepts to explain the determinants of choice behavior in animals. Thus, in this chapter, we will focus on three major issues: What are the effects on behavior of intermittent reinforcement; how do organisms make choices among alternative operants and outcomes; and how can concepts from economics be used to help us understand choice behavior?

Schedules of Intermittent Reinforcement

We know from the last chapter that when a response (lever press or key peck) regularly produces reinforcement, the response increases in probability. But we also know that human experience does not characteristically include reinforcement each time a given response occurs. What happens to behavior when it is reinforced intermittently, as most human behavior presumeably is? Behavior theorists have found that how behavior is affected depends upon how the intermittent reinforcement is arranged. The study of the effects of intermittent reinforcement on behavior is referred to as the study of *schedules of reinforcement*. A reinforcement schedule is simply a rule that specifies how often, and under what conditions, a particular response will be reinforced.

All schedules of reinforcement have one thing in common: Reinforcement depends upon the occurrence of at least one response. In schedules where each response is reinforced—sometimes called regular reinforcement, but more often called *continuous reinforcement (CRF) schedules*—a single response is all that is required for reinforcement. With other schedules, reinforcement may depend upon something in addition to a particular response, either the passage of a certain amount of time (*interval schedules*) or the occurrence of a certain number of previous responses (*ratio schedules*). Each of these types of schedules can be subdivided. The intervals required for reinforcement may be either fixed (where each interval is the same) or variable. Similarly, ratios may be fixed (each reinforcement depending upon the same number of responses) or variable. These four types of schedules—*fixed interval, variable interval, fixed ratio* and *variable ratio* are the most basic types of reinforcement schedules.[1]

Fixed Interval (FI) schedules: When reinforcement is arranged on a fixed interval schedule, a single response after the passage of a fixed amount of time produces reinforcement. If the value of the interval is one minute (FI 1-min), then one lever press or key peck, a minute or more after the interval has begun, produces reinforcement. Responses *during the interval* do nothing. The passage of the interval by itself does nothing. Reinforcement depends upon both the passage of time and a single response. If the experimental subject could tell time, then it could simply relax until a minute was up and then make a single response, thereby producing a maximum amount of reinforcement with a minimum amount of effort. While organisms do not perform quite this efficiently on FI schedules, they do learn to predict the length of the interval.

Variable Interval (VI) schedules: On variable interval schedules, reinforcement also depends upon the passage of time and a single response. But unlike FI schedules, the time between reinforcements

1. The research program that first provoked real interest in the study of schedules of reinforcement was conducted by C.B. Ferster and B.F. Skinner, (1957).

on VI schedules varies from one reinforcement to the next. The value of the VI schedule is the average time between reinforcements. Thus, for example, a VI 2-min schedule might make the first reinforcement available after one minute, the next two minutes later, the next four minutes later, the next 30 seconds later and so on. Although it is possible to obtain reinforcement for each response on a VI schedule, simply by waiting for the inter-reinforcement interval to elapse, there is no way for the subject to predict the length of a particular inter-reinforcement interval. This difference between VI and FI schedules results in a striking difference in the pattern of responding maintained by the two types of schedules.

Fixed Ratio (FR) schedules: On a fixed ratio schedule, reinforcement depends upon the completion of a certain number of responses; time is irrelevant. If the value of the ratio is fifty (FR 50), every fiftieth response is reinforced. If the subject responds rapidly, reinforcements may be only seconds apart, and if the subject responds slowly, rein-

A duck trained to retrieve rings by looping them around its neck. *The reinforcement schedule is a fixed ratio 4, that is, the duck must retrieve 4 rings for each reinforcement. (Courtesy of Animal Behavior Enterprises)*

forcements may be many minutes apart. The passage of time does not make reinforcement any more likely.

Variable Ratio (VR) schedules: On a variable ratio schedule, the number of responses required for reinforcement varies from one reinforcement to the next. On a VR 50 schedule, the animal might first have to make 60 responses, then 50, then 85, then 50, then 15, then 70, then 40 and so on. The value of the VR schedule specifies the *average* number of responses required for reinforcement.

Having defined the different basic schedules of reinforcement, we will examine their effects on behavior. To do so, we must first determine that behavior does in fact continue to occur when it is reinforced in accord with one of these schedules. If these schedules can maintain behavior, the next issue to address is whether their effects on behavior are different.

Intermittent Schedules and the Maintenance of Behavior

Imagine a rat that has just been trained to press a lever for food. After it has obtained 50 reinforcements, we decide to expose it to an intermittent reinforcement schedule. We choose an FR 200 schedule, that is, every 200th lever press will produce food. What will be the effect of this schedule? If you examine Figure 4–1 (p. 73), you might predict that the FR 200 schedule will not maintain responding. Instead, the rat will probably have stopped pressing the lever long before it has made 200 responses and earned even a single FR reinforcement. This phenomenon, as we have seen, is called extinction. It would also occur if we were to shift a rat from a CRF schedule say to an FI 10-minute schedule. Thus, it might appear that the power of reinforcement schedules to maintain responding is severely limited. Contrary to appearances, however, it is quite possible to sustain responding on schedules that require many hundreds of responses for a single reinforcement, or many minutes to elapse between reinforcements. The trick is to bring the animal to the target schedule gradually. Thus, rather than shifting from CRF to FR 200, one might shift from CRF to FR 3, then to FR 10, then to FR 20, then FR 50 and so on. One would wait before making each shift until the animal was responding on the current ratio fairly reliably, without frequent pauses.

Why should it be that an abrupt transition from CRF to FR 200 cannot maintain behavior while a gradual transition can? The answer to this question lies in a phenomenon known as the *partial reinforcement effect*. It is now well-established that if reinforcement is discontinued (extinction), it will take longer for an animal to stop responding if its responses had previously been intermittently reinforced than if they had been regularly reinforced.[2] This effect probably results from the fact that when extinction follows regular reinforcement, one can quickly learn that conditions have changed. Indeed, a single unreinforced response is enough to tell you that things are not as they were. In contrast, when extinction follows partial reinforcement, it is more difficult to tell that conditions have changed. After all, in the past, many responses have occurred without reinforcement despite the fact that reinforcement is still occasionally forthcoming. Imagine using sweets as a reinforcer to induce a child to do homework. Every night the child obtains candy or ice cream when the homework is done. After a while, you decide that the child should be doing homework without the promise of a reinforcer so you end the contingency. It will take the child only one night to discover that the rules of the game have changed. In contrast, if the child had been getting reinforcement every four or five nights, discovery that reinforcement had been discontinued would take much longer.

Let us see how the partial reinforcement effect can explain why gradual transitions to schedules that deliver reinforcement infrequently can maintain behavior while abrupt transitions cannot. Suppose we shift a rat from CRF to an FR 3. It presses the lever and no food comes. Extinction has begun, but it will press the lever a few more times before it gives up. Once it does persist for a few more presses, it will satisfy the FR requirement and obtain another reinforcement. After a while, it will become accustomed to this schedule, and press away with no hesitation. Now, you change the ratio to an FR 10. Again, extinction will begin. But this time, the rat, already accustomed to intermittent reinforcement, will take longer to discover that conditions have changed. It will make at least 10 lever presses before it quits. Since the tenth press will produce food, lever pressing will continue. As we increase the ratio, more and more responses are required before an animal can distinguish extinction from the previous ratio. This means that cessation of responding will take longer and

2. For a discussion of the partial reinforcement effect, see Amsel (1962;1967) or Mackintosh (1974).

longer to be complete. And this means that the animal will persist long enough to obtain food on the new ratio. Through this process, reinforcement can be made increasingly infrequent and still maintain responding. While there are limits to how many responses an organism will make for a single reinforcer, the limits are very large indeed.

Patterns of Behavior Maintained by Intermittent Schedules

Now that we know that schedules of reinforcement do indeed maintain operant behavior, we can ask about how they do so. Are the patterns of behavior maintained by different schedules different, and if so, in what way? To explore this question, we need a new measuring instrument—the *cumulative record*. Cumulative records provide a visual representation of the pattern of responding in time (see Figure 5–1). A pen rests on a piece of paper which is moved by a motor at a constant speed. As the paper moves beneath the pen, the pen makes a horizontal line on the paper. The pen is connected electrically to the switch behind the response key (or lever), so that each time the switch is closed, the pen moves up vertically, by a small, fixed amount. Thus, each response moves the pen up a notch, and each instant of time moves the pen horizontally. The resulting curve traced by the pen depicts responses (y or vertical axis), over time (x or horizontal axis). The slope of the curve at any point (y/x) indicates the rate at which responses are occurring at that point.

Typical cumulative records of responding maintained on the four basic reinforcement schedules are depicted in Figure 5–2. The downward marks of the pen indicate occurrences of reinforcement. It is clear from Figure 5–2 that the different schedules produce strikingly different patterns of responding. Variable ratio and variable interval schedules are similar in that they produce relatively constant patterns of responding in time. They differ in that variable ratio schedules maintain higher rates of responding than variable interval schedules. Similarly, fixed ratio schedules generate higher rates of responding than fixed interval schedules—when the organism is responding at all. The most noticeable characteristic of both FR and FI schedules is that for some time after each reinforcement there is no responding.

How can we account for these different patterns of behavior maintained by the four schedules? Let us first consider the differences between fixed (FR and FI) and variable (VR and VI) schedules. Why

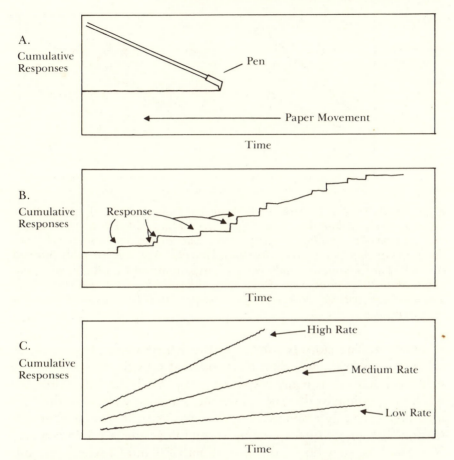

Figure 5–1. Schematic Drawings of Cumulative Records. *In A, the pen is moving across the paper and no responses are occurring. In B, the animal is making an occasional response. In C, the three lines represent steady patterns of responding at high, medium, and low rates. The actual rates can be read from the record as the slope of the lines.*

does an animal pause at the start of each FR or FI? We can explain this pausing by looking at what the occurrence of reinforcement tells the animal about when the next reinforcement will be coming. Consider an animal responding on an FI 1-minute schedule. It makes the response, and food is delivered. The food delivery signals a long delay before food again becomes available. Thus, the animal does not respond. As time passes, and the 1-minute interval progresses, food availability becomes more likely. Thus, the animal resumes its

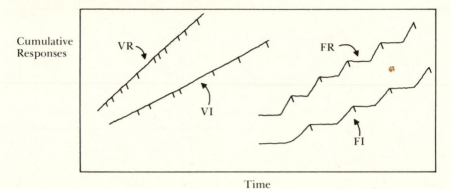

Cumulative
Responses

Time

Figure 5–2. Typical Patterns of Responding Generated by the Four Basic Reinforcement Schedules. *The downward strokes indicate reinforcements and the rate of responding at any point in time is represented by the slope of the curve at that point. Note that variable-ratio (VR) and variable-interval (VI) schedules maintain steady rates of responding, with VR response rate higher than VI response rate. Fixed-ratio (FR) and fixed-interval (FI) schedules maintain patterns of responding characterized by a pause after each reinforcement.*

responding. The story is similar on the FR schedule. On an FR 50 schedule, for example, when food comes it tells the animal that the next food delivery is many responses away. With the FR, unlike the FI, letting time pass does not move the animal any closer to the next food delivery; only responses can do that. Thus, it is somewhat surprising that animals ever resume responding after a reinforcement. Nevertheless, they do. In the case of both FR and FI schedules, animals learn to discriminate the time period right after a reinforcement (in which the chances of another reinforcement are zero) from time periods more removed from the last reinforcement. It is only in these latter periods that responding resumes.

In contrast, with the variable schedules, the occurrence of a reinforcer is not a sign that another one will not be available for a while. Because the interval or ratio varies from reinforcement to reinforcement, it is possible that sometimes a reinforcement will follow almost immediately on the preceding one. Thus, there is no discrimination to be made between time periods just after reinforcement and later periods, and response rate is relatively steady.

Now let us consider why ratio schedules sustain higher rates of responding than interval schedules. To understand this effect, we must evaluate what responding at different rates does for an animal on ratio or interval schedules. Imagine first an animal responding on a VR 50 schedule. Suppose the animal makes one response every ten seconds. If it does, it will take 500 seconds (more than 8 minutes) to make 50 responses. Thus, on average, it will obtain food once every eight or so minutes. Now suppose the animal responds once a second. If it does, it will obtain food every 50 seconds on the average. In short, on a ratio schedule, the faster an animal responds, the more often it gets food. The relation between rate of response and rate of food delivery is a direct one.

This is not the case on interval schedules. If responses are being reinforced on a VI 1-minute schedule, an animal will not get food more than once a minute, on average, no matter how fast it responds. It does the animal little good to respond rapidly. Thus, there is a selective advantage to a rapid responding on ratio schedules that is absent on interval schedules. This selective advantage probably explains why ratio schedules sustain higher response rates than interval schedules.[3]

Schedules of Reinforcement in the Natural Environment

This chapter began by suggesting that intermittency is much more characteristic of reinforcement in the natural human environment than is continuous reinforcement. The study of schedules of reinforcement amounts to a study of the effects of different types of intermittency on behavior. How well do the basic schedules of reinforcement characterize intermittent reinforcement in the real world?

It is not too difficult to find examples of human behavior that is maintained by one or another of the basic reinforcement schedules, and when such examples are found the pattern of behavior maintained is remarkably like the records in Figure 5–2.

Fixed Ratios

It used to be quite common for factory workers to be paid on a piecework basis: Every hundred suits pressed, or hems sewn, or transmissions installed produced a certain payoff. These fixed ratio schedules generated very high rates of responding, with brief pauses after each ratio, as shown in Figure 5–2. This kind of salary arrange-

3. See Morse, 1966.

ment was very desirable to management for a variety of reasons. It maintained high outputs. In addition, it made wages a direct part of unit costs. When business was good, and much was produced, employees earned high wages. When business was bad, employees were given less work, completed fewer ratios, and earned less money. Employers were not required to pay constant wages (as by the hour) independent of whether there was a great deal of work or only a little.[4]

Employees found the piecework system undesirable. This was partly, but not exclusively, because their wages would rise and fall uncertainly from week to week. What really made piecework undesirable is that the schedule made employees work too hard to earn their wages. The schedule generated behavior at a rate which left workers nervous and exhausted at the end of the day. It was the daily strain of working at high speeds, and hesitating to rest or go to the bathroom since taking time out would cost money, which made ratio schedules aversive.

If working at high speeds was aversive, one might wonder why employees did not simply slow down. To ask this question is to assume that individuals have autonomous control over their actions. The view of the behavior theorist is that the source of control over behavior lies largely in the environment, not in the individual. That people work at high rates which they find aversive is no surprise; that is simply the effect of ratio schedules on the behavior of people. The faster one responds, the more frequent is reinforcement. Slowing down costs. Even if one is willing to decrease the frequency of reinforcement by decreasing response rate, one cannot intentionally slow down to a comfortable rate. The ratio schedule will generate a high rate. One's only alternative is to escape the situation. This, indeed, is what more and more employees have done as their unions have been able to exercise control over management. Piecework systems have been replaced by hourly wage systems. It is difficult for one to change the pattern of behavior which is generated by a reinforcement schedule, but one can change the schedule.

Pigeons apparently have the same reaction to ratio schedules as people do. If a pigeon that is pecking a lit key for food reinforcement on a ratio schedule is given the opportunity to peck another lit key, the sole consequence of which is to turn off the light on the ratio key

4. The relation between the central principles of behavior theory and the workplace is discussed in detail in Chapter 9.

briefly, the pigeon will reliably peck this key to "escape" from the ratio. There is no alternative source of food, so this behavior gains nothing but temporary respite from the ratio schedule. Moreover, the pigeon could conceivably gain its respite by simply not pecking the lit ratio key, or by pecking it at a moderate rate. But it does not. It pecks to escape the aversive ratio key, but when that key is lit, despite the aversiveness of the schedule, the pigeon's behavior conforms to the pattern depicted in Figure 5–2.[5]

Variable Ratios

In the case of variable ratio schedules, there appears to be a natural environment example which fits the laboratory case perfectly. Slot machines in gambling casinos are programmed to pay off on variable ratio schedules. The passage of time between coin insertions has no effect on the likelihood of payoff; only responses are relevant. As anyone who has ever fed coins into slot machines or watched others do so can attest, this reinforcement schedule generates a high and steady rate of responding.

Variable Intervals

Variable interval schedules also appear to be relatively easy to find in the human environment. Imagine trying to complete a telephone call when the line is busy. Reinforcement depends on both a response (dialing the number) and the passage of time; the more time passes, the more likely it is that the number you want will not be busy. Consider also the way in which most parents attend to the cries of their young children. While some parents reinforce each response, most expect their infants to occupy themselves periodically without parental attention, and allow their infants to fuss for a while before attending to them. The requirement for reinforcement is both the passage of time, and the occurrence of a response (crying). The schedules operative in both of these situations generally result in a steady rate of responding as depicted in Figure 5–2.

Fixed Intervals

It is difficult to find pure examples of fixed-interval schedules operating in the natural environment. While there are a large number of situations which are fixed-interval like, most of them differ in one

5. Appel, 1963.

or more important respects from FI schedules as studied in the laboratory. Consider a few examples. Most people are paid salaries at regular intervals—one week, two weeks, or a month. The schedule in operation seems to be an FI. But what is the response which is actually reinforced? Perhaps it is walking to the pay window or to one's mailbox. Reinforcement depends upon both the passage of a fixed amount of time and the occurrence of this response. Thus, walking to the pay window is reinforced on an FI schedule. But reinforcement also depends upon behavior during the interval. Walking to the pay window is reinforced only if one has done his job all week long. On FI schedules, behavior during the interval is irrelevant.

As another example, consider cooking, or, more accurately, checking on the progress of the items being cooked. The required cooking time of most dishes is fixed, and checking on stews or breads or roasts before that time has elapsed has no effect. Once the time has elapsed, checking the progress of the item is reinforced. Thus, cooking seems like a perfect example of an FI. But consider what would happen if the required cooking time were one hour and one checked after two hours. The dish would be overcooked and ruined. Thus, reinforcement for "checking the roast" depends upon a response after time X, *but before time Y*. On ordinary FI schedules, this additional requirement is not present. Nevertheless, the behavior of the cook often does conform to the FI pattern depicted in Figure 5–2. Early in the interval, one does not check the roast. As the interval progresses, checking the roast occurs with increasing frequency. It is possible to construct somewhat artificial examples of FI schedules in the natural environment. In general, however, schedules of this type are only FI-like, usually because behavior during the interval between reinforcements really does matter in one way or another.

In summary, one can find natural examples of reinforcement schedules that are either exact or close parallels to the schedules studied in the laboratory. And when such parallels are identified, the patterns of behavior maintained by these natural schedules are very similar to the patterns observed in laboratory studies.

The Study of Choice: Concurrent Schedules of Reinforcement

At the beginning of this chapter, we suggested that a central element of human behavior that is not adequately captured in simple operant conditioning experiments is choice. Our actions almost always represent choices among alternatives. Should we study history or biology? Should we study at all, or go to the movies? Should we go out to dinner, or see a play? Should we call on this customer or that one? Our past history of reinforcement for studying often contributes to determining whether or not we study, just as the rat's past history of reinforcement for lever pressing determines whether or not it will press the lever. But what also contributes to determining whether or not we study is what the possible alternatives are, and presumably what reinforcement history is associated with them. While the rat may be characterized as choosing, each moment, whether or not to press the lever, there are no serious alternatives to lever pressing available in the conditioning chamber. The food produced by lever presses has no competition from other possible reinforcers.

Behavior theorists have been cognizant of the significance of choice in human activity, and have attempted to study choice behavior experimentally. What characterizes the study of operant choice behavior is the focus on how the likelihood of a given class of operant behavior is affected not just by *its* reinforcement history, but by the reinforcement history associated with other possible classes of operant behavior. In a typical choice experiment, a pigeon might be confronted with two lit response keys, say one yellow and one blue. Pecks at the two keys might produce food according to two independent VI schedules of reinforcement. A well-trained pigeon in such a situation will peck a few times on one key, then switch to the other, then switch back to the first, and so on, obtaining reinforcement for pecks on both keys. Procedures of this type are referred to as *concurrent schedules,* which are more generally defined as two or more schedules that operate simultaneously and independently, each for a different response. By studying the behavior of animals exposed to concurrent schedules of reinforcement, we can begin to evaluate how the availability of an alternative source of reinforcement influences a given operant behavior.

Suppose, for example, we expose a pigeon to a single VI 3-minute schedule of food reinforcement for pecking. It comes gradually to peck the key at a steady, moderate rate of perhaps 40 pecks per minute. Now, we introduce a second key, this one associated with a VI 1-minute schedule. The pigeon will begin pecking this key, and gradually, over time, it will peck less and less at the first key. What this simple demonstration shows is that the frequency of operant behavior can be altered even if the schedule of reinforcement that is maintaining it is not altered. What affects the frequency of the operant in this case is the frequency of reinforcement available for another operant.

The behavior of animals exposed to concurrent VI schedules of this type is remarkably reliable. It turns out that responses are emitted to the two keys (or levers) in direct proportion to the frequency of reinforcement obtained for these responses. If we call the response keys A and B, then

$$\frac{\text{Responses (R) on A}}{\text{Responses on A} + \text{Responses on B}} = \frac{\text{Reinforcements (r) on A}}{\text{Reinforcements on A} + \text{Reinforcements on B}}$$

or

$$\frac{R_A}{R_A + R_B} = \frac{r_A}{r_A + r_B} \qquad [1]$$

The relative frequency of responding on an alternative matches the relative frequency of reinforcement for responses on that alternative. This relation is called the *matching law*.[6]

This matching law provides a roughly accurate description of the behavior of a wide variety of organisms in a wide variety of choice situations. It is as true of lever-pressing rats as of key-pecking pigeons; it is as true of situations involving aversive stimuli as of situations involving food.[7] Also, the matching law applies not just to reinforcement frequency, but to other aspects of reinforcement as well. If one varies the magnitude of reinforcement available for responses on each of two keys or levers, relative frequency of responding matches relative magnitude of reinforcement. That is,

$$\frac{R_A}{R_A + R_B} = \frac{M_A}{M_A + M_B} \qquad [2]$$

where M = magnitude of reinforcement. And if one varies the delay of reinforcement between two alternatives, relative frequency of responding matches the reciprocals of the delays. That is,

$$\frac{R_A}{R_A + R_B} = \frac{\dfrac{1}{D_A}}{\dfrac{1}{D_A} + \dfrac{1}{D_B}} \qquad [3]$$

6. See Herrnstein, 1970; deVilliers, 1977.
7. deVilliers, 1974.

where D = delay of reinforcement.[8] Thus, if one schedule provides eight seconds of food availability for each reinforcement, while the other provides four seconds, and both schedules provide reinforcements with the same frequency, an animal will prefer the first to the second by a ratio of about two to one. Similarly, if one schedule provides reinforcement with a two second delay while the other provides it with a four second delay, the animal will prefer the first to the second by the same two to one ratio.

The Matching Law in Operation

The matching law tells us how factors such as frequency, magnitude and delay of reinforcement independently affect choices. It also provides a framework for studying these variables in combination. For example, it might be the case that if frequency, magnitude and delay of reinforcement were manipulated simultaneously that the following equation would describe the result:

$$\frac{R_A}{R_A + R_B} = \frac{r_A \times M_A \times 1/D_A}{(r_A \times M_A \times 1/D_A) + (r_B \times M_B \times 1/D_B)} \qquad [4]$$

A particularly impressive example of the study of these variables in combination investigated the joint effects of reinforcement magnitude and reinforcement delay on choice.[9] Consider pigeons faced with the following choice: If they peck a green key, they obtain four-seconds of access to food, but they must wait four-seconds to get it. If they peck a red key, they get two seconds of access to food, but they get it immediately. Which of these alternatives should pigeons prefer? We can answer this question by using the matching law. To do so, we must assume that even immediate reinforcement involves some delay, since it takes the pigeon time to get its beak to the feeder. So let us assume that the pigeon's choice is between 4 seconds of food delayed 4 seconds and 2 seconds of food delayed 0.1 seconds. According to the matching law:

8. Chung and Herrnstein, 1967; Catania, 1963; for a review, see Catania, 1966.
9. Rachlin and Green, 1972.

$$\frac{\text{Responses Red}}{\text{Responses Red} + \text{Responses Green}} = \frac{\dfrac{\text{Reinforcement Time in Red}}{\text{Delay in Red}}}{\dfrac{\text{Reinforcement Time in Red}}{\text{Delay in Red}} + \dfrac{\text{Reinforcement Time in Green}}{\text{Delay in Green}}}$$

or

$$\frac{\text{R red}}{\text{R red} + \text{R green}} = \frac{\dfrac{\text{T red}}{\text{D red}}}{\dfrac{\text{T red}}{\text{D red}} + \dfrac{\text{T green}}{\text{D green}}} \qquad [5]$$

By substituting the values of T and D used in the experiment, we get:

$$\frac{\text{R red}}{\text{R red} + \text{R green}} = \frac{\dfrac{2}{0.1}}{\dfrac{2}{0.1} + \dfrac{4}{4}} = \frac{20}{21} = .95 \qquad [6]$$

Thus, the matching law predicts that pigeons will prefer the smaller, immediate reward to the larger, delayed one.

But now suppose that this choice between red and green is only a part of a larger procedure, one depicted in Figure 5–3. Here, a trial begins with pigeons faced with two white keys. If they peck the right key 15 times, all the lights in the box go out for 10 seconds (10 second delay). Then the two keys come on again, one red and one green. A peck on the red key immediately produces 2 seconds access to food while a peck on the green key produces 4 seconds access to food, after a delay of 4 seconds (the direct choice between red and green that we just worked through). If they peck fifteen times on the left, white key all the lights also go off for 10 seconds. But now, when the lights come back on, only the left key is lit, with green light. A peck on the green key produces 4 seconds of food after a 4-second delay.

What might we expect the pigeons to do on this procedure? We already know that if given the choice between red and green (bottom right of Figure 5–3), pigeons vastly prefer small, immediate reinforcement to large delayed reinforcement. Thus, when the keys are white, pecks at the left key will force the pigeons into a relatively unpreferred state of affairs (large delayed reward), while pecks at the right will give them the opportunity to choose a more preferred state of affairs (small, immediate reward). Thus, we might think pigeons

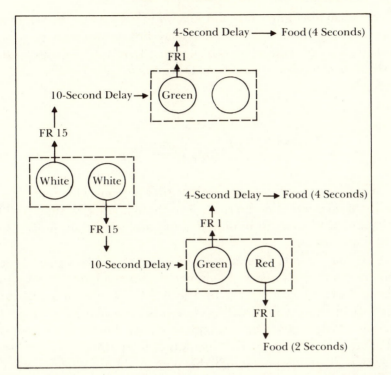

Figure 5–3. Diagram of a Procedure to Study Effects of Magnitude and Delay of Reinforcement on Choice. *Animals are initially confronted with a choice between two white keys. Fifteen pecks on the left key commits them, 10 seconds later, to the availability of 4 seconds of food with a 4-second delay. Fifteen pecks on the right key gives animals a choice, 10 seconds later, between 4 seconds of food with a 4-second delay and 2 seconds of food immediately.*

will prefer the right, white key because only pecks at it give them access to the red key. What does the matching law have to say?

We know that the relevant equation is this:

$$\frac{R_{\text{left}}}{R_{\text{left}} + R_{\text{right}}} = \frac{\dfrac{T_{\text{left}}}{D_{\text{left}}}}{\dfrac{T_{\text{left}}}{D_{\text{left}}} + \dfrac{T_{\text{right}}}{D_{\text{right}}}} \qquad [7]$$

What are the values of T and D to be plugged into the equation? The values of T are the same as before, 4 and 2 seconds. But the values of

D have changed. For while the pigeon is pecking at the white keys, there is going to be a 10 second delay before the keys turn red or green no matter which key the pigeon chooses. Thus, we must add 10 seconds to both the values of D we used before. That gives us:

$$\frac{R_{left}}{R_{left} + R_{right}} = \frac{\frac{4}{10+4}}{\frac{4}{10+4} + \frac{2}{10+0.1}} \approx .60 \tag{8}$$

Thus, the matching law predicts that pigeons will choose the left key about 60 percent of the time even though left key choices will not give them access to the reinforcement conditions they prefer (small, immediate reward).

The matching law seems to have made an unlikely pair of predictions. It is telling us that a pigeon will prefer the left white key to the right one even though pecks on the left key put it in a situation in which 4 seconds of food with a 4-second delay is the only possible outcome. When given an immediate choice between that outcome and another one (immediate 2 seconds of food) the pigeon prefers the other one. Thus, even though the pigeon should prefer immediate small reinforcement to delayed large reinforcement (red to green), if we make it commit itself far enough in advance (left white key vs. right white key) it will choose a delayed large reinforcement over an immediate small one.

The results of the experiment confirmed these predictions based on the matching law. When choosing between red and green, pigeons pecked red virtually all the time. But when choosing between left and right white keys, they pecked left 65 percent of the time.

The variable which will determine which white key the pigeon prefers (everything else held constant) is the time interval between the left-right choice and the red-green choice. There should be some duration between these choices at which pigeons will be indifferent to left or right. We can guess at this duration by turning again to the matching law:

$$\frac{R_{left}}{R_{left} + R_{right}} = .50 = \frac{\frac{4}{X+4}}{\frac{4}{X+4} + \frac{2}{X+0.1}} \tag{9}$$

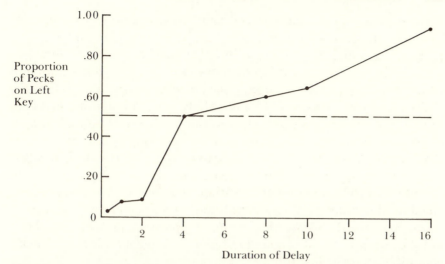

Figure 5–4. A Test of the Matching Law. *The figure depicts the proportion of left-key choices as a function of the delay imposed between early choice and later reinforcement. The point of indifference between left and right keys falls just where the matching law predicts—at 4 seconds delay. (After Rachlin & Green, 1972.)*

By solving for X in this equation, we find the value of X at which pigeons should peck left and right white keys with equal frequency is 4 seconds. When the experimenters systematically varied the time between the initial choice between left and right and the later choice between red and green, they obtained the results presented in Figure 5–4. The prediction, based upon the matching law, was exactly confirmed—that with a delay of 4 seconds between the initial choice and the final response, pigeons should be indifferent between left and right keys.[10]

This particular instance of the matching law has potential practical application. We could characterize the behavior of the pigeon when it is confronted with a choice between red and green as a choice of a less useful outcome (2 seconds food) over a more useful outcome (4 seconds food) because the former is immediate. We get the pigeon to choose the more useful alternative when the commitment occurs so far in advance that both outcomes are substantially delayed. Then, the relative immediacy of one outcome over another becomes unimportant. One can imagine many human choices as between immediate,

10. Rachlin and Green, 1972.

small reinforcement, and delayed large reinforcement. Consider for example, the choice between going to the movies and studying on a particular evening. We could imagine that going to the movies involves a small, but immediate reinforcement (an evening's entertainment) while studying involves a large, delayed reinforcement (a good exam grade). Given the choice at 7:45 P.M. between studying and an 8 P.M. movie, the student, like the pigeon, might choose the small, immediate reinforcement. But if the choice were required at 9 A.M., so that now both reinforcers were going to be delayed, the student might choose to study. If we arranged contingencies so that people had to commit themselves to one or the other outcome well in advance, the chances of commitment to studying rather than going to the movies might increase. It is possible that many problems in "self-discipline" or "self-control" might be ameliorated if contingencies involving early commitment were instituted.[11]

Operant Behavior and Economics

The matching law seems to be an extremely powerful predictive tool. We can use it to evaluate how organisms will allocate their behavior when confronted with a variety of alternatives offering different combinations of frequency, magnitude and delay of reinforcement. The matching law brings us much closer to an account of human behavior in the everyday environment than simply observing how different reinforcement schedules maintain responding. It does so by explicitly acknowledging, and building into experimental settings, the fact that the occurrence of any given behavior represents a choice among alternatives. It tells us that even choice is orderly and predictable.

Viewed through the lens of the matching law, questions about choice become questions about how organisms allocate their limited resources. When those organisms are pigeons or rats the resources in question are behaviors. When those organisms are people, the limited resources may be behavior as well. But people have another type of limited resource available. That resource, of course, is money. And issues relating to how people decide to allocate their limited resources, both in behavior and in money, have traditionally been the province

11. See Rachlin, 1974.

of the discipline of economics. It is therefore not surprising that in the last few years, behavior theorists have begun to apply concepts developed in economics to their own domain. The matching law is coming to be viewed as a special case of the operation of economic principles that are far more general. We will sketch some of these recent applications of economic principles to operant behavior with an emphasis on two issues. We will be looking at the implications of these new developments for the matching law, and we will be looking at how the economic analysis brings behavior theory still closer to an account of human behavior in the natural environment.[12]

The Idea of Demand

One of the central concepts in economics is the idea of *demand*. Informally, the demand for a given commodity is the amount of that commodity that will be purchased, or consumed, at a given price. In economics, one is typically interested in how demand for a commodity is affected by changes in the price of that commodity. Thus, for example, suppose a typical family purchases 2½ pounds of bread per week, when bread costs 50¢ a pound. What will happen to that family's consumption as the price of bread rises to $1, $2, or even $3 a pound? We could plot bread purchasing as a function of the cost of a pound of bread. Such a plot, like the one in Figure 5–5, is called a *demand curve*.

The striking thing about this curve is how little consumption is affected by price. Even though the cost of bread increases by a factor of 6, consumption of bread decreases only a little, and the amount of money spent on bread each week rises steadily. When consumption of a commodity is relatively unaffected by its price, demand for that commodity is said to be *inelastic*. Most of the commodities we view as necessities of life are characterized by inelastic demand curves like the one in Figure 5–5.

In contrast, consider the demand curve in Figure 5–6, this time for movies. Plotted in Figure 5–6 is a hypothetical relation between the price of a movie and the number of movies seen per week. When movies cost $3, the average person sees one movie per week. As the price of movies increases, the movies seen drops precipitously. By

12. See Allison, Miller and Wozny, 1979; Hursh, 1980; Lea, 1978; Rachlin, Green, Kagel and Battalio, 1976; and Staddon, 1979, for some important, general discussions.

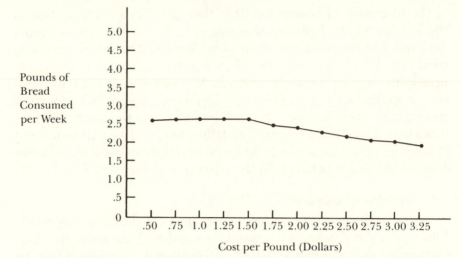

Figure 5–5. Hypothetical Demand Curve for Bread. *As the price of bread increases from 50 cents per pound to $3 per pound, the amount of bread consumed decreases slightly. Because consumption of bread is relatively unaffected by price, demand for bread is said to be inelastic.*

the time the price of movies has increased to $8, the person has virtually stopped seeing them. A demand curve like the one in Figure 5–6, in which consumption is dramatically affected by price, is said to reveal demand that is *elastic*. Most of the commodities we tend to view as luxuries might fall on demand curves like the one in Figure 5–6.

What have demand curves to do with operant conditioning, and more specifically, with the matter of choice? To answer this question, we must first decide what is the equivalent of the price of a commodity in typical choice experiments. Pigeons and rats do not have money. What they do have is responses. Key pecks and lever presses are their coin of the realm. Thus, the behavioral equivalent of price might be the schedule of reinforcement—the number of responses, or amount of time, that must be "spent" to purchase a reinforcer.

In typical choice experiments, the reinforcer used is food, a necessity of life and a commodity for which demand is relatively inelastic. Moreover, the reinforcer is typically the same for both alternative operants. The two alternatives may differ in the frequency, magnitude or delay of food they offer, but they both offer food. Under these circumstances, we can expect that demand will be insignificant

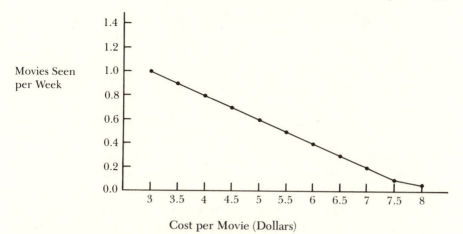

Figure 5–6. Hypothetical Demand Curve for Movies. *As the price of movies increases from $3 per movie to $8 per movie, the number of movies per week drops. Because consumption of movies is markedly affected by price, demand for movies is said to be elastic.*

in determining choice, since whatever the demand curve may be, it will be the same for both alternatives.

But such a circumstance is a highly artificial one. Human choices are rarely between two schedules that offer the same reinforcer. More commonly, people must choose between different reinforcers. The matching law might provide a device for finding out the relative value of two different reinforcers by measuring an organism's choice responses for them. Thus, if a rat were indifferent between an alternative that offered one pellet of dry food every minute and one that offered a piece of chocolate chip cookie every five minutes, we might be tempted to suggest that a piece of chocolate chip cookie was five times as valuable to the rat as a dry food pellet.

It is when the matching law is extended to account for choices among different types of reinforcers that the concept of demand becomes relevant. To see this, consider the following experiment.[13] Rats were given the opportunity to press two levers. Presses on one lever produced food pellets. Presses on the other lever produced a burst of electrical stimulation of the rat's brain in an area sometimes called a "pleasure center." It is called a pleasure center because rats, and other animals, will engage in high rates of operant behavior to produce such stimulation. When lever presses produced either food

13. Hursh and Natelson, 1981.

or brain stimulation on FR 2 schedules, the rats vastly preferred the brain stimulation to food. They produced nine brain stimulations for each food pellet. This fact, according to the matching law, would suggest that brain stimulation is much more valuable than food. But this is not the case. When the FR was increased to eight, for both reinforcers, the amount of food the rats produced was unchanged. In contrast, the amount of brain stimulation produced dropped precipitously, to a point where the rats were producing more food than brain stimulation. If one had only the data from the FR 8 to examine, one would assume that food was more valuable to the rat than brain stimulation.

In truth, it makes no sense to say that one of the reinforcers was more valuable than the other. What distinguished the two reinforcers was their elasticity. Food is inelastic; it is a necessity. Brain stimulation is elastic; it is a luxury. When both are cheap (FR 2), demand for brain stimulation exceeds demand for food. But as they grow more expensive (requiring more responses), the demand curve for brain stimulation drops precipitously (as in Figure 5–6), eventually falling below the curve for food. Thus, the concept of demand, elastic and inelastic, is essential for us to understand the pattern of the rat's choices between these reinforcers as the price of both of them changes. It follows that in general, when choices are between different commodities, making sense of an organism's pattern of preference will depend upon knowing what the demand curves for those commodities look like. Understood in this way, the matching law holds only when the demand curves for both reinforcers are the same, or similar, in form.

Demand and Income

In discussing demand elasticity, we said that when demand for a commodity is elastic, the amount consumed will decrease as price increases. Strictly speaking, this is not quite accurate. Suppose the price of movies increases from $3 to $9, as in Figure 5–6. But suppose that your income increases from $200 per week to $600 per week. Under these conditions, the cost of movies, as a proportion of your total income, has remained the same. Not surprisingly, demand for luxuries (commodities with elastic demand) only decreases dramatically when the price *as a proportion of income* increases. The absolute price of a commodity is less important than its relative price—its price relative to your income.

How is the concept of "income" embodied in the operant conditioning experiment? Remember, the rat or pigeon's "money" is its operant responses. Thus, its income would be the number of responses it has available. In most operant conditioning experiments, this quantity is not fixed. An experimental session might last a fixed amount of time, or until a fixed number of reinforcers has been earned. But the number of responses that occur within the session is left free to vary. Thus, if the cost (schedule) of a reinforcer were to go up, an animal could always adjust to this change by increasing its rate of responding. In essense, in the typical operant conditioning experiment, the amount of income available to the animal is under its control.

Conditions like this will minimize the effects of demand on choice, because increases in absolute price need not imply increases in relative price. To create a situation that is more closely analogous to the typical human one, one would have to establish a procedure in which animals had only a fixed number of responses available per session (income). Now, changes in price (schedule) of reinforcers might have dramatic effects on choice, as a function of the elasticity of the demand for the reinforcers.

A few experiments of this type have now been done.[14] In one such experiment, baboons were given a choice between food and heroin infusion. Under experimental conditions that were typical in that there was no constraint on the number of responses that could occur in a session, neither food nor heroin demand seemed terribly elastic. That is, neither food choices nor heroin choices were very dramatically affected by price (FR requirement). Then the procedure was changed. The baboons were given a fixed income of responses per day that could be allocated either for the purchase of heroin or for the purchase of food. Now, the differential demand for the two reinforcers made its presence felt. When both reinforcers were cheap, the baboons chose each of them roughly equally. As the cost (schedule) increased, demand for heroin dropped while demand for food stayed constant. Food demand was inelastic while heroin demand was elastic, a difference that could only be revealed when the animals' income was kept controlled by the experimenter.

This example shows again how the matching law is relatively uninfluenced by demand in typical experimental settings. The lack of influence results from the lack of constraint on income (responses).

14. Elsmore, 1979; Rachlin, Green, Kagel and Battalio, 1976.

When income is constrained, a circumstance much more like everyday circumstances than the typical operant experiment, demand becomes critically important.

Substitutability of Commodities

There is another central economic idea that has much to do with choice behavior. The matching law, and the typical experimental situations used to study it, acknowledge that how well a reinforcer will maintain an organism's behavior depends upon what else is available in a situation. Thus, a VI 3-minute schedule of food reinforcement may maintain a great deal of responding in isolation, but very little responding if a VI 10-second schedule of reinforcement is also available. The matching law offers a precise specification of how alternative sources of a given reinforcer will affect the power of a particular source to sustain responding.

But consider for a moment whether it makes sense that the effect of an alternative reinforcer will be the same no matter what the relation is between the alternative reinforcer and the original one. Suppose we are interested in determining what kinds of manipulations will reduce people's use of private automobiles (and gasoline) in commuting to work. We could increase the price of gasoline, but the demand for gasoline is relatively inelastic, since people must get to work. We could offer people a choice between gasoline and gasohol (a mixture of gasoline and alcohol). Under these conditions, we might expect that as the price of gasoline increased relative to the price of gasohol, people would allocate increasing resources to gasohol. These two substances, gasoline and gasohol, *substitute* very well for one another. Alternatively, we might improve the availability of reliable, inexpensive, public transportation. Again, public transport and private transport substitute well for one another. But suppose, instead, we increased the availability of cheap, convenient, downtown parking. What effect would this have on the use of private automobiles? Presumably it would increase their use, because using private automobiles and having convenient parking available are *complements;* the more you have of one, the more you want of the other. Finally, suppose we offered people a host of amusements—movies, theater, restaurants, and so on—as alternatives to gasoline on which to spend their money. These reinforcers are neither substitutes nor complements to gasoline use; they are relatively independent of it.[15]

15. This example is modified from Hursh, 1980.

The point is that to determine the effect of introducing an alternative reinforcer on behavior already maintained by a reinforcer, we must know something about the relation between the reinforcers. When they are substitutes, interaction between the alternatives will be great, and the more attractive we make one of them, the less the other will be chosen. If they are complements, interaction will again be great, but now, the more attractive we make one, the *more* of the other will be chosen. Finally, if they are neither substitutes nor complements, interaction will be minimal. Now let us consider the typical operant choice experiment. The reinforcers for the two alternatives are the same—food pellets. They are maximally substitutable. Thus, it follows (as the matching law tells us) that the more attractive we make one alternative (in terms, say, of price, or reinforcement schedule), the more it will be chosen over the other. But what the principles of substitutes and complements tell us is that this typical experimental outcome is just a special case—one that holds only for substitutable reinforcers. If we give animals a choice between food and water, we obtain a quite different pattern of results. What we find is that the more attractive we make one alternative, the more an animal consumes of *both* alternatives. This is because food and water complement each other. A thirsty animal will eat less and a hungry one will drink less. As we alleviate one or the other of these needs, an animal's consumption of the complementary commodity will go up.[16] Thus, the matching law cannot be generalized to cases involving complementary reinforcers.

Open and Closed Economic Systems

Our discussion of the application of economic concepts to operant behavior has shown us that the matching law, which seemed to be an extremely general formulation, is actually a rather restricted one. The matching law holds most clearly when the alternative reinforcers are substitutable, when demand for the reinforcers is inelastic, or if elastic, similar, and when income is not fixed by the experimental procedure. By allowing us to see the matching law as restricted in these ways, these economic concepts cast the typical methods of operant conditioning experiments in a new light. They suggest variables that must be studied (substitutability, elasticity, income) which have previously been neglected. We can illustrate the way in which these economic concepts make us aware of issues that have previously been ignored

16. See Hursh, 1978; Rachlin, Green, Kagel and Battalio, 1976, for example.

by introducing one further concept to the analysis of operant conditioning experiments.

That is the concept of an *open* or *closed economic system*. Imagine being in a department store trying to decide whether to spend your money on some new clothes or some record albums. Your income is fixed, and we might expect to be able to say something about how the price of these items, together with their respective demand curves, will influence your purchasing decision. If the demand for both is relatively elastic, we might expect that as the price of one increases, your demand for it will decrease, resulting in your choice of the other item. But suppose that your uncle is in the record business, so that if you are willing to wait a little while, he will give you any record you want, for free. Under these conditions, we might expect that knowing all there is to know about income, demand, and price would not be much help in predicting what you will purchase. The reason is that because of your uncle, record albums are not really a part of this system of economic concepts. You have an alternative source of this commodity to which economic considerations do not apply. A circumstance like this is described as an *open economic system*. It is to be contrasted with a *closed economic system*, in which access to commodities occurs only through the expenditure of income. The interplay we have described between income, demand and price is only expected to occur in a predictable fashion if the economic system is a closed one.

Why bother with making this distinction, when in the lives of most people, the economic system is distinctly closed? Few of us have uncles who actually give us free access to commodities we really want. But in typical operant conditioning experiments, this distinction is an extremely important one. When one experiments with animals as subjects and food as the reinforcer, one first deprives the animals of food, often until their body weight has been reduced to some fixed proportion of normal weight. Once this is done, the animals are given experimental sessions every day. They are weighed after the sessions and if they have not obtained enough food to maintain their body weight at the desired level, they are given a food supplement between sessions. This feature of experimental procedures is so standard that it is almost never mentioned in papers that report experimental methods and results. Everyone does experiments this way.

Our economic analysis tells us that this feature of standard conditioning experiments is not just incidental. Rather, it is very significant. It turns what would otherwise be a closed economy, during experimental sessions, into an open one. Just as you might decide to purchase clothes rather than records, the pigeon or rat has an "uncle" (the experimenter) in the food business. If it is willing to wait a little while, it can have all the food it needs for free, without expending its income. In short, economic analysis tells us that what goes on during an experimental session should be significantly affected by whether food supplements are available afterwards.

And does it make a difference that food is made available between sessions? The answer is decidedly yes. Suppose we are interested in determining how rate of responding is affected by the value of the schedule of reinforcement. We might expose animals to a series of FR schedules, and a series of VI schedules and see how response rate changes as the schedule changes. If we did this, we might observe data like those plotted in the top of Figure 5–7.[17] Panel A shows that as the FR increases in size, response rate first increases, then decreases. Panel B shows that with VI's there is a steady decrease in responding as the VI increases. Since, as the schedule value increases, an animal must increase its rate of response to obtain the same quantity of food in a session, these curves indicate that animals will obtain less food as the cost of food goes up. The demand for food seems to be elastic.

But both of these curves were taken from standard procedures, in which supplemental feeding occurs between sessions. If instead, we eliminate these supplemental feedings, closing the economic system, there is a very dramatic change in the animal's behavior. As panels C and D indicate, when the system is closed, rate of responding continues to increase as the schedule value increases, whether the schedule is a VI or an FR. Thus, the demand for food is inelastic, at least when the economic system is a closed one.

The manipulation that produced the data in panels C and D, in contrast to A and B, was a trivial one. What was manipulated was a feature of procedure that had become so standard that researchers had not even really considered it as a potential variable. As we can see, it is not merely a potential variable, but a potent one.

The evidence we have reviewed in this section strongly suggests

17. Data in panel A are from Felton and Lyon, 1966; data in panel B are from Catania and Reynolds, 1968; data in panel C are from Collier, Hirsch and Hamlin, 1972; and data in panel D are from Hursh, 1978.

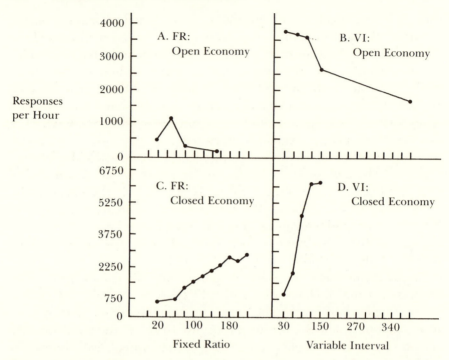

Figure 5–7. The Effect on Response Rate of an Open or a Closed Economy. *In panels* A *and* B, *the economy is open, and response rate tends to decrease as the schedule value increases. In panels* C *and* D, *the economy is closed, and response rate increases as schedule value increases.* (*see note 17*).

that operant behavior is economic in nature. The rules by which animals allocate their resources in choosing among alternatives seem to be the same as the rules people use in making similar decisions. To the extent that economics provides us with a framework for understanding human choice, it may also underlie some principles of behavior theory since behavior theory seems to embody, in the laboratory, so many of the factors that are central to economic analysis.

This chapter attempted to bring behavior theory a few steps closer to conditions that exist in the natural environment. Behavior in the natural environment is not always reinforced, and usually involves choices among alternatives. As we have seen, behavior theorists have studied the effects of partial reinforcement, and the determinants of choice. Some of the principles that have emerged from this study are these:

1. Behavior can be maintained by intermittent reinforcement. There are different types of intermittent reinforcement, called schedules of reinforcement, and each of them maintains behavior in characteristic patterns.

2. Schedules of reinforcement in the natural environment can be found that closely parallel the types studied in the laboratory. And behavior is maintained by these schedules in similar fashion in both settings.

3. The determinants of choice can be summarized for a variety of circumstances by the matching law. The matching law tells us that the allocation of responses among alternatives will match the relative frequency, magnitude and delay of reinforcement offered by the alternatives.

4. However, recent efforts to bring concepts from economics into the laboratory have revealed that the matching law is just a special case of the operation of far more general, economic principles. These principles involve the interplay of demand elasticity, income, price, and commodity substitutability, in open and closed economic systems. These principles capture all the phenomena explained by the matching law, as well as a wide range of others that the matching law cannot explain.

Chapter 6

Stimulus Control of Operant Behavior

WHEN an animal is performing an operant response for food, it is not performing that response in a vacuum. A variety of stimuli occur throughout the animal's engagement with the task. In our discussion of operant conditioning in the last two chapters, we completely ignored such stimuli and their possible significance. In this chapter, we discuss the role that such environmental stimuli play in influencing the occurrence of operants. There is more to the determination of operant behavior than just the simple relation between operants and their consequences.

There are two major ways in which environmental stimuli, aside from biologically significant reinforcers, influence the occurrence of operants. First, organisms learn that operants may be reinforced only in the presence of certain environmental stimuli, and they learn what those stimuli are. Second, they learn that under some conditions, these environmental stimuli, which are of no biological significance to the organism, may come to function as reinforcers. The first of these influences is referred to as the process of *discrimination and generalization*. The second is referred to as *conditioned reinforcement*. Both of them depend for their influence upon a Pavlovianlike relation between environmental stimuli and reinforcers. We will first identify each of these types of phenomena, and indicate their importance to behavior in the natural environment. Then we will discuss their underlying principles.

Discrimination

Suppose we expose a pigeon to a procedure in which a pecking key is lit with red light. Pecks at the key produce food reinforcement,

A rat performing a complex discrimination. *Reinforcement is delivered only if the rat jumps at the "odd" card, the one that differs from the others. (Photo by Frank Lotz Miller from Black Star)*

on a variable interval schedule. After the pigeon has learned to peck the key, and is pecking at a steady rate, we change the procedure. Periodically, the color of the key changes from red to green, stays green for a while, then changes back to red. While the key is green, pecks are never reinforced. Initially, the pigeon will peck at green just as it does at red. But over time it will learn that reinforcement is not available when the key is green. It will learn only to peck when the key is red. When such learning occurs, we say that the animal has learned a discrimination. It has learned that key pecks are reinforced, but only under a particular set of environmental conditions, when the response key is red.

Of all the phenomena studied in operant conditioning laboratories, discrimination is the most pervasive in daily life. No one makes responses that are reinforced in all circumstances. People are consistently required to learn the circumstances in which a particular response will be reinforced. The child learning to cross city streets must learn more than how to step on and off curbs without tripping. He or she must learn that crossing the street is appropriate when the light is green, but not when it is red, and that crossing at the end of the block is appropriate while crossing in the middle is not. The child being taught to cross the street already knows the difference between red and green, as does the pigeon. What must be learned is the difference in the *relation* between each of these stimuli and the consequences of crossing the street. This is what is meant by discrimination. The study of operant discrimination is principally concerned with uncovering the processes by which operant behavior comes under the control of environmental objects or events.

Generalization

While discriminative control of operant behavior may be ubiquitous, it is imperfect. Frequently, behavior that is reinforced under one set of environmental conditions will occur under other, similar conditions. Thus, the pigeon that has learned to peck a red key but not a green key is likely to peck the key if it is orange. The pigeon might do this because of the similarity between orange and red. On the other hand, the pigeon might refrain from pecking when presented with a yellow key, because of its similarity to green. In each case, the pigeon's pecking, or lack of it, has *generalized* to conditions that are new, but similar to the original training conditions. Indeed, how much an animal will respond to a new stimulus is related in an orderly way to how similar this new stimulus is to the training stimulus. As an example, in one experiment pigeons were trained to peck a key when a tone 1000 Hertz (Hz) in pitch was being played. They were then presented with tones of different pitch. The number of responses to these new tones is presented in Figure 6–1. It is clear that with

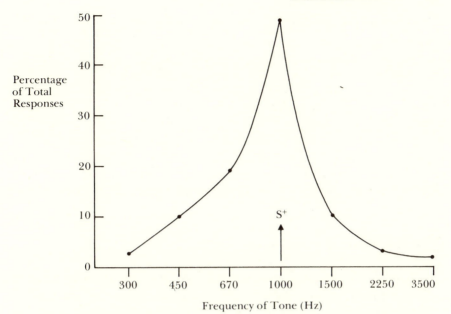

Figure 6–1. Excitatory Generalization Gradient for Tone Frequency in a Pigeon. *The S+ had been a 1,000-Hz tone. The points represent the percentage of all responses made during the generalization test which were made to each particular stimulus. (After Jenkins & Harrison, 1960.)*

increases in the difference between training tone and test tone, responding to the test tone decreased. The result is a *generalization gradient,* which has the greatest number of pecks at the training stimulus (S+), and falls off in orderly fashion as distance from the training stimulus increases.[1]

This phenomenon of *generalization* is as common a characteristic of human behavior as discrimination. Thus, if one purchases a used car that turns out not to perform as promised, one might generalize this negative experience to all used car dealers, and never purchase a used car again. Alternatively, one might generalize to all cars, used or new, manufactured by the company that made the lemon that was purchased.

The process of generalization is much like the process of induction that characterizes scientific inquiry. As we saw in Chapter 4, science

1. Jenkins and Harrison, 1960.

seeks to explain a particular event as an instance of a general principle, that is, it seeks to subsume individual events under appropriate generalizations. Such generalizations in science may be invalid, just as they may be invalid in ordinary experience (the used car dealer may be honorable and the particular manufacturer may be reliable and the purchaser may just have had a stroke of bad luck). When we discuss generalization as a feature of operant behavior, we are concerned with identifying the variables that determine whether generalization occurs, in what direction it occurs (for example, across all used car dealers, or across all cars made by the given manufacturer), how broad it is, and how organisms come to make generalizations that are appropriate and accurate.

Conditioned Reinforcement

Until now, when discussing reinforcement or punishment, we referred to environmental events of biological significance. Food, water and electric shock have clear and immediate biological effects. However, most human behavior does not produce such biologically important stimuli. Our actions produce money, or good grades, or smiles of approval from parents or peers. Are these events reinforcers? If they are not, the applicability of principles of behavior theory to human affairs will surely be limited, indeed. If they are, how do they become reinforcers? Behavior theorists claim that such stimuli are reinforcers, and that they become reinforcers as a result of conditioning. Thus, they are called *conditioned reinforcers*.

Suppose we train a pigeon to peck a key for food. Just prior to each food delivery, a tone is sounded briefly. As a result of such a pairing of the tone with food, the pigeon will peck the key if key pecks produce the tone, but no food. Thus, the tone is now effective as a reinforcer of key pecks. Behavior theorists suggest that a similar process may underlie the effectiveness of social approval or money as reinforcers. Suppose your child begins doing household chores. You reliably tell her what a good job she has done, and give her a piece of cake, or some ice cream as a reward. After a number of such episodes, you may discover that just telling her what a good job she has done is sufficient to make her eager to do more. The approval may now be reinforcing because it has previously been paired with the ice cream. Similarly, money may come to be an effective reinforcer as a result of being paired with the stimuli it is used to purchase. Once these pairings have occurred, money may sustain behavior even when the pairings are discontinued. If this account of how stimuli like money and social approval come to be reinforcing is accurate, the explanatory power of behavior theory is greatly enlarged.

Discrimination, Generalization, Conditioned Reinforcement and Pavlovian Conditioning

We have said that discrimination, generalization, and conditioned reinforcement have Pavlovian-like properties. But so far, we have not mentioned Pavlovian conditioning. What does Pavlovian conditioning have to do with discrimination, generalization and conditioned reinforcement? Consider the diagrams of typical Pavlovian conditioning, discrimination and conditioned reinforcement procedures in Figure 6–2. In the Pavlovian conditioning procedure, the red light is the CS

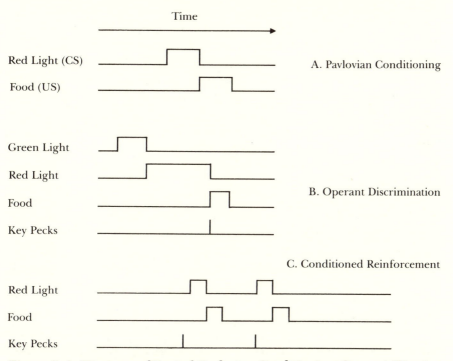

Figure 6–2. Diagrams of Typical Pavlovian Conditioning, Operant Discrimination, and Conditioned Reinforcement Procedures. *The important point to notice is that in all three procedures, the relation between the red light and food is the same.*

and food is the US. In the operant discrimination procedure, the red light is the stimulus in the presence of which pecks are reinforced, called the S^+ (the green light is called the S^-). These two procedures are different in very important ways. Foremost among them is that in the Pavlovian conditioning procedure, food (the US) comes no matter what the pigeon does, while in the operant discrimination procedure food will only come if the pigeon pecks. Nevertheless, if we look at just the relation between the red light and food, it is the same in both procedures. Red is a signal that food is coming. The same is true of the conditioned reinforcement procedure. We might view this procedure as one in which key pecks are required to produce an entire Pavlovian conditioning trial (red light as CS and food as US). Thus, it is clear that at least superficially, both operant discrimination and conditioned reinforcement procedures involve Pavlovian conditioning relations. To find out whether the resemblance between Pavlovian conditioning, discrimination and conditioned reinforcement is more than superficial requires empirical investigation. After all, a Pavlovian CS tells an organism what is about to happen to it while an operant discriminative stimulus tells an organism what it has to do. Thus, while both stimuli are signals, they are signals giving quite different sorts of information. To know whether this difference is critical, we must examine whether the kinds of factors that influence Pavlovian conditioning (see Chapter 3), also influence operant discrimination learning and conditioned reinforcement. Let us turn first to a discussion of the phenomena of discrimination and generalization.

The Process of Discrimination

What are the conditions that determine whether animals will learn discriminations, whether environmental stimuli will come to exert discriminative control over behavior? To answer this question, we need a device or procedure with which to detect such control if it is present. Such a device is provided by the generalization test.[2] As

2. The generalization test has been a most popular method in recent years for making inferences about the discriminative control of responding by particular stimuli. But this test is not the only method, and not always the best one (Mackintosh, 1977). Alternative tests for discriminative control include removing the hypothesized controlling stimulus altogether and looking for cessation of responding, or transferring the hypothesized controlling stimulus to a new situation and looking for more rapid learning from animals experienced with the stimulus than from inexperienced animals.

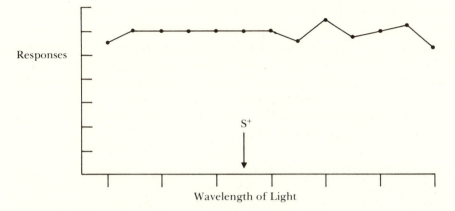

Figure 6–3. Hypothetical Generalization Gradient. *The gradient is flat and indicates lack of control over responding by wavelength of light.*

Figure 6–1 shows, an animal trained with a particular stimulus as S⁺ responds to other, similar stimuli. However, it responds less and less to those stimuli as they become less and less similar to S⁺, that is, the generalization gradient has a peak at S⁺. The fact that responding changes as the stimulus changes implies that the stimulus is controlling the response. Suppose one administered a generalization test for color to a pigeon that had been trained to peck a green key for food, and obtained a gradient like that in Figure 6–3. The gradient is completely horizontal, or flat. Apparently, the pigeon generalizes completely from green to all colors. When flat generalization gradients such as these are observed, we infer that the stimulus dimension being varied (in Figure 6–3, key color) is not controlling the pigeon's behavior. No matter how the wave length or color is altered, the animal's behavior remains pretty much unchanged. Why might this be? What can account for the failure of a stimulus to control operant responding?

Predictiveness and Redundancy

To answer this question, let us review some conclusions we reached in Chapter 3 on Pavlovian conditioning. In order for conditioning to occur, a differential (predictive) contingency must exist between the CS and the US; that is, conditioning occurs if the US is more likely in the presence of the CS than in its absence, but does not occur if the US is no more likely in the presence of the CS than in its absence. If more than one predictive CS is present, then conditioning will occur to the CS that is most predictive. If a number of equally predictive CSs are present, then conditioning might occur to all of them. Alternatively, the presence of one especially salient CS might *overshadow* conditioning to any of the others.

How do these facts relate to the case of the pigeon pecking the green key? Suppose that in order for a discriminative stimulus to exert control over operant responding, it must be a differential predictor of reinforcement availability, just as an effective Pavlovian CS is a differential predictor of the US. Does the green key meet this criterion? Considered in contrast to stimuli outside the chamber, it does. Reinforcement is available in the chamber, but not outside it. Therefore, green is a differential predictor of food availability. But green is not the *best* predictor of reinforcer availability. The green key shares its predictive relation to reinforcer availability with the houselight, the wire mesh floor, the sound of the exhaust fan and a host of other stimuli that are present in the chamber and absent outside it. Any one or more of these stimuli might overshadow the green light and effectively control pecking. Suppose, for example, the pigeon's responding were controlled by the brightness of the key and not by its color. If this were true, then a generalization test in which stimuli were different colors but the same brightness would be presenting the same *effective* stimulus to the pigeon again and again. Though the objective stimulus would be changing as color changed, the aspect of the stimulus that was exercising control would remain constant. Control of key pecking by brightness could be revealed in a second generalization test, one in which the color of the key remained green but its brightness was varied. Such a test might yield the gradient in Figure 6–4. If so, one could conclude that the stimulus controlling pecking was the brightness of the light on the key and not its color.

When there are a number of equally predictive signals for reinforcer availability, each providing the same information as the other, we call them *redundant*. When such redundant stimuli are present, which of them will control responding is influenced by a number of factors. First of all, one stimulus may be inherently more salient than the others, and overshadow them. For example, in one study, pigeons were trained to peck a lit key for food in the presence of a tone. Both the tone and the key light were always present as redundant signals

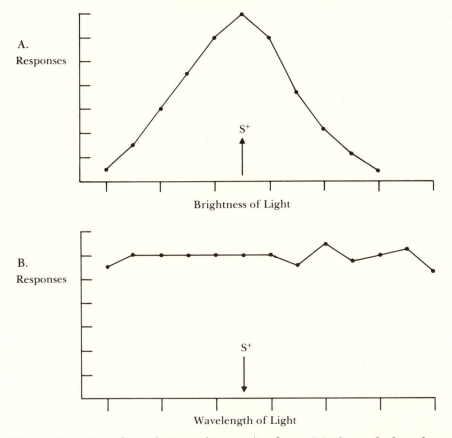

A.
Responses

S⁺

Brightness of Light

B.
Responses

S⁺

Wavelength of Light

Figure 6–4. Hypothetical Generalization Gradient. (A) *The peaked gradient indicates control of responding by intensity or brightness of light. Contrast this with the flat gradient in Figure 6–3 (reprinted here—B), which indicates lack of control of responding by color.*

for food. After this training, generalization tests for tone frequency yielded flat gradients like the one in Figure 6–3. In contrast, a second group of pigeons was trained to peck a key in the presence of the tone, but in total darkness. For this group, generalization tests for tone frequency yielded gradients like the one in Figure 6–4.[3] Clearly,

3. Rudolph and Van Houten, 1977.

for the first group of pigeons, the key light overshadowed the tone in controlling pecking.

To suggest a plausible analogy to this experiment, consider the lecturer learning which members of the audience to focus on while speaking. She learns to discriminate attentive from inattentive members of her audience, and to look only at the attentive ones, because their alert nodding glances are reinforcing. But suppose that all the attentive listeners sit in the front of the room. Now there will be redundant positive stimuli—a part of the room and a set of attentive faces. If the room cues were to overshadow the face cues, we might expect this lecturer to focus on the front of the room even when she addressed a different audience.

The relative salience of a stimulus may also be influenced by an organism's past experience. Suppose a pigeon has had previous experience in which a tone was a signal for reinforcer availability. The pigeon is then exposed to a procedure in which a tone and a light are redundant signals. It is likely that the tone will control responding. Without the prior experience with the tone, the light might well control responding. In a confirming experiment, two groups of pigeons were trained to peck a lit key for food in the presence of a 1000 Hz tone. Key light and tone were redundant signals. Prior to the experiment, one of the groups had received prolonged experience in which the delivery of the daily ration of food to the pigeons in their home cages was signalled by the 1000 Hz tone. When, after training, both groups were given generalization tests for tone frequency, the group with no pre-experimental experience with the tone produced a flat gradient, as in Figure 6–3 while the group with pre-experimental experience produced a peaked gradient, as in Figure 6–4.[4] Thus, prior experience in which a stimulus is a non-redundant signal seems to insure control by that stimulus in situations in which it competes with other equally predictive stimuli, a phenomenon very much like the blocking effect (see Chapter 3, pp. 53–55).

In summary, we have seen that in situations in which a number of different stimuli bear an equally predictive relation to the availability of food, the particular stimulus that will effectively control responding is largely beyond experimental control. The inherent salience of dif-

4. Thomas, Mariner and Sherry, 1969. For further supporting evidence, see Lawrence, 1949, 1950.

ferent stimuli, and the relevant past experience of the experimental subject, will combine to determine what the effective stimulus will be. The experimenter is not helpless though. The way to insure that a particular stimulus will control responding is to make that stimulus the best predictor of reinforcer availability. And the way to do this is by discrimination training.

Discrimination Training as a Stimulus Selector

Consider the following experiment. One group of pigeons was trained to peck a green key with a white, vertical line superimposed on it. After some training, they were given a generalization test with lines which differed from the vertical in 22.5 degree steps. The resulting flat gradient of generalization is presented in Figure 6–5A.

A second group of pigeons was given discrimination training. The vertical line on a green background was the S$^+$; key pecks in its presence produced food. The green key by itself was the S$^-$; pecks in its presence did not produce food. After the pigeons had learned to peck the S$^+$ and not the S$^-$, a generalization test for line orientation was administered. The resulting sharply peaked gradient is depicted in Figure 6–5B.

Finally, a third group of pigeons was given discrimination training in which green plus vertical was the S$^+$ and red without a line was the S$^-$. The subsequent generalization test for line orientation produced the flat gradient depicted in Figure 6–5C.[5]

Let us attempt to explain these results. The flat gradient in Figure 6–5A suggests that some stimulus other than the line was controlling pecking. Since the line and the green key color and a host of other stimuli were all equally predictive of reinforcer availability, control of responding by the line could have been overshadowed by many different things.

This possibility was eliminated for the pigeons whose data are in Figure 6–5B. For this group, pecks were only reinforced when the line was present. Green was also present at this time, as were other aspects of the situation, like the houselight and the exhaust fan. However, green was also present during periods when pecks were not reinforced. Thus, discrimination training established the vertical line

5. Newman and Baron, 1965.

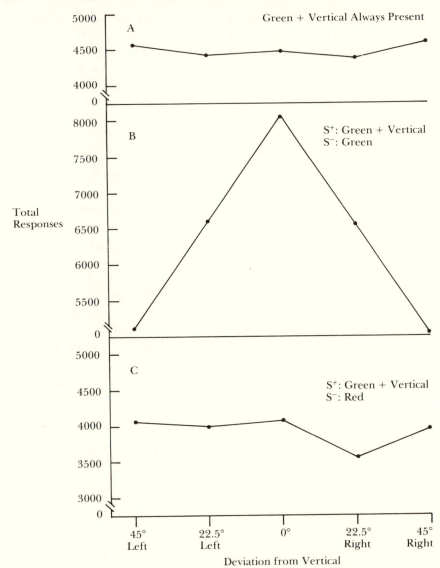

Figure 6–5. Effect of Discrimination Training on Stimulus Selection. *Each part of the figure presents a generalization gradient for line orientation for a different group of pigeons. Group A was simply trained to peck a green key with a white vertical line for food. Group B had green + vertical as an S⁺ and green without vertical as an S⁻. Group C had green + vertical as S⁺ and red without vertical as S⁻. (After Newman & Baron, 1965.)*

as the *best predictor* of reinforcement, with the result that the line controlled pecking, as witnessed by the peaked generalization gradient.

The discrimination training received by the group whose data are in Figure 6–5C also established the vertical line as a better predictor of reinforcement than most other aspects of the situation. Environmental stimuli such as the houselight and exhaust fan noise were present during S^- periods as well as S^+ periods. Thus, these stimuli should have been eliminated from competition with the line for control of responding. Notice, however, that the line was not the *best* predictor of reinforcement; the green key was equally good (S^- was both the absence of the line and red on the key). The resulting flat generalization gradient suggests that green overshadowed the line and controlled pecking when the two stimuli were equally predictive of reinforcement.

We see, therefore, that discrimination training can be used to insure control of responding by a particular stimulus. It accomplishes this by establishing that stimulus as the best predictor of reinforcement. All other aspects of the environment that might potentially control responding are present all the time, both when reinforcement is available and when it is not. The S^+ is only present when reinforcement is available.

Discrimination Training and Incidental Stimuli

The effects of discrimination training need not always be so dramatic, shifting control of responding entirely from one aspect of the situation to another (as suggested by the data in Figure 6–5). It is also possible that in the absence of discrimination training, numerous background or *incidental stimuli* share control of responding so that each of a variety of generalization tests will yield moderately peaked gradients, and that discrimination training eliminates control by all stimuli but the S^+, with the result that the generalization gradient for the S^+ is sharpened.

In a test of this proposition, some pigeons were trained to peck a key for food in the continual presence of a 1000 Hz tone.[6] A generalization test with other tonal frequencies produced the gradient depicted in the Figure 6–6A. Other pigeons learned a discrimination: the 1000 Hz tone signalled reinforcer availability (S^+), and no tone

6. Jenkins and Harrison, 1960, 1962.

signalled non-reinforcement (S⁻). This group produced the generalization gradient depicted in Figure 6–6B.

A final set of pigeons also learned a discrimination: The 1000 Hz tone was S⁺ and a 950 Hz tone was S⁻. This group produced the generalization gradient in Figure 6–6C.

Based upon the preceding discussion, we would conclude that the flat gradient in Figure 6–6A is the result of the overshadowing of the tone by other, equally predictive but more salient, "incidental"

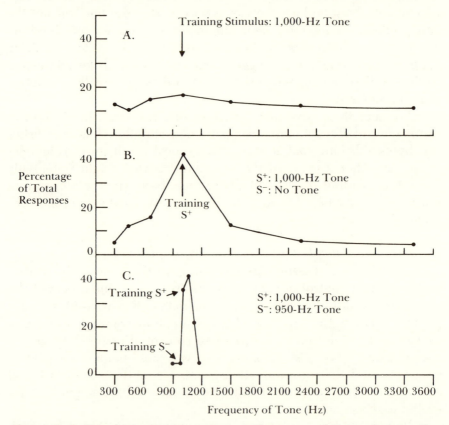

Figure 6–6. Discrimination Training as a Sharpener of Generalization Gradients. *The figure presents the percentage of all responses made during generalization testing which were made in the presence of each different tone. The gradient in* A, *after nondiscriminative training, is flat. The gradient in* B, *after discrimination training with a 1,000-Hz tone as* S⁺ *and no tone as* S⁻, *is peaked. The gradient in* C, *after discrimination training between 1,000 Hz* (S⁺) *and 950 Hz* (S⁻) *is even more peaked. (After Jenkins & Harrison, 1962.)*

stimuli. Discrimination training makes the tone a better predictor of reinforcement than any other stimulus, and the result is the peaked gradient in Figure 6–6B indicating how the tone controls responding. But what aspect of the tone is exercising control? Is it pitch, or loudness, or loudness and pitch in combination? For the group of pigeons whose data are in Figure 6–6C even this source of competition among potential controlling stimuli is eliminated. The only difference between S^+ and S^- is pitch (1000 Hz vs. 950 Hz). Not only is the tone a better predictor of reinforcement than incidental stimuli, but the frequency or pitch of the tone is a better predictor of reinforcement than any of its other characteristics. As a result, the generalization gradient for tonal frequency produced by this group is even more peaked than the one in Figure 6–6B.

Let us summarize the data in Figure 6–6 as a way of summarizing the entire section. When there is no best predictor of reinforcement, almost any aspect of the experimental situation might control responding (Figure 6–6A). When the presence of a tone is established as the best predictor of reinforcement, then one or more aspects of the tone will control responding, and control by incidental stimuli will be eliminated (Figure 6–6B). When the frequency of the tone is the best predictor of reinforcement, then that *specific* aspect of the tone will control responding and control by other aspects of the tone will be eliminated (Figure 6–6C). In general, the way to assure control of responding by any particular aspect of a situation is to make that aspect the best predictor of reinforcement.

The problem of bringing behavior under the control of a particular stimulus or class of stimuli is analogous in many ways to the problem scientists face in deciding which generalization is the appropriate one for explaining a particular phenomenon. The scientist observes a red ball and a green cube dropped from the same place at the same time. They land together. Should the scientist's generalization invoke the colors of objects and the noises they make, the shapes of the objects, their material composition, or what? A way to discover which generalization is appropriate is systematically to manipulate various properties of the balls, and observe which manipulations leave which regularities unchanged. This amounts to finding which antecedent event is best correlated with the consequent event of interest—in this case, finding the best predictor. But finding the best predictor is precisely what discrimination training entails. When there are multiple, redundant predictors, behavior may be controlled by any of them.

Similarly, when there are multiple, redundant antecedent events, our generalizations may invoke any of them. In sum, the model of discrimination learning we are suggesting here has organisms behaving as informal scientists.

Attention

If we were to describe the results in Figure 6–6 less formally, we would be inclined to say that discrimination training teaches animals to *pay attention*. It teaches them which parts of the environment to focus on, and which parts to ignore. When a tone is S^+ and no tone is S^-, the animal learns to pay attention to the tone. When a 1000 Hz tone is S^+ and a 950 Hz tone is S^-, then the animal learns, more specifically, to pay attention to the frequency of the tone. There is a long history of attempts to investigate attention as a critical part of the process of discrimination learning, and we turn now to a discussion of some of the issues involved in the study of attention.

What does it mean to say that an animal is "paying attention" to a stimulus aside from that the animal's responding is controlled by that stimulus? Can we somehow separate paying attention from the more general characteristic of an animal's behavior in a discrimination learning experiment that it responds appropriately in the presence of the S^+ and S^-?

These questions have been confronted by numerous investigators over the years. A number of different answers have been proposed, but many have the same general character. Discrimination learning is conceived as a two-part process: One must learn what stimuli are relevant or what to pay attention to; and one must learn to do specific things in the presence of specific stimuli.[7] As an example, consider a young child learning to cross city streets. What the child must learn is that traffic lights are the relevant stimuli, and that he or she may walk when the light is one color but not when the light is a different color. Thus the child must learn both what to pay attention to (the color of the traffic light), and what action is appropriate in the presence of what stimulus (crossing is appropriate when the light is green, but not when it is red).

---

7. See Lovejoy, 1968; Mackintosh, 1975; Sutherland, 1965; Sutherland and Mackintosh, 1971; Trabasso and Bower, 1968; Zeaman and House, 1971.

Transfer of Training

Attempts to show that "paying attention" is a separable part of discrimination learning have often involved experiments on *transfer of training*. Animals trained on one kind of discrimination problem are then given a different kind, and the measure of interest is the extent to which training on the first problem affects, or transfers to, learning the second one.

In one kind of transfer of training experiment, two groups of subjects first experience different discrimination problems. For example, both groups might receive circles or squares that are red or green. For Group 1, red stimuli are S^+ and green stimuli are S^-, regardless of shape. For Group 2, squares are S^+ and circles are S^-, regardless of color. As the animals master the discrimination, we might imagine the learning process involving the following components:

1. For Group 1, color is relevant and shape is irrelevant. That is, color is predictive of reinforcement availability while shape is not. For Group 2, shape is relevant (predictive of reinforcement) and color is not.

2. For Group 1, given that color is relevant, specifically, red predicts reinforcement and green predicts the absence of reinforcement. Therefore, responses should only occur when red is present. For Group 2, squares predict reinforcement and circles its absence. Therefore, responses should only occur when squares are present.

Alternatively, the discrimination process might involve only a single component—learning specifically about S^+ and S^- and not also about the dimensions (color or shape) which they possess.

This phase of the experiment, and a second test phase, are depicted in Figure 6–7. What might we expect the effects of Phase 1 to be when the groups are exposed to Phase 2, in which blue is the S^+, yellow is the S^- and diamonds and triangles are irrelevant? Note first that the specific stimuli being employed are all different in Phase 2 than in Phase 1. However, the relevant dimension in Phase 2 is color—the same dimension that was relevant in Phase 1 for Group 1, but a different dimension from what was relevant in Phase 1 for Group 2. If learning a discrimination involves learning to attend to the relevant dimension as well as learning which specific stimulus is S^+, Group 1, having already learned to attend to color, should learn faster in Phase 2 than Group 2. If, on the other hand, discrimination learning involves simply learning to respond to S^+ and not S^-, neither group should be helped more than the other by past experience, since the

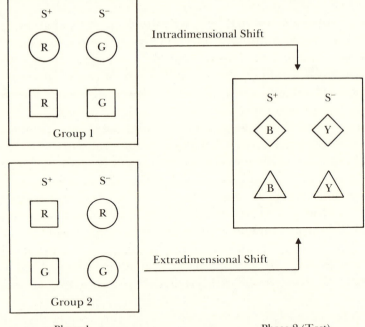

Phase 1   Phase 2 (Test)

Figure 6–7. The Intradimensional Shift vs. the Extradimensional Shift.
*Groups 1 and 2 must learn to respond to blue (S⁺) and not yellow (S⁻) in
Phase 2, after prior training. Group 1 has previously learned to respond to
red (S⁺) and not green (S⁻). For this group, the new problem represents an
intradimensional shift. S⁺ and S⁻ are different in Phase 2 from Phase 1, but
they are on the same dimension (color). Group 2 has previously learned to
respond to squares but not circles. For this group, the new problem represents an extradimensional shift. Both the specific S⁺s and the dimension on
which they fall are different in Phase 2 from Phase 1.*

specific S⁺ and S⁻ (blue and yellow) were not a part of the previous
training.

These experiments are described as pitting *intradimensional shift*
(different values on the same dimension; blue and yellow instead of
red and green, as in Group 1) against *extradimensional shift* (different
relevant dimensions; colors as S⁺ and S⁻ instead of shapes, as in Group
2). The reliable observation in rats, pigeons, monkeys, children, and
adults is that the intradimensional shift is learned faster than the
extradimensional shift, providing support for the view that discrimi-

nation learning involves learning to pay attention to relevant (predictive) stimulus dimensions.[8]

Complex Discrimination

Our discussion of discrimination and generalization has emphasized the similarity in the process by which stimuli come to control operant behavior and the process by which stimuli come to trigger Pavlovian conditioned responses. In making this case, we have chosen rather simple examples of discrimination learning. The stimuli are always simple, easy to detect, discrete, and ordered on some continuum (e.g., tonal pitch or color). Very few of the discriminations people are required to make have these characteristics. The stimuli are complex and multi-faceted, the relevant facets are not easy to detect, and it is not clear that the relevant features of many discriminative stimuli fall on any physical continuum. We respond differentially to friendly and unfriendly faces. What makes a friendly face? We respond differentially to true and false information claims. What makes an information claim recognizably true and what do such true claims have in common? What reason is there to believe, in short, that discriminative control over human behavior bears any important resemblance to the kinds of situations we have been discussing?

One way to address this issue is by identifying some examples of animal discrimination in the laboratory which have many of the complexities of human discrimination. Since these complex laboratory cases can be understood with the theoretical tools we have already been developing, they inspire a measure of confidence that human discrimination in the natural environment can also be understood with these tools. While these examples of complex laboratory discrimination do not constitute proof that we have an account of human discrimination, they are encouraging.

8. For demonstrations, see Mackintosh and Little, 1969; Shepp and Eimas, 1964; Shepp and Schrier, 1969; and Wolff, 1967. There are also other kinds of transfer of training studies which point to paying attention as a critical component of discrimination learning. See Kendler and D'Amato, 1955; Kendler and Kendler, 1962 for examples, and Sutherland and Mackintosh, 1971, for a critical discussion.

Discriminating Relations

There has long been evidence that animals exposed to discrimination training can learn to respond to the relations between the stimuli in the situation. If, for example, a bright light is S^+ and a dim one is S^-, they can learn to choose the brighter stimulus. When they are later tested by being presented with a choice between two new stimuli, they go to the brighter one. An impressive demonstration that animals can learn to respond to relations comes from work on what is called the *intermediate size problem*. Suppose animals are trained with a 150 cm² square as S^+, and 100 and 200 cm² squares as S^-. They must learn to choose the 150 cm² square. But what are they learning? Are they learning that the 150 cm² square is the positive stimulus, or that the middle-sized stimulus is positive? To find out, we present them with three new stimuli, squares 200, 250 and 300 cm² in area. In such tests, animals reliably choose the middle stimulus.[9]

Another experimental demonstration that animals learn about relations among stimuli, and not the absolute values of the stimuli is the following: Rats were exposed to cards that were divided in half. The bottom half of each card was an intermediate shade of gray. The top half of the cards was either one of three lighter shades or one of three darker shades. The animals had to learn to make a left turn when the top of the card was darker than the bottom and a right turn when the top of the card was lighter than the bottom. The procedure is diagrammed in Figure 6–8. After learning, they experienced a number of test trials. On these trials, the bottom of the card was no longer an intermediate gray, but one of the other six shades. Sometimes, for example, two of the darker stimuli were arranged with the lighter of the two on top. The animals had learned to make a left turn in the presence of each of these stimuli. However, they had learned to make a right turn when confronted with the pattern light above dark. Which response did they make? One response would indicate that their responding was controlled by absolute stimulus properties and the other would indicate that their responding was controlled by relations among stimuli. In the overwhelming majority of such test trials, the animals' responses were appropriate to the relation between the stimuli and not their absolute characteristics.[10]

Though discriminations like these are considerably more complex

9. Gonzales, Gentry and Bitterman, 1954.
10. Lawrence and DeRivera, 1954.

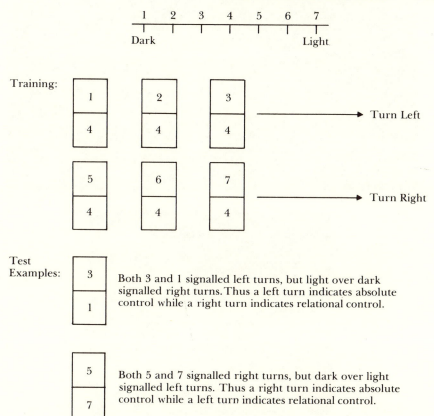

Figure 6–8. A Test of Control of Responding by Stimulus Relations. *A procedure studied by Lawrence and DeRivera, 1954, which provided support for the relational view of discrimination learning is diagrammed schematically.*

than the ones we discussed earlier in the chapter, they still have the characteristic that the relevant property to be discriminated is discrete and easy to identify physically, a feature which is absent from many human discriminations. There is now some evidence available that pigeons can learn discriminations even when the relevant properties of the stimuli are extremely difficult to identify physically. The evidence comes from the study of what are called *natural concepts* in pigeons.[11] In these experiments, photographs were taken of ordinary city street scenes, and pigeons were presented with slides. In one set

11. Herrnstein, Loveland, and Cable, 1976; Herrnstein, 1979.

Figure 6–9. Discrimination of Natural Objects by Pigeons. *Pigeons were presented with slides of ordinary street scenes, and were required to discriminate them by the presence or absence of either water, trees, or a particular person. This figure presents examples of some typical stimuli presented. A positive example of water is in A and a negative is in B. A positive example*

of a tree is in C and a negative is in D. A positive example of the particular person is in E and a negative is in F. In all cases, the majority of pigeons responded correctly to these stimuli (from Herrnstein, Loveland, and Cable, 1976). Photographs by Richard Herrnstein © copyright, 1976.

of slides, 40 contained a tree or part of a tree somewhere in the picture and 40 did not. In another set, 40 contained water somewhere in the picture and 40 did not. In the final set, 40 contained a view of a particular person somewhere in the picture and 40 did not. Different groups of pigeons learned these three discriminations, with either tree, water, or the person as S$^+$. Key pecks when the S$^+$ were present produced food while pecks when an S$^-$ was present did not. The pigeons learned the discriminations to an impressive degree of accuracy. Still more impressive, when they were given new slides to respond to, they were just as accurate on first presentation, as they had been with the training slides. That these discriminations were extremely difficult, and required discriminative skills similar to the ones people must use in everyday life, can be seen in Figure 6–9, which presents examples of typical S$^+$s and S$^-$s in each of the three categories.

Significance of Discrimination

We have now concluded our discussion of discriminative control of operant behavior. It is a phenomenon of major significance if principles of behavior theory are ever to produce an account of phenomena outside the laboratory. Intelligent human behavior involves not just learning the right thing to do, but learning the appropriate circumstances for doing it. And appropriate circumstances include not just the training situation, but generalization to relevantly similar new situations. Too much generalization would lead to inappropriate behavior in many situations, and too little generalization would lead to a kind of machine-like, inflexible organism that had to be given explicit training whenever a new situation arose. Thus effective discrimination walks a fine line between overgeneralizing and undergeneralizing what was learned in the training situation.

What does the laboratory have to teach us about discriminative control? How are studies of discriminative control in the restricted experimental environment applicable to problems of discriminative control in complex, natural settings? In some ways, applicability is quite limited. Laboratory studies of generalization teach us that an animal is more likely to emit a response in the presence of a stimulus that is similar to the training stimulus than in the presence of a stimulus that is quite distinct from the training stimulus. This is an important principle with enormous predictive power. The problem is this: In the laboratory, it is easy to specify whether a stimulus is similar to a training stimulus or not; training stimuli are typically chosen specifically to lie on a continuum which provides the means of judging similarity. Stimuli in the natural environment are not so neat. Is the classroom similar to the library? Is it more similar to the home? Is the mental hospital ward similar to the local community? If not, on what dimensions is it different and how can it be made more similar? Without knowing what dimension of a stimulus situation is relevant for comparison, it is impossible to assess stimulus similarity.

Suppose, for example, a teacher came to you as an expert behavior theorist and asked for advice in dealing with a child who created frequent disturbances in the classroom. You might devise a program for modifying this child's behavior and carry it out in periodic, therapeutic sessions with the child. Your program might be successful in eliminating the child's disruptive behavior with you. But how can you be sure that the child's modified behavior will carry over, or generalize, to the classroom? To be sure of this, you would need to know what the controlling classroom stimulus was, and be sure to design your modification program so that it included that stimulus. It should be apparent that identifying controlling stimuli in a complex, human social situation is not so simple an affair as it is in the laboratory.

Nevertheless, studies of generalization in the laboratory may provide a means for assessing stimulus similarity in the natural environment. If one assumes the general shape of generalization gradients as a given, then one can use the probability of responding in situations which differ from the training situation as an index of stimulus similarity. If the probability of responding is low, then the situation is judged as different from the training situation. If the probability of responding is high, then the situation is judged as similar to the training situation. The logic of this kind of analysis is exactly the reverse of what is done in the laboratory. There, the degree of stimulus similarity is known, and the shape of the generalization function must be determined. Once this is done, however, the generalization function itself may be used as an index of stimulus similarity in the natural environment. If such a strategy proves reliable, it will represent an enormous contribution to our understanding of behavior in the natural environment.

There is another very clear lesson to be learned from the laboratory. In the absence of explicit discrimination training, discriminative control is left to chance. Any of a host of different stimuli which stand in the same relation to reinforcement may control responding. To insure control of responding by a particular stimulus, one must arrange the situation so that that stimulus is the best predictor of reinforcement. The way to do this is to establish a discrimination, with the target stimulus as S^+ and its absence, or some other stimulus, as S^-. In this way, the control of behavior by incidental stimuli will be minimized, and the likelihood of overgeneralization will be reduced.

Conditioned Reinforcement

The phenomenon of operant discrimination is one very significant example of how Pavlovian relations between stimuli and reinforcers influence operant behavior. We turn now to another example, which is perhaps just as significant: *conditioned reinforcement*. Pigeons, rats and dogs work in experimental settings to produce food or water or to avoid shock. People rarely engage in behavior that produces or avoids biologically significant stimuli directly. Many people are virtually never deprived of food or water. If one is to account for human behavior in terms of reinforcement principles one must look elsewhere for the reinforcers. Likely reinforcers in the natural environment are money, social approval, love, status, and power. The obvious influence of stimuli like money on human behavior challenges the behavior theorist to develop an account of how money might come to reinforce behavior. Thus, the generality of principles of behavior theory may depend upon our understanding of conditioned reinforcement.

Establishing a Conditioned Reinforcer

As we saw in Figure 6–1, a conditioned reinforcer looks like a Pavlovian CS procedurally. An animal engages in an operant response for reinforcement, and each reinforcer is preceded by a biologically neutral stimulus, like a light flash or a tone. As a result of this pairing of neutral stimulus with reinforcer, the neutral stimulus acquires the capacity to sustain operant behavior on its own.

In one of the earliest demonstrations of conditioned reinforcement, rats' lever presses produced a clicking sound and food. Then lever pressing was observed when presses produced the click only. These animals pressed the lever more than animals for which lever presses did not produce clicks.[12] This experiment is an example of how, by conditioning, a neutral stimulus (click) can be used to maintain an operant response. What is there about the relation between click and food that seems to make the click a conditioned reinforcer?

Because conditioned reinforcers look procedurally like Pavlovian CSs, it is not surprising that issues we discussed in the chapter on Pavlovian conditioning reappear in a discussion of conditioned reinforcement. The earliest interpretation of the conditions necessary for Pavlovian conditioning isolated temporal contiguity between CS and US. Subsequent research and theoretical analysis led to a revision of our understanding. Informativeness or predictiveness of the CS was also necessary; temporal contiguity was not sufficient in itself. The same is true for establishing a stimulus as a conditioned reinforcer.

Consider the following experiment. Rats already trained to press a lever for food experienced trials with the lever absent in which food presentation was preceded by two stimuli, S1 and S2 as depicted in Figure 6–10A. For one group of rats (Group B), S1 was also occasionally presented alone, without S2 or food, as in Figure 6–10B. After this training, the rats were placed in a situation in which lever presses produced only S1 for some animals and only S2 for others. Based upon what we now know about the importance of the predictiveness of stimuli in conditioning situations, what would we expect the results of such an experiment to be? Let us consider first the rats (Group A) who experienced only the stimulus sequences depicted in Figure 6–10A. S1 and S2 both reliably preceded food. However, since S1 appeared a half-second before S2, the appearance of S2 was redundant; all the information available regarding food was carried by S1. If the predictiveness of a stimulus is essential to its conditioned reinforcing power, we would expect these rats to have responded more when responses produced S1 than when responses produced S2.

Now consider the second group of rats (Group B). When S1, S2 and food occurred in sequence, S2 was again redundant. However, some of the time only S1 occurred. As a result of these extra trials, S1 no longer made S2 redundant; sometimes S1 was followed by food but sometimes it was not. Now, S2, which was always followed by food, was the best predictor of food. If the predictiveness of a stimulus is crucial to its conditioned reinforcing power, we would expect these rats to have responded more in extinction for S2 than for S1.

12. Bugelski, 1938.

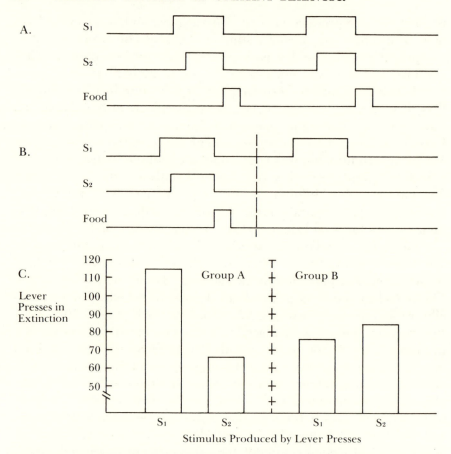

Figure 6–10. Effects of the Informative Value of Stimuli on Their Effectiveness as Conditioned Reinforcers. A *depicts the S_1–S_2–food sequence received
by Group A. B depicts the two types of sequence received by Group B. C
depicts responses in extinction for both groups when lever presses produced
either S_1 or S_2. (After Egger & Miller, 1962.)*

   As can be seen in Figure 6–10C, the predictions based upon the
predictiveness hypothesis were confirmed experimentally. Rats in
Group A, which experienced only S1-S2 food trials, pressed more for
S1 than S2. Rats in Group B, which sometimes experienced S1 alone,
pressed more for S2 than S1.[13] Note that this experiment cannot be
taken to show that predictiveness is *necessary* for a stimulus to become
a conditioned reinforcer. What it does show is that the more predictive
a stimulus is, the more effective it is.

   13. Egger and Miller, 1962.

Observing Responses

Imagine a pigeon pecking a white key for food. Sometimes food is available on an FI schedule and sometimes food is available on an FR schedule. In either case, the key remains white. Usually, FI and FR schedules sustain different rates and patterns of responding (see Figure 5–2, p. 100). However, in this situation, there is no way to tell which schedule is in effect at any given time. If the pigeon had some way of telling, it might produce response patterns appropriate to the operative schedule.

Suppose we give the pigeon a way of telling. We light up a second key. If the pigeon pecks this key (called the observing key) the light on the first key turns red if the FI is in effect, and green if the FR is in effect. This procedure is diagrammed in Figure 6–11. By pecking the observing key, the pigeon gets no closer to reinforcement, but it can find out what schedule of reinforcement is in effect on the operant key. Pecks on the observing key are called *observing responses* because they yield information without having any direct effect on the delivery

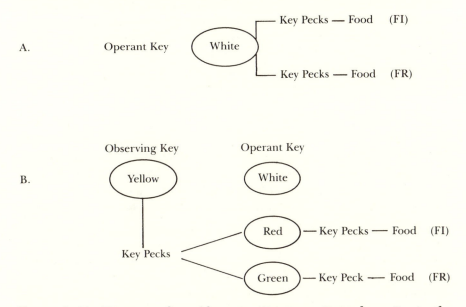

Figure 6–11. Diagram of an Observing Response Procedure. *In* A, *the pigeon's pecks at a white key are sometimes reinforced on an FI schedule and sometimes reinforced on an FR schedule, and the pigeon has no way of telling which schedule is in effect at any time. In* B, *by pecking at a second, observing key, the pigeon can change the color of the operant key to red or green, depending upon whether the FI or FR schedule is operating.*

of food itself. If observing responses are maintained, the stimuli they produce are presumably reinforcing because of the information they provide about food availability on the operant key.[14]

There is now abundant evidence that animals will make observing responses to get information about the availability of food or the likelihood of shock. For example, in one experiment, pigeons were faced with a choice. Pecks on either of two keys were reinforced on either an FI 10-second or an FI 40-second schedule. Which schedule was in effect was determined by the experimenter. If the subject pecked one of the keys, that key would turn red if the FI 10-second schedule was in effect, and green if the FI 40-second schedule was in effect. If the pigeon pecked the other key, the key would turn yellow no matter what schedule was in effect. Pecks on either key served equally well to satisfy the FI requirement and produce food. The only consequence of key selection was information about what schedule was in effect. The pigeons showed a very strong preference for the key that provided information.[15] The same effects have been obtained when the reinforcement schedule was either FR 10 or FR 90.[16] It should be noted that, with FR schedules, knowing which one is in effect can make no difference in how much work is required, or how much food is obtained. The occurrence of the reinforcer is completely unaffected by the animal's choice; the only consequence of choice is information. It seems on the surface that the reduction of uncertainty is sufficient to make a stimulus a conditioned reinforcer.

Good versus Bad Information

There are alternative explanations of animals' apparent preferences for predictive stimuli. It is possible that predictive stimuli will be reinforcing only if the news provided by the stimuli is relatively good. Stimuli that provide information may derive reinforcing value not solely from the information they provide but also from their association with the events they predict. If they predict relatively undesirable events, they may not be reinforcing. Imagine turning in assignments to a teacher who provides no feedback when the assignments are satisfactory and lots of feedback, on request, when they are unsatisfactory. The only news you can get from your teacher is bad news. It is possible that given the choice between no information and

14. Wyckoff, 1952.
15. Bower, McLean and Meachem, 1966.
16. Hendry, 1969.

bad information, you will choose no information. This is the essence of the view we are presently exploring.

There is some evidence to support the view that stimuli are reinforcing only when they provide good news—that is, only when they predict events that are positive. In one experiment, pigeons were exposed to a VI schedule of food reinforcement for pecking. During a random, unsignalled proportion of the time, pecks produced electric shock on an FR schedule. When observing responses produced signals for both shock-free periods and shock periods, high rates of observing responses were recorded. But when observing responses only produced signals for shock periods, many pigeons did not make observing responses, and those that did, did not sustain them.[17] Note that a procedure that only signals shock periods provides just as much information as a procedure which signals both shock and shock-free periods. The absence of the signal for shock when an observing response occurs is itself a signal for no shock. Nevertheless, observing responses were not maintained on this procedure. This failure is presumably the result of the fact that the only stimulus actually produced by the observing response was correlated with an aversive situation, with bad news.

Thus, it appears that pure information may not be sufficient to endow a stimulus with reinforcing power and maintain observing responses. A crucial component of the control of observing responses may be that the stimuli they produce be associated with something positive.

Token Reinforcers

We suggested earlier that any account of human behavior based upon operant conditioning principles would have to depend heavily upon the role of conditioned reinforcement. Most human behavior does not produce food or water or avoid noxious stimuli directly. Human behavior produces money, social approval or scorn, and so on. Why does money sustain behavior? It is tempting to argue that it is the association of money with things like food, clothing, and shelter which gives money its power, that money is simply a conditioned reinforcer. But in many respects, the relation between money and

---

17. Dinsmoor, Flint, Smith and Viemeister, 1969. For a detailed argument supporting this view, see Fantino, 1977.

the things it buys is very indirect; the delay between obtaining money and obtaining food may be days or weeks long. Animal studies of conditioned reinforcement provide no hint that money is sufficiently powerful to bridge such long delays. Indeed, conditioned reinforcing effects in the laboratory are fragile. Thus, we will need some direct evidence that money can be established as a conditioned reinforcer as a result of being paired with unconditioned reinforcers before any arguments about the role of conditioned reinforcers in the control of human behavior can be taken seriously. Such evidence is available.

Some of the earliest investigations of conditioned reinforcement involved procedures in which chimpanzees responded for tokens (poker chips) which could subsequently be exchanged for food. It was assumed that if responding was maintained by token reinforcement, this would be evidence that tokens acquire reinforcing value because they are paired with food. Among the interesting findings which came out of these studies were the following:

1. Some chimpanzees worked as hard for tokens (exchangeable for grapes) as they did for grapes.

2. Chimpanzees would work for tokens even if a delay of one hour was imposed between obtaining the token and exchanging it for food, provided they could hold onto the tokens during the delay period.

3. Chimps would learn a new response for token reinforcement, even if a delay was imposed between obtaining the token and exchanging it. With no delay, the chimps learned as rapidly with token reinforcement as with food reinforcement.

4. When chimps housed in pairs were simply given tokens, struggles for dominance, begging, and even stealing of tokens were observed.[18]

More recent research has shown that when responses produce tokens according to some schedule of reinforcement, a pattern of responding appropriate to the schedule develops. Responding in chimps can be maintained on an FR 125 for tokens, even when 50 tokens must be accumulated (6250 responses) before exchange for food is permitted.[19] Results of this sort make plausible the claim that conditioned rein-

18. Wolfe, 1936; Cowles, 1937.
19. Kelleher, 1957; 1958.

A chimp trained to deposit tokens to produce food reinforcement. (*Courtesy of Yerkes Regional Primate Research
Center, Emory University*)

forcement, at least in the form of tokens, maintains behavior in the
same way money does.

What makes the case particularly convincing is research that has
been carried out in applied settings. Token reinforcement has become
a popular instrument for behavior modification and control in both
mental hospitals and schools. For example, token reinforcement has
been introduced into hospital wards that house long-term psychiatric
patients. These patients were reluctant to engage in the most rudi-
mentary forms of activity prior to the introduction of tokens. They
would not feed, clean or dress themselves, and they engaged in virtually no social interaction. When the tokens were introduced, they
were required to obtain food, cigarettes, chewing gum, and the handful of other commodities that interested the patients. And the patients

were required to work for the tokens. At first required work was exclusively self-maintenance activity like grooming and dressing, but eventually, other kinds of activity involving the running of the ward were added. Thus, in the hospital ward setting, tokens had the status of money. They had to be earned, and could be used to purchase reinforcers. Restructuring the daily routines of long-term hospital patients in this way has resulted in substantial increases in the rate of patient discharge from the hospital (see Chapter 8, pp. 211–223 for a more complete discussion).[20]

Whether the effectiveness of tokens can be understood strictly in terms of principles of conditioned reinforcement is unclear. In the most typical cases, the responses that earn tokens are just the first part of a sequence of responses required for reinforcement to occur. After the tokens are collected, they must be exchanged for the unconditioned reinforcer. Thus tokens are not simply paired with the reinforcer (as a CS is paired with a US). They do not simply tell the organism what is coming. They also tell the organism wht to do, that is, they tell the organism to stop making the responses that produce tokens and start making the responses that cash them in. In this respect, tokens are like discriminative stimuli, telling the person what operant response will be appropriate at a given moment. Thus, tokens may be effective because they are conditioned reinforcers, or because they are discriminative stimuli, or because they are both.

In this chapter, we discussed the phenomena of operant discrimination, generalization, and conditioned reinforcement. The critical features of these phenomena may be summarized as follows:

1. The study of discrimination and generalization is primarily concerned with uncovering the processes by which operant behavior comes under the *control* of environmental objects and events.

2. In any situation, there are a large number of stimuli which may control responding, many of which are only incidental to the specific experimental task.

3. When a number of stimuli are equally predictive of reinforcer availability, they may share control over the operant. Alternatively, one stimulus may be more salient than the others and overshadow them in controlling responding.

20. Some of the pioneering work with token economics has been done by Ayllon and Azrin, 1968, and by Staats, 1975. See also Atthowe and Krasner, 1968.

4. In any situation, the stimulus that is the best predictor of reinforcer availability can be expected to control responding. Explicit discrimination training allows the experimenter to determine which stimulus will control responding by insuring that the most informative relation is between that stimulus and reinforcement.

5. Discrimination learning involves learning to pay attention to relevant (predictive) aspects of the situation and learning to ignore irrelevant (unpredictive) aspects of the situation.

6. Responding that is under the control of a particular stimulus will also occur in the presence of other, similar stimuli. This is the phenomenon of stimulus generalization.

7. A stimulus can become a conditioned reinforcer, and sustain responding on its own, if it provides reliable information about the occurrence of an unconditioned reinforcer.

This discussion of stimulus control of operant behavior concludes our presentation of the basic principles of behavior theory. We have presented those principles sympathetically, and perhaps implied that a complete understanding of the full range of human activity in terms of behavior theory awaits only the working out of some minor details in the laboratory.

But there are problems with behavior theory, problems that challenge its completeness, even as an account of the behavior of animals in standard conditioning experiments. In the next chapter, we turn to a discussion of these problems, and of a theoretical alternative to behavior theory that may be able to explain them.

Chapter 7

Misbehavior of Organisms

THE principles of behavior theory discussed thus far seem, at the very least, to tell us about some of the ways in which the behavior of organisms can be influenced. For researchers in behavior theory who see the ultimate goal of their enterprise as elucidating *some* of the influences on organisms, it is perfectly sensible to continue studying the subtleties of Pavlovian and operant conditioning, and developing increasingly refined and accurate generalizations. But many behavior theorists have aspirations that are much grander than the elucidation of *some* principles of behavior. For them, the goal of the project is a comprehensive account of behavior. For them, behavior theory should eventually be able to encompass most of the important influences on behavior, and be able to produce explanations of behavior no matter in what environment it occurs. In particular, behavior theory should eventually be able to produce explanations for the behaviors of an organism in its natural environment. This goal raises two fundamental questions for evaluating the significance of behavior theory. First, are there important influences on behavior in the natural environment that are not recognized by behavior theory? If so, it would mean that behavior theory is incomplete. The next issue to address would then be whether it could be made complete simply by adding supplementary principles to the principles of Pavlovian and operant conditioning that are already in hand.

Second, are the influences investigated by behavior theory significant in the natural environment? It is possible that behaviors that appear to be under purely operant or Pavlovian control in the laboratory might not be under such pure control in nature. If this were true, we might conclude that there is something special about the conditions of behavior theory experiments on which pure operant or

Pavlovian control depends. It might turn out, for example, that operant principles fully controlled behavior only in conditions that mimicked laboratory conditions. If so this would serve to emphasize a point we made in Chapter 2 (p. 43): We cannot infer from the fact that a behavior is under one kind of control in the laboratory that it is under the same kind of control in all circumstances.

We raise these possibilities because in this chapter we present evidence that both of them are true. There is evidence for important influences on the behavior of animals that behavior theory does not acknowledge. And there are demonstrations that behavior under strict operant control in one set of circumstances is not in others. Depending on the prevailing circumstances, a behavior may be subject predominantly to Pavlovian control or to operant control. It may be that it is only under the special conditions of the operant experiment that operant influence on behavior is the dominant one.

Is the Pigeon's Key Peck an Operant?

If one had to pick a behavior that was under strict operant control, a likely candidate, based upon the evidence presented in Chapters 4 through 6, would be the pigeon's key peck. In those chapters, we discussed only a small handful of the countless demonstrations that key pecking is controlled by contingencies of reinforcement and punishment. Yet in recent years, evidence has been accumulating that under some circumstances key pecking is influenced by Pavlovian contingencies. Moreover, this Pavlovian influence is sufficiently powerful that it can dominate the influence of operant contingencies that are also present.

Suppose we place hungry pigeons in a conditioning chamber, and give them access to food at regular intervals. We might operate the feeder once every 15 seconds. What effect should these food deliveries have on the behavior of the pigeons? Since no particular behavior is required for the delivery of food, we might not expect any systematic change in what the pigeons did over time. If so, we would be wrong. When an experiment like this was conducted, with the experimenters observing the behavior of the pigeons with great care, it turned out that all pigeons exposed to the regular delivery of food eventually ended up pecking. They would reliably peck at one or another feature of the conditioning chamber as the time to the next food delivery drew near.[1]

How can we account for this reliable change in the pigeons' behavior? We might try to appeal to some sort of operant influence. Perhaps the pigeons happened to be pecking early in training just when food was delivered, and this accidental contingency between pecking and food increased the future likelihood of pecking. Aside from the implausibility of the prospect that every pigeon would happen to be pecking when food came, the experimenters actually observed what the pigeons were doing at times of food delivery, and found that they were engaged in a wide range of activities other than pecking. Nevertheless, over the course of training, these other activities tended to drop out, and pecking became ever more probable. We can not explain this finding by appealing to operant principles. However, we can explain it by appealing to Pavlovian principles. If we deliver food to a dog at regular intervals, the dog will eventually start to salivate in advance of the food. The dog seems to be making Pavlovian conditioned salivation responses in the absense of a CS for food. When this phenomenon occurs, it is called Pavlovian *temporal conditioning*. There actually is a CS, the passage of time. As long as food is delivered at regular intervals, the dog learns to associate the time period just prior to food delivery with food, and comes to salivate during that time period.

We can treat the pigeons' key pecking just prior to food delivery as a similar instance of Pavlovian temporal conditioning. It differs from temporal conditioning of the dog only in that the conditioned response is pecking. But this pecking is precisely the response that appears to be under strict operant control in operant conditioning experiments.

Autoshaping

In the last experiment we discussed, hungry pigeons were periodically presented with food. We could turn this procedure into a standard Pavlovian one by presenting a stimulus just prior to each food delivery. When experiments of this type are performed, with a response key illuminated for a few seconds before food, pigeons end up reliably pecking at the response key. This phenomenon has come

1. Staddon and Simmelhag, 1971.

to be called "autoshaping" (automatic shaping). Instead of training pigeons to peck a key, one can simply expose them to an autoshaping procedure. Pairings of key light and food will typically have pigeons pecking the key within 50 to 100 trials.[2]

What is this autoshaping phenomenon? It seems again to be a straightforward instance of Pavlovian conditioning. The lit key is the CS, and the food is the US. The conditioned response, pecking, is precisely the same as the response investigators have taken to be a prototypic operant. Research on autoshaping has made it clear that the phenomenon is an example of Pavlovian conditioning. First, just as with more traditional examples of Pavlovian conditioning (see Chapter 3), the form the autoshaped peck takes is influenced by the nature of the reinforcer, or US. Thus, when food is the US, pigeons "eat" the key, while when water is the US, they "drink" the key.[3] Photographs of a pigeon autoshaped to peck a key with either food or water as the US are presented in Figure 7–1. The form of the key peck is clearly different in the two cases, with the beak wide open when food is the reinforcer, and almost closed when water is the reinforcer. Similar consummatory responses have been observed in other species exposed to autoshaping procedures. When rats receive food signalled by the insertion of a lever into the box, or by illumination of tiny lights in the lever, they sniff, lick and chew on the lever, just as they would at food.[4]

Second, the development of autoshaped key pecking seems governed by the same aspects of the stimulus-reinforcer relation that govern more traditional occurrences of Pavlovian conditioning. We saw in Chapter 3 that the key to Pavlovian conditioning was an informative relation between CS and US; the CS must be a differential predictor of the US for conditioning to occur. The same is true of autoshaping.[5]

These data are impressive support for the view that autoshaping reflects Pavlovian conditioning in operation, that at least under some circumstances, pecking is subject to Pavlovian control. Thus, any notion that pecking is an example of a pure operant is false. But the autoshaping situation is one in which no operant contingency is pre-

2. Brown and Jenkins, 1968; see Hearst and Jenkins, 1974; Locurto, Gibbon and Terrace, 1980; and Schwartz and Gamzu, 1977, for reviews.

3. Jenkins and Moore, 1973.

4. Peterson, Ackil, Frommer and Hearst, 1972; Stiers and Silberberg, 1974.

5. Gamzu and Williams, 1971, 1973.

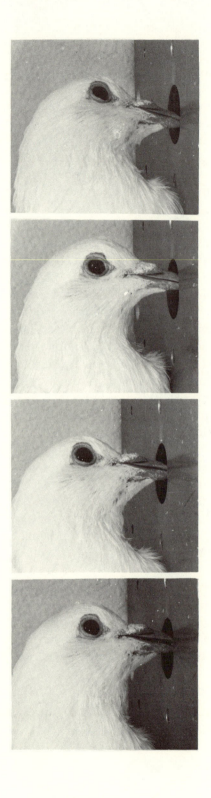

sent. Suppose a Pavlovian autoshaping contingency were combined with an operant one. Would the operant contingency be dominant?

The Omission Effect

A procedure that combines Pavlovian and operant contingencies, called the *omission procedure,* is diagrammed in Figure 7–2. A response key is periodically illuminated for six seconds. If no key peck occurs during this time, the key light is extinguished and food is presented. However, if a key peck occurs, it turns out the key light, ending the trial, and prevents food. Thus, the Pavlovian autoshaping contingency is combined with a *negative* operant contingency. Key pecks prevent food delivery, and if pecking is subject to control by this operant contingency, pigeons should quickly stop pecking. Pecking is the only thing they can do that is guaranteed not to be followed by food.

Nevertheless, the pigeons do not stop pecking. The bottom of Figure 7–2 presents cumulative totals of responses over 800 trials for 13 different subjects. All subjects responded on at least 10% of the trials, some responded on more than 50% of the trials, and one responded on 90% of the trials.[6] The fact that key pecking reliably occurred under these conditions indicates not only that pecking can be controlled by both Pavlovian and operant contingencies, but that in at least some circumstances, the Pavlovian contingencies dominate the operant ones. This is not to say that pecking is completely insensitive to operant contingencies in autoshaping situations. Indeed, there is evidence that when pigeons are presented with two keys as identical Pavlovian signals for food, and pecks on one of the keys have no effect, while pecks on the other prevent food, the pigeons direct most of their pecks at the key without the negative operant contingency.[7] The

6. Williams and Williams, 1969.
7. Schwartz and Williams, 1972.

Figure 7–1. Key pecking for food and water. (A) *The pictures show a pigeon's beak movements as it pecks a key that has been paired with water. The movements resemble those the bird makes when it drinks. (B) These pictures show quite different beak movements made when the bird pecks a key that has been paired with food. Now the movements resemble those the animal makes when it eats. (Photographs by Bruce Moore, from Jenkins and Moore, 1973)*

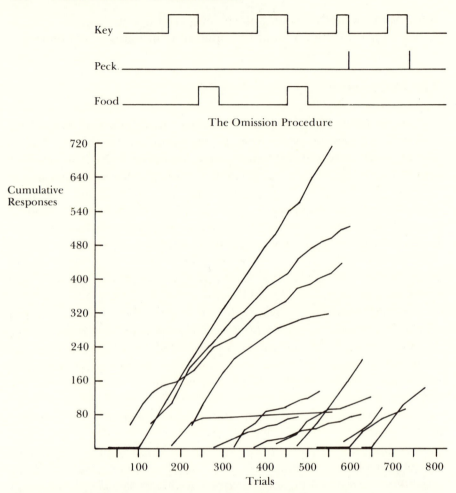

Figure 7–2. The Omission Phenomenon: Maintenance of Key Pecking in the Face of Negative Consequences. *The omission procedure is diagrammed at the top of the figure, and cumulative responses of pigeons exposed to the procedure are presented at the bottom. (After Williams & Williams, 1969.)*

lesson of the autoshaping and omission phenomena is that pecking, which seems like a pure operant in some circumstances, is actually subject to both operant and Pavlovian control. If we were to generalize this to other operants, the lesson would be that the mere fact that pure operant control can be demonstrated in one experimental setting is no guarantee that it will occur in all experimental settings, or in natural ones.

Misbehavior of Organisms

We have now shown that one of the problems we posed for the comprehensiveness of behavior theory is real. Successful operation of operant contingencies in one experimental context does not imply their general significance. There is other evidence that is consistent with the evidence from autoshaping and omission experiments. It comes from the work of two former associates of B.F. Skinner's, Keller and Marion Breland, who used their training in behavior theory to establish a prosperous animal training business. In 1961, they published a whimsical but significant paper, "The Misbehavior of Organisms," which recorded their occasional training failures, in which organisms "misbehaved."[8] What they meant by "misbehavior" was that the contingencies of reinforcement which they introduced into given situations did not entirely succeed in controlling what the animal did.

Let us consider a few of their examples:

The Dancing Chicken

The chicken walks over about 3 feet, pulls a rubber loop on a small box which starts a repeated auditory stimulus pattern (a four-note tune). The chicken then steps up onto an 18-inch, slightly raised disc, thereby closing a timer switch, and scratches vigorously round and round over the disc for 15 seconds, at the rate of about two scratches per second, until the automatic feeder fires in the retaining compartment. The chicken goes into the compartment to eat, thereby automatically shutting the door. The popular interpretation of this behavior pattern is that the chicken has turned on the "juke box" and "dances."

The development of this behavioral exhibit was wholly unplanned. In the attempt to create quite another type of demonstration which required a chicken simply to stand on a platform for 12 to 15 seconds, we found that over 50% developed a very strong and pronounced scratch pattern, which tended to increase in persistence as the time interval was lengthened. (Another 25% or so developed other behaviors—pecking at spots, etc.) However, we were able to change our plans so as to make use of the scratch pattern, and the result was the "dancing chicken" exhibit described above.

In this exhibit the only real contingency for reinforcement is that the chicken must depress the platform for 15 seconds. In the course of

8. Breland and Breland (1961) coined the expression "misbehavior of organisms" as a parody on B.F. Skinner's seminal *Behavior of Organisms* (1938).

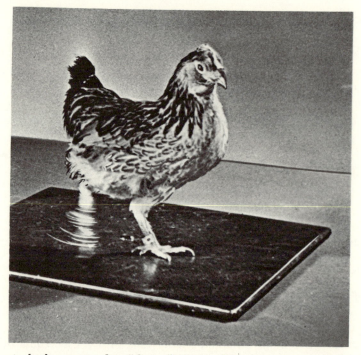

A chicken trained to "dance" after pulling on a string which turns on the music. (*Courtesy of Animal Behavior Enterprises*)

a performing day (about 3 hours for each chicken) a chicken may turn out over 10,000 unnecessary, virtually identical responses.[9]

The Miserly Raccoon

The response concerned the manipulation of money by the raccoon (who has "hands" rather similar to those of the primates). The contingency for reinforcement was picking up the coins and depositing them in a 5-inch metal box.

Raccoons condition readily, have good appetites, and this one was quite tame and an eager subject. We anticipated no trouble. Conditioning him to pick up the first coin was simple. We started out by reinforcing him for picking up a single coin. Then the metal container was introduced, with the requirement that he drop the coin into the container. Here we ran into the first bit of difficulty: he seemed to have a great deal of trouble letting go of the coin. He would rub it up against the inside of the container, pull it back out, and clutch it firmly for several

9. Breland and Breland, 1961, pp. 681–682.

seconds. However, he would finally turn it loose and receive his food reinforcement. Then the final contingency: we put him on a ratio of 2, requiring that he pick up both coins and put them in the container.

Now the raccoon really had problems (and so did we). Not only could he not let go of the coins, but he spent seconds, even minutes rubbing them together (in a most miserly fashion), and dipping them into the container. He carried on the behavior to such an extent that the practical demonstration we had in mind—a display featuring a raccoon putting money in a piggy bank—simply was not feasible. The rubbing behavior became worse and worse as time went on, in spite of nonreinforcement.[10]

The "dancing chicken" danced though it was not trained to do so. As the Brelands point out, the chicken expended substantial unnecessary effort. The reinforcement contingency was not responsible for this activity, and one suspects that a reinforcement contingency would not eliminate it. The coin rubbing of the raccoon was not merely unnecessary: It interfered with responses that would have produced food. Nevertheless, the raccoon continued to manipulate the coins until the Brelands abandoned the project.

These examples and others reported by the Brelands are perplexing because they demonstrate the failure of reinforcement contingencies to control behavior. Why do the reinforcement contingencies fail? What other than contingent reinforcement could be responsible for the "misbehavior" of the chicken and the raccoon?

In the case of the chicken, a behavior increased markedly in frequency without reinforcement being contingent upon its occurrence; in the case of the raccoon, behavior upon which reinforcement was contingent was suppressed. Thus, reinforcement is neither necessary nor sufficient to bring about increases in a behavior's frequency. Nevertheless, in certain situations—for example, the standard conditioning chamber—making reinforcement contingent upon a given behavior does seem to be both necessary and sufficient to increase the behavior's frequency. Presumably, the conditioning chamber is designed so that behavior patterns like those observed by the Brelands are prevented from occurring.

We might attempt to reconcile the Breland's findings with behavior theory by seeking to explain their examples of "misbehavior" with Pavlovian principles. Consider the "dancing" chicken. Perhaps

10. Breland and Breland, 1961, p. 682.

The pig that went to market. *The picture shows a pig trained with operant techniques to push a market cart. This is an example of successful operant control produced by Breland and Breland, without intrusion of misbehavior. (Courtesy of Animal Behavior Enterprises)*

the chicken's scratching is a reflex action in response to the presence of food. If so, scratching would be a chicken's parallel of salivation in a dog. As such, it would presumably be the kind of behavior that principles of Pavlovian conditioning are intended to explain. Could this possibly be the case? Could scratching, like salivation, be a reflex? If so, it poses no special problem for behavior theory. Scratching may not look like salivation, being comprised of skeletal action rather than glandular secretion. But then pecking is also skeletal, and there is no reason to believe that Pavlovian principles must be restricted to non-skeletal activities.

The raccoon's behavior is somewhat more difficult to accommodate within behavior theory. Handling the coins and depositing them produced reinforcement, and the reinforcement seemed to control the behavior. Then, mysteriously, the reinforcement contingency apparently lost control. If it did lose control, did some other contingency gain it? Consider the possibility that a Pavlovian relation developed, and this relation overpowered the operant one. Perhaps rubbing bits of food together is a reflexive response to food presentation, like salivation, pecking, and maybe scratching. And perhaps the coins, as informative signals for food, became Pavlovian CSs. If so, the raccoon might have rubbed the coins as a result of the same process that induces dogs to salivate at tones, and sometimes, pigeons to peck at keys. The raccoon's "misbehavior" could thus be seen as another case in which Pavlovian contingencies dominated operant ones.

On this interpretation, neither of the Breland's examples are instances of "misbehavior." Instead, they are instances of control by Pavlovian contingencies, in situations where one might have expected control by operant ones. Thus, the responses might be surprising, but they are not incompatible with behavior theory principles.

While the Breland's findings are not necessarily incompatible with behavior theory principles, they raise once again the problem that because operant control can be demonstrated in one situation does not imply it occurs in all situations. Indeed, the case of the raccoon shows that even in the same situations, operant factors may control behavior at one point in time but not another. The Breland's findings, along with the autoshaping and omission phenomena, create difficulties for evaluating the domain of applicability of Pavlovian and operant principles, both separately, and in combination. For if the raccoon's behavior is to be explained in terms of the joint effects of Pavlovian and operant principles, this means that any situation offers the potential for such joint influence. And this possibility very much complicates the task of behavior theory. How is one to determine what the effects of operant contingencies are, if any experimental situation in which you study them might also permit Pavlovian influence? And how is one to determine in which situations operant principles dominate, and in which Pavlovian, if both may be dominant in the same situation at different times?

Thus, autoshaping, omission and the misbehavior phenomena create difficult methodological problems for behavior theory, even if we interpret each of these phenomena in terms of principles that are a part of behavior theory. The difficulty is compounded if it turns out that some of these phenomena depend on principles that are foreign to behavior theory. For if this is the case, as we pointed out in the beginning of the chapter, behavior theory's claim to comprehensiveness would be seriously undermined.

In discussing some of their findings, the Brelands expressed the view that understanding them would require principles from outside the domain of behavior theory:

> Here we have animals, after having been conditioned to a specific learned response, gradually drifting into behaviors that are entirely different from those which were conditioned. Moreover, it can easily be seen that these particular behaviors to which the animals drift are clear-cut examples of instinctive behaviors having to do with the natural food-getting behaviors of the particular species.[11]

Thus, for the Brelands, misbehavior reflected the operation of principles that had nothing to do with Pavlovian or operant conditioning—indeed, nothing to do with learning at all. Misbehaviors were instances of *instinctive* behavior, behavior that characterizes all members of a given species, and occurs independent of experience, under appropriate environmental conditions. This instinctive behavior is genetically determined, and clearly outside the province of behavior theory. Moreover, the fact that these behaviors occurred under highly artificial conditions, and at the cost of food to hungry animals, suggested to the Brelands not only that instinct was a significant determinant of animal behavior, but also that it might completely dominate Pavlovian and operant factors if given the opportunity to occur at all.

Behavior theory is fundamentally about learning—about the modification of behavior as a result of experience. The claim that its principles are comprehensive implies that most of the behavior of a mature organism, whether a pigeon or a person, is a consequence of learning. Either a behavior itself is learned, or its occurrence depends upon learned connections between it and environmental (for example, discriminative or reinforcing) stimuli. Thus principles of behavior theory are intended to account for the acquisition, maintenance and context-sensitivity of an organism's behavior. The principles that are to provide this account are the principles of Pavlovian and operant conditioning.

In light of this emphasis of behavior theory, a suggestion like the Brelands' constitutes a serious challenge. If a significant portion of an organism's behavior is genetically determined, then it is outside the province of behavior theory, and behavior theory is incomplete. But

---

11. Breland and Breland, 1961, p. 683.

in addition to this problem, the Breland's position poses a second one. For once we acknowledge that some of an organism's behavior is outside the province of behavior theory, how can we determine whether the behavior we observe in a given experiment is actually controlled by operant or Pavlovian contingencies, and not by those genetically determined factors?

Thus, behavior theory is faced with a second serious methodological problem. If it wants to obtain general principles of operant or Pavlovian control, behavior theory not only must be concerned that successful operant control in one situation need not imply successful operant control in others—but also with preventing genetically determined behavior patterns from occurring in experimental situations.

To some extent, the experimental methods of behavior theory have been developed with these difficulties in mind. But behavior theory has not been sufficiently sensitive to these problems to prevent unanticipated influences from slipping into experimental settings unnoticed. Let us examine how behavior theorists have attempted to handle these problems, and what methods might be used to handle them even more effectively.

Discovering General Laws of Behavior

Imagine a visitor from another planet about to embark on the study of human behavior. Having no preconceptions about the nature of the human organism, his first step in the investigation might be careful observation. The observation would reveal a host of physical and behavioral characteristics that distinguish people from other organisms. It would quickly become clear to this visitor that if one is to find out about people, one must study them directly. Though it would certainly be more convenient to do research with smaller, more docile, more easily cared for organisms, the differences among different types of organisms would seem so pronounced that it would be hazardous to study one organism to find out about another.

This attitude is shared by most nonpsychologists. While many people believe that one can learn about some aspects of humans through the study of nonhumans (for example, the structure and function of a large number of body organs), their confidence in species continuity stops short at the level of thought, feeling, and action. Current practice in behavior theory belies this popular belief. Much of what behavior theorists think they know about human behavior comes from the study of the behavior of nonhumans. They are confident that the behavior of pigeons in the laboratory is an accurate representation of the behavior of both pigeons and people outside the laboratory. Why?

From the outset, behavior theory has been guided by the assumption that general, that is, transspecies and transitutational, laws of behavior exist. Just as one can learn about the human eye by studying the eye of a horseshoe crab, so one can learn about human behavior by studying the behavior of the pigeon or the rat. But even while adopting the assumption of species similarity, behavior theory has always been mindful of species differences. If one merely observes the pigeon in its natural environment and expects one's observations to provide general principles of behavior, one is likely to be disappointed. Many of the things that pigeons do reflect behavior processes unique to the pigeon and its close relatives. While sometimes what the pigeon does may be a reflection of general principles of behavior, at other times it may reflect systems of action that are specific to the species, and genetically determined. The difficult problem is to separate the species-specific characteristics from the general ones. The best way to do this is to bring the pigeon into an artificial laboratory environment that prevents species-specific behavior patterns from exerting their influence, just as in order to investigate the force of gravitation, the physicist constructs an artificial laboratory situation within which the action of non-gravitational forces is prevented. For this reason, behavior theory has employed research methods that attempt to neutralize the unique genetic contributions to the behavior of a species. If one successfully eliminates these genetic influences what remains to be observed are behavior patterns whose principles will generalize across species.

Unbiased Environments

How does one eliminate these genetic influences? What methods will yield general principles of behavior control? Studies of evolution and natural selection teach us that what shapes a species is selection pressure from the environment. Though changes in the genetic constitution of members of a species may occur at random, they are not passed on at random. Some genetic alterations yield organisms poorly suited for survival in the natural environment while others yield organisms especially well-suited for survival and reproduction. Thus, pressure from the environment ultimately yields organisms whose central characteristics are particularly well-attuned to that environment. Therefore, if one studies the behavior of organisms in the natural environment, one is likely to observe a great many genetically determined behavior patterns that are specifically adapted to that environment and not derived from experience with that environment. If one's interest is in general principles of behavior rather than principles unique to the pigeon or the rat, one's task is greatly simplified when the animals are studied in an environment in which genetically determined behavior patterns are irrelevant. In short, to maximize the chances of obtaining principles of behavior control that are true for all organisms, one should study behavior in an artificial and unbiased experimental environment. If the environment is artificial and unbiased, it will not call forth genetically determined, specially adapted patterns of behavior.

What does it mean to say that the experimental environment is artificial and unbiased? Consider an historical example. B.F. Skinner's earliest research was concerned with hunger and its effects on reflexes. To study this problem, Skinner and others attempted to measure general activity levels and the frequency and form of responses which were specific components of the feeding system. Such measurements were difficult to make, partly because it was difficult to quantify changes in the state of these activities over time. What was needed was a reliable measuring instrument. Skinner's search for such an instrument led to what is commonly known as the Skinner box, in which rats are trained to press a lever for food. He was not at this time particularly interested in the acquisition or control of lever pressing; he was interested in hunger. Lever presses were easy to count, and by counting them, one could tag changes in the strength of the animal's feeding related behaviors.[12]

There was nothing about lever presses that made them especially appropriate to measure hunger. One could as well count chain pulls or paw swipes or a host of other things. All that was special was that the response produced food. By measuring the frequency of the response, one could measure the animal's need for food and, in this way, one could learn about hunger. More significantly, one could

12. Skinner, 1932. Also, see Herrnstein, 1974.

compare hunger to other states of need in the animal. Suppose one wanted to assess the relative impact of hunger and thirst on an animal's behavior. If one were measuring specific feeding and drinking activities, a comparison of hunger and thirst would be difficult. Since feeding and drinking activities are different, an attempt to compare them would present the proverbial problem of comparing apples and oranges. How many bites of food, for example, are equivalent to how many licks of water? If one were, instead, measuring neither feeding nor drinking, but some third activity, like lever pressing, a direct comparison of the two different need states would be easier. Since lever pressing bears no relation to either feeding or drinking prior to the experiment, we can take it to be an unbiased estimator of both. This is precisely what it means to describe one's experimental situation as unbiased.

With this example in hand, let us extend the notion of unbiased methods to aspects of the experimental environment other than the response one is measuring. Suppose one is interested in Pavlovian conditioning or operant discrimination learning. What should one use as a CS or discriminative stimulus? While the stimulus one uses must be something the animal is able to detect, it should not be something antecedently related to the US or to the reflex. Thus, if one is studying conditioned fear, with shock as the US, it might well be a bad idea to use as a CS a model of one of the organism's natural enemies. Such a stimulus may well produce fear, but the fear may result from the fact that a relation between the predator and danger exists prior to any experimental manipulation. If so, such an experiment will tell us little about conditioned fear in general. Instead of using a picture of a predator as a CS, we use a light, or a tone, stimuli that the experimenter can show were not related to danger before our experiment. That the relation between CS (tone) and US (shock) is unbiased enhances the chances that the conditioning phenomenon one observes will be a consequence only of the relations among stimuli and behaviors introduced and manipulated by the experimenter, and will not be specific to either the species or the situation being studied.

Successfully creating unbiased environments would eliminate the problem that genetic factors might be influencing experimental results, since unbiased environments would presumably neutralize these genetic factors. However, it would not address the problem (represented by phenomena like autoshaping and omission, and perhaps by some examples of misbehavior), that Pavlovian and operant influences might both be present in situations thought to be pure instances of one or the other. To handle this problem, additional methodological care is needed.

Substitutability

Consider the raccoon trained to manipulate coins for food. Is this a pure example of operant conditioning, or are Pavlovian factors also operating? To be sure that the effect is purely operant, we must require not only that stimulus-behavior-reinforcement relations be unbiased, but also that members of each class be *substitutable* for one another. Suppose for example we conduct a series of experiments with raccoons. The set of stimuli from which we choose consists of a tone, a flashing light and a triangle. The set of behaviors we study includes turning around in a circle, pressing a lever, and manipulating coins. The set of reinforcers includes food and water. Substitutability holds only if we obtain the same empirical relations between stimulus, behavior and reinforcer, no matter which stimulus, behavior and reinforcer we choose. When substitutability does not hold, operant influence may still be present, but it will not be the only influence present. It might well be, for example, that for the raccoon, lever pressing and coin manipulating are not substitutable for each other, because only the latter is influenced by Pavlovian contingencies. It is clear that this need for substitutability enormously increases the amount of experimental work that must be done before one can arrive at firm conclusions about operative principles.

To see how complicated the behavior theorist's task is, consider Figure 7–3. Figure 7–3 is a limited characterization of the world of the rat, divided into the classes "stimuli," "operants," and "reinforcers." Suppose one does Experiment 1: In the presence of a bright light, lever presses produce food. The rat learns to press the lever at a high rate. Does this fact reflect a general principle or is there something special about the situation which makes some of its elements nonsubstitutable? To begin to answer this question, we do Experiment 2; a dim light is substituted for the bright one. Suppose it turns out that while rats still press the lever in Experiment 2, they do so at much lower rates than in Experiment 1. What are we to conclude from this result?

Two possibilities are apparent. First, it is possible that there is

Stimuli	Operants	Reinforcers

Lights
  Bright
  Dim
  Colored
Tones
  Soft
  Loud
Buzzers
Clicks
Temperature
Air puffs
Tastes Etc.
	Lever Pressing
	Wheel Running
	Alley Running
	Biting
	Licking
	Rearing
	Tail Flicking Etc.
		Food
		Water
		Sex
		Temperature
		Shock
		Poison
		Loud Noise Etc.

Experiment 1: Bright Light —— Lever Press —— Food Experiment 2: Dim Light —— Lever Press —— Food Experiment 3: Dim Light —— Wheel Run —— Food Experiment 4: Bright Light —— Wheel Run —— Food Experiment 5: Bright Light —— Wheel Run —— Water Experiment 6: Dim Light —— Wheel Run —— Water Experiment 7: Bright Light —— Lever Press —— Water Experiment 8: Dim Light —— Lever Press —— Water		

Figure 7–3. Outline of Concrete Procedures an Experimenter Might Use to Determine the Substitutibility of an Experimental Situation. *The eight listed experiments serve to highlight the meaning of "substitutible." It does not mean that all stimuli (or operants or rewards) are interchangeable. It does mean that the difference between any two stimuli (for example, bright and dim light) will be the same regardless of the operant or reward being used.*

some special relation between brightness and lever pressing. If so, we would be forced to conclude that Experiment 1 did not yield general principles. Second, it is possible that a bright light will maintain higher rates of *any* operant than will a dim light. To test this possibility, we do Experiments 3 and 4. Wheel running is reinforced by food in the presence of either a dim light (Experiment 3) or a bright one (Experiment 4). Suppose the results of these experiments parallel the results of Experiments 1 and 2; wheel running occurs at a higher rate in the presence of a bright light than in the presence of a dim one. Now, we can conclude that the relation between brightness of a light and the frequency of an operant is general; bright lights are more effective as discriminative stimuli in maintaining behavior than are dim ones. If, on the other hand, it turned out that rats ran more in wheels in the presence of dim lights than in the presence of bright ones, we would have to conclude that there was a significant interaction between members of the category "stimuli" and members of the category "operant"; in short, we would have to conclude that our experiments involved nonsubstitutable elements and were not yielding general principles.

But again, assume that Experiments 3 and 4 confirm the principle suggested by Experiments 1 and 2, that bright lights control higher rates of responding than dim ones. Can we conclude at this point that our experimental situation is substitutable, and that the principles derived from it are general? Not quite yet. It is possible that the results of all four experiments are unique to situations in which food is the reward. Thus, we do Experiments 5 through 8. If it turns out that substituting water for food does not change the effect of brightness on responding, we may then reasonably conclude that all eight experiments involved substitutable elements and yielded general principles. It may seem that the procedures required to determine the substitutability of the elements in a situation are unnecessarily cumbersome. What must be considered, however, is what such a set of experiments accomplishes. If one does Experiments 1 through 8, and they work in the manner stipulated, one can then use just this set of experimental situations to uncover principles of learning and behavior control which should characterize virtually all situations, or at least all situations involving substitutable stimuli, operants, and rewards.[13]

By the criterion of substitutability, the autoshaping and omission phenomena make it clear that the pigeon's key peck is not substitutable, at least not always. Because pecking is subject to Pavlovian control as well as operant, substituting a different operant for it might well change the phenomena one observes.[14] As a result, the assumption of behavior theory that the study of key pecking reveals principles of pure operant control that can be generalized to all operants of all organisms becomes suspect.

Indeed, a research program like the one outlined in Figure 7–3 has never really been carried out. Behavior theorists have typically assumed that they were working with substitutable and unbiased operants, stimuli and reinforcers and were thus discovering general principles. The phenomena we have discussed provide a few indications that they have not been. There are many other, similar phenom-

13. One would also have to perform a similar series of experiments on a different species to be sure that the principles derived from the first series extend to animals other than rats.

14. For evidence that this is true, see Schwartz and Gamzu, 1977.

ena that have been uncovered in recent years. And what these phenomena have suggested to researchers is that perhaps when organisms learn in nature, their learning is not characterized by relations between substitutable stimuli, operants and reinforcers. Rather, learning in nature might typically involve relations among events that are nonsubstitutable. And these nonsubstitutable relations may have a more significant influence on behavior than principles of behavior theory do.

Taste Aversion Learning

A rat is permitted access to a flavored solution, say vanilla. After drinking the solution for a few minutes, the rat is sublethally poisoned. It takes 20 minutes or so for the poison to act, and the poison makes the rat sick. A day or so later, the rat, now fully recovered, is given access again to the vanilla-flavored solution. The rat avoids the solution. Apparently, the rat has learned, in only one trial, to associate a flavor (vanilla) with poison. Not only has the rat learned in one trial, but it has learned even though the interval between taste and illness was 20 minutes long. In fact, rats can learn to avoid a flavor when the interval between taste and illness is 12 hours long.[15] This phenomenon is referred to as taste aversion learning.[16]

Is taste aversion learning special? It appears to be an example of Pavlovian conditioning: The taste is a CS and the poison is a US. But Pavlovian conditioning does not usually occur in one trial, and CS-US separations of 12 hours will not usually produce conditioning. To what could we attribute these aspects of taste aversion? Perhaps they result from the unusual potency of the CS or the US. But evidence that an account like this will not do comes from the following experiment. Rats were exposed to a procedure in which whenever they licked at a tube containing a flavored solution, the lick produced both a click and a light flash. Thus, at the same instant the rats experienced a taste, a light and a noise. Some of the rats were subsequently poisoned; other rats received painful shock to the feet. After a number of such trials, the drinking of the rats was evaluated with a procedure

15. See Revusky and Garcia, 1970.
16. For early findings, see Richter, 1953; Rzoska, 1953; Garcia, Kimmeldorf and Hunt, 1961. For recent reviews, see Revusky and Garcia, 1970; Rozin and Kalat, 1971; Barker, Domjan and Best, 1978.

in which the light and noise were separated from the taste. On one day licks at a tube produced the flavored solution, but no light or noise, while on the next day, licks at a tube produced light and noise, but tap water instead of the flavored solution.

The results of this experiment are presented in Figure 7–4. The number of licks at the tube per minute are presented for both pre-tests with audiovisual and taste cues separated and post-tests (after conditioning) with audiovisual and taste cues separated. The top part of Figure 7–4 presents data from rats that experienced poison as a US; the bottom part presents data from rats that experienced shock. It is clear that with poison as a US, taste dominated noise and light as a CS. The rats showed no change in drinking from the "bright, noisy"

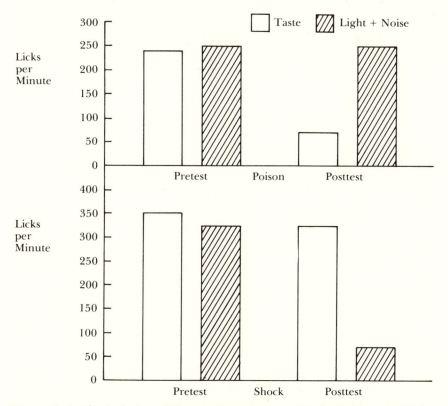

Figure 7–4. The Relation of Cue to Consequence. *With poison as a US (top figure), rats associate the poison with taste and not with light or noise. With shock as the US (bottom figure), the reverse is true. (After Garcia & Koelling, 1966.)*

tube between pre- and post-tests, and a substantial decrease in drinking from the taste tube. On the other hand, with shock as the US, exactly the reverse was true. There was no decrease at all in drinking the flavored water, and a substantial decrease in drinking the "bright, noisy" water. Moreover, shock was just as effective in suppressing drinking as was poison.[17] We must conclude that taste aversion learning reflects neither the power of taste as a CS, nor the power of poison as a US, but the power of the two in combination. When the combination is broken (as when shock is the US), we find almost no conditioning to the taste. Thus, the phenomenon of taste aversion learning seems to depend upon a special relation that exists between tastes and illness. A taste as a CS does not seem to bear the same unbiased relation to illness that a tone as a CS bears to shock. While tones, lights, and dozens of other stimuli are presumably substitutable for one another in combination with shock, they are not substitutable for tastes, in combination with either shock or poison, without producing dramatic alterations in experimental results.

Are Behavior-Environment Relations Biased?

The experiments on taste aversion do not manifest substitutability of stimuli. Rather, they seem to point to a different principle, one we will call *belongingness*.[18] Taste and poison seem to go together. Taste and pain to the feet do not, nor, for that matter, do audio-visual stimuli and stomach illness. The notion of belongingness should strike an intuitive chord. If, after eating a fine dinner out, you go home and get sick to your stomach, it is likely that you will associate the illness with something you ate. You will not associate illness with the color of the wallpaper in the restaurant, or with the music played by the violinist, or with the floral pattern on the china you ate from, or with the people who accompanied you, or with the ride home. Each of these other stimuli bears the same temporal relation to your illness as does the food. Yet surely it will be the food, and not any of the

17. Garcia and Koelling, 1966.
18. Initially coined by E.L. Thorndike many years ago, the term belongingness is now sometimes used to refer to biased relations among stimuli or responses and stimuli (see Schwartz, 1974). Since the discovery of belongingness in taste aversion learning, numerous other examples of belongingness have been demonstrated in the laboratory. See Shettleworth, 1972; Seligman and Hager, 1972; Hinde and Hinde, 1973.

other cues, that you will subsequently avoid. As it turns out, what the rat learns from the taste aversion experiment is similar to what you might learn from the restaurant. The rat seems built to behave as if "it must have been something I ate."

What is the import for behavior theory of the phenomenon of belongingness evidenced in taste aversion learning? What is the significance of the evidence we have reviewed, that many familiar conditioning phenomena are at least in part the result of special relations between behavior and environmental events, that standard experimental methods have failed to eliminate? Efforts to establish unbiased experimental situations have not been entirely successful. In the light of such evidence, what should the behavior theorist do?

One possibility is that better methods can be developed which eliminate the bias introduced by belongingness. Such a strategy is consistent with the view that the goal of behavior theory—to discover laws which generalize across species and across situations—is a reasonable one, but that the means to the goal must be improved. Alternatively, one could see the evidence for belongingness as indicating that the search for general laws is a mistake. Since much of the behavior of animals seems powerfully controlled by belongingness relations, one might decide to study these specialized relations in each species. Underlying this choice is the view that most interesting behavior in the natural environment bears a special relation to important environmental events.

The issue we are confronting is this: *Are behavior-environment relations unbiased?* If most of the behavior of organisms is the result of unbiased relations, then there is no particular difficulty in claiming that the "laws of behavior," while not universal, are still quite general. Indeed, one could acknowledge the existence of nonsubstitutable kinds of learning, and of "misbehavior," and take these phenomena as a forceful and dramatic *justification* for attempting to create an artificial, unbiased environment in the laboratory. If one views substitutable learning as playing a significant role in shaping the behavior of organisms, especially complex organisms, then phenomena such as taste aversion only point out how important it is to make experimental situations truly unbiased, rather than vitiating the effort to create an unbiased experimental situation altogether. If one is interested in general principles of behavior and not in principles peculiar to the rat or pigeon, and if one believes that significant general principles can be identified, then unless one studies behavior in unbiased situations, one will have great difficulty separating the general principles from the species-specific ones. This point of view was explicitly expressed by Skinner even before the assumption that behavior is unbiased had been seriously challenged:

> In any case, behavior in a natural habitat would have no special claim to genuineness. What an organism does is a fact about that organism regardless of the conditions under which it does it. A behavior process is none-the-less real for being exhibited in an arbitrary setting.[19]

Suppose, on the other hand, one assumes that most of what an organism does is the result of biased relations, that is, constrained by the organism's genetically-determined character. An implication of this view is that one can hardly hope to learn about people by studying pigeons. Indeed, if one studies the behavior of pigeons in a sufficiently artificial environment, one will not even learn very much about them. This view is an explicit challenge to the views that have dominated behavior theory. It seems critical, therefore, to address the question, are behavior-environment relations biased? A proper evaluation of the phenomena observed in the conditioning chamber will depend upon how we answer that question.

Taste Aversion and Bias

Let us reconsider a hypothetical event. Suppose you go to a restaurant for the first time. You are impressed right away by the fresh flowers, the delicate china, the ornate chandeliers, and the colorful landscapes that hang on the walls. You enjoy a number of courses, some familiar and some novel. In all, you have a thoroughly delightful experience. Later that night, you become sick to your stomach. To what will you attribute your illness? Of course, you will conclude that it was something you ate. It would not occur to you to attribute your illness to the paintings on the wall or to the chandeliers. In addition, we can speculate that you will not associate your illness with all of the things you ate, or with a random subset of them. In all likelihood, you will associate your illness with *novel* foods that you ate. After all, you may have eaten *coq au vin,* and Caeser salad, and chocolate mousse many times before without getting sick. But you may never have eaten snails before. Thus usually, something novel will get the

19. Skinner, 1966, p. 1208.

blame.[20] Despite the fact that a host of different stimuli share the same temporal relation to your illness, you will be biased to form an association between the illness and only one or a few of those stimuli.

That you will be biased in forming an association is not controversial. It is a fact of behavior. Indeed, the existence of biases may be the surest sign that an organism learns. Bias can be a reflection that one's response to a current set of events is influenced by one's experience with similar events in the past. Thus you might associate a novel food with illness because past experience with familiar foods (not followed by illness) rules them out of consideration. An account of present associative bias based upon past learning experience would pose no special problem for behavior theory. Principles of generalization, attention, and discrimination could be used to provide a reasonably complete and coherent picture. For example, if a pigeon is trained to peck a green key for food, and subsequently given a choice between a green key and a key illuminated with a white triangle, it will peck the green key. Or, if a rat that has been exposed to pairings of light and shock is then exposed to pairings of the same light coupled with a tone prior to shock, the rat will show associative bias and associate the shock exclusively with the light. The light and tone bear identical relations to the shock, just as the food and the plate on which it is served bear identical relations to illness. Nevertheless, light and tone will not share equally in the association with shock.[21] This kind of bias is what behavior theory is substantially about.

The problem posed by the phenomenon of taste aversion is not that it demonstrates associative bias, but that it may demonstrate a bias that does not depend upon past experience. That is, the bias may be built into the rat, and perhaps into the person. It is this kind of bias that behavior theory has systematically avoided. It is a bias whose underlying mechanisms will not be revealed by the methods of behavior theory.

Constraints on Learning

The systematic exploration of built-in associative bias is known as the study of "constraints on learning."[22] At first glance, this may

20. Revusky and Bedarf, 1967.
21. Kamin, 1969.
22. See Shettleworth, 1972; Hinde and Hinde, 1973.

seem a paradoxical title. Constraint implies limitation or restriction. Constrained learning is somehow less adaptable, less flexible, than unconstrained or unbiased learning. Yet what seems so dramatic about the taste aversion learning phenomenon is its superiority over unconstrained, or unbiased, learning. Taste aversions are learned in one trial, and they are learned over long delays between taste and illness. Such characteristics make taste aversion strikingly different from most instances of learning about tones and shock, or lights and food.

A careful analysis will reveal that "constrained" is just the right description for taste aversion learning. Imagine a wild rat that habitually feeds on a particular kind of food in a particular garbage dump. One day someone tosses some mildly poisonous, tasteless, odorless dye into the garbage. The dye coats the rat's food supply, increasing its brightness. The rat eats its diet, and subsequently gets sick. The rat will not associate its illness with the *taste* of the food, because the taste is familiar. Moreover, by virtue of its associative bias, the rat will have great difficulty associating its illness with the new brightness of the food. As a result, it may return to the dump repeatedly, and eat the tainted food repeatedly, and become sick repeatedly. The very selectivity that allows the rat to learn rapidly and effectively about something vitally important under ordinary circumstances (the relation between taste and illness), will under these unusual circumstances, prevent the rat from learning. If the association of taste and illness were an unbiased one, like the association of tone and shock, the rat might learn much more slowly to avoid dangerous foods under most circumstances than it ordinarily does. However, it would learn just about as well to avoid foods on the basis of their color as on the basis of their taste. Thus, the phenomenon of taste aversion does reveal a constraint on learning. It may be that any time one finds that an organism can learn one kind of thing with special facility, one will find in the same organism a special *infacility* to learn other, similar things.

The word "constraint" also points us to what may be the most significant difference between built-in associative bias and bias that is based upon past learning experience. What is the product of past experience can presumably, within limits, be undone by future experience. We can eliminate the pigeon's bias for green over triangles by extinguishing key pecks to green. We can eliminate the rat's bias for light over tone by presenting light alone and following it with shock. We may not be able to eliminate the rat's bias for tastes over colors as signals for poison.

Why has behavior theory systematically avoided the study of

built-in associative bias over the years? The reason is that behavior theory has taken as its task an analysis of the flexibility of organisms. There are important respects in which all dogs are alike, and all people are alike, and dogs are different from people, not as a result of experience but as a result of built-in, biological characteristics of different species that set limits on the effects experience can produce. But behavior theory has not been interested in these limits. It has been interested in understanding what, within these limits, makes one dog different from another, or one person different from another. It has taken as its task the explanation of the enormous variety of human knowledge, actions and goals. Such variety, it is assumed, must result from the diversity of individual experience.

It is hardly a startling claim that there are biological limits on what an organism perceives and what it does. The external environment appears to your pet dog fundamentally different than it does to you. Similarly, you and your dog are capable of quite different movement patterns. The structure of your muscles, joints and motor nervous system simply permits you to do things that dogs cannot, and conversely. The study of constrained learning merely extends these obvious aspects of species difference to a less obvious domain—the domain of learning. It is claimed that there are significant biological constraints on the kinds of things different species are able to learn. The point of this claim is not just that there are quantitative differences among species in learning, for this also is obvious. Rather, the point is that there are qualitative differences—that different species will find different kinds of things easy to learn as a result of their genetic make-up.[23]

Examples of constrained learning point to the limitations of behavior theory's comprehensiveness. Pavlovian and operant contingencies may be important influences on the behavior of virtually all organisms. But what constrained learning tells us is that they are not the only influences. Taste aversion learning is but one instance of constrained learning—one that caught the attention of behavior theorists because of its striking differences from ordinary Pavlovian conditioning. There are many other examples. Indeed, the study of constrained learning is the province of an entire discipline, known as *ethology*.[24] Ethologists assume that constrained learning is character-

23. Keil, 1981, makes a similar argument for some aspects of human behavior.
24. See Eibl-Eibesfeldt, 1970; Hinde, 1970; Tinbergen, 1951; von Frisch, 1967; Wilson, 1975.

istic of organisms, and attempt to study it both by observing the behavior of animals in nature, and by placing animals in experimental settings that capture important aspects of their natural environments. Ethologists contend that how, when and what an organism will learn is rigidly constrained by the genetic endowment of the species. Organisms inherit a kind of genetic blueprint or master plan. The blueprint rigidly specifies some aspects of an organism's behavior, and more loosely specifies other aspects. Room is left for experience to influence the final, adult character of the behavior. But the blueprint permits learning only under a limited set of conditions and only about a limited set of things, so that even when experience can influence an organism, the range of its effects will be relatively small. Moreover, and perhaps most important, the process by which an organism gains from experience will be specialized. Different species will learn different things in different ways.

We can compare the ethological notion of a behavioral blueprint to the blueprint of a building. The blueprint divides a building into rooms in an inflexible way. The "categories" of the building are specified in advance. Within each category, or room, experience can have its influence. The room can be furnished in a large number of ways. But the structure of the room—its size, its shape, its location in the building—imposes constraints on how it will be furnished. Some rooms, like bathrooms and kitchens, have their ultimate character even more rigidly specified by the blueprint than other rooms. The locations of sinks, ovens, toilets, and so on, impose major limitations on how the room will look when it is furnished.

Nearly 300 years ago, the famous British philosopher John Locke spoke of how a mind is furnished:

> Let us then suppose the Mind to be, as we say, white Paper, void of all Characters, without any *Ideas;* How comes it to be furnished? Whence comes it by that vast store, which the busie and boundless Fancy of Man has painted on it, with an almost endless variety? Whence has it all the materials of Reason and Knowledge? To this I answer, in one word, from *Experience.* [25]

The philosophical tradition following Locke laid the foundation, in many respects, for behavior theory, which differs from the views of ethologists in that for them, how the rooms of the mind are furnished

25. Locke, 1690.

has something to do with experience, but has much more to do with the structure imposed on the rooms, prior to any experience, by the form of the building. Thus, if one really wants to understand the major characteristics of a building or the behavior of an organism, one focuses on the structure that determines what the rooms are, and not the experience that determines how they are furnished. For the ethologist, Pavlovian and operant conditioning processes certainly play a role in determining the behavior of an organism and, as such, should be understood. However, entirely different kinds of learning also play a role in determining adult behavior, and the blueprint can tell us what kinds of learning will occur under what kinds of conditions. Behavior theory may tell us about some of the ways in which organisms learn when they do learn, but an understanding of the blueprint will tell us when they learn and what they will learn about. Thus, for the ethologist, it will not be possible to make behavior theory comprehensive simply by adding some supplementary principles to it.

As we said, the methods of ethologists have revealed many instances of constrained learning, either in the natural environment, or in semi-naturalistic experimental settings. In addition, it has become clear in recent years that constrained learning occurs even in the seemingly unbiased environment of the operant conditioning chamber. To choose just one example, research in the last decade on avoidance learning has made it clear that perhaps the most significant determinant of whether, and how rapidly, an organism will learn to avoid shock is the nature of the avoidance response the experimenter requires (see Chapter 4).[26] If the experimenter chooses an avoidance response that is a part of the organism's built-in responses to danger, avoidance is learned rapidly, even if the Pavlovian or operant contingencies that are operative are far from optimal for learning to occur. In contrast, if the required avoidance response is a part of some other behavior system that is incompatible with responding to danger, the organism may never learn, even if the operative Pavlovian and operant contingencies are optimal.

For an example of this, consider training pigeons to peck a key to avoid shock. We now know, from studies of autoshaping and omission, that pecking is a part of the pigeon's feeding repertoire. Key pecking can be produced as a Pavlovian response to food. In one experiment that attempted to train pigeons to peck a key to avoid

26. Bolles, 1970.

shock, the pigeons were first exposed to a series of trials in which a green light appeared on a key for six seconds and was followed by food. If they pecked the key while it was lit, the trial immediately ended without food. This was the omission procedure discussed above (p. 165). After a number of experimental sessions, when the pigeons had come to peck the key reliably (and thus prevent food), the procedure was changed. Now, for the first time, after six seconds of key illumination, the pigeons received a painful electric shock instead of food. Pecks on the key prevented the shock just as they had earlier prevented food. This is an avoidance procedure of the type described in Chapter 4. The only difference between omission and avoidance procedures is the reinforcer. If the reinforcer is food, it is an omission procedure and if the reinforcer is shock, it is an avoidance procedure. When pigeons were shifted to avoidance from omission, they stopped pecking the key! When the procedure was changed so that some trials (when the key was green) were omission and others (when the key was red) were avoidance, pigeons pecked reliably to avoid food but not to avoid shock. This experiment provides a rather clear indication that there is something special about the relation between pecking and food. Not only does pecking occur in a feeding situation even when it costs the pigeon food, but pecking does not occur in a danger situation when it will save the animal from shock.[27] It is only when one chooses an avoidance response that is in the middle ground— neither especially well suited for learning nor especially unsuited for it—that Pavlovian and operant contingencies of the sort discussed in Chapters 3 through 6 have a dominant influence. Thus, the comprehensiveness of behavior theory principles may be restricted to just those circumstances in which stimuli, operants and reinforcers are unbiased and substitutable—circumstances that organisms are neither well-designed nor poorly designed for.

We have presented evidence in this chapter that the comprehensiveness of behavior theory is limited, in two distinct ways. First, there is evidence for important influences on behavior that are outside the domain of behavior theory. Second, there is evidence that because operant principles are dominant in one situation does not mean they will be dominant in others. Thus, the conditioning chamber can not

27. Schwartz, 1973; see Bedford and Anger, 1968; MacPhail, 1968; Hineline and Rachlin, 1969, for other examples.

be taken as a model of all environments. It must be demonstrated empirically that the principles obtained inside the conditioning chamber also hold outside it.

The behavior theorist might respond to these challenges to comprehensiveness by arguing that the significance of behavior theory principles *has* been demonstrated outside the conditioning chamber. He or she could point to many demonstrations that principles of Pavlovian and operant conditioning control human behavior in a wide range of nonexperimental settings. If this argument is true, it defuses to a great degree the seriousness of evidence for genetically determined influences on behavior. For, even if the behavior of nonhumans is rigidly constrained by genetic factors, and thus, the conclusions we draw about pigeons and rats from conditioning experiments must be limited, the behavior of people seems strikingly flexible and adaptable to changing environmental conditions. Thus, the principles of behavior control developed by behavior theory may have broad and crucial applicability to human behavior, at the same time that their applicability to the behavior of pigeons and rats is circumscribed.

It is certainly plausible that genetic constraint is less significant for human behavior than it is for pigeon behavior. Since genetic constraint has been the focus of some of the challenges to behavior theory addressed in this chapter, one might be tempted to conclude that the persuasiveness of behavior theory as a way of understanding human nature is relatively unaffected by these arguments about the limits to its generality. Thus, to evaluate both types of challenge to the comprehensiveness of behavior theory, we must evaluate attempts to apply it to human behavior. If one can show that behavior theory principles can be used to modify and control human behavior, one's confidence in the relevance of behavior theory to human behavior would be enhanced. So let us turn to a discussion of attempts to apply principles of behavior theory to human behavior.

Chapter 8

Applications of Behavior Theory

THE sciences attempt to provide us with conceptual schemes with which to understand the phenomena in their domains. How do we evaluate those schemes? What kinds of evidence do we use to judge whether the picture of the world provided by modern physics or chemistry should be embraced or rejected? There are no simple answers to these questions. The criteria we use for evaluating a conceptual scheme often depend upon our interests. If we are physicists or chemists or philosophers of science, we may demand that a new conceptual scheme be simpler, more elegant, and more general than its predecessors. It should be able to incorporate phenomena that its predecessor could not, and direct further inquiry in new and interesting directions. If we are engineers, or industrial chemists, we may find conceptual elegance aesthetically appealing, but our main professional interest will be in the power of a new conceptual scheme to generate accurate predictions about the behavior of the materials (engines, bridges, organic compounds) we work with. Finally, if we are ordinary lay people, we may expect a new conceptual scheme to yield technological developments that have an impact on daily life. That is, we may expect conceptual innovations to have practical consequences. This is not to suggest that we should expect technological advance to be an immediate or transparent result of conceptual advance. Sometimes the relation between conceptual and practical development will be oblique, and often, it will be delayed. Nevertheless, we usually demand that a new conceptual scheme will have eventual practical consequences if we are to take it seriously.

One reason for our expectation that conceptual advance in science will have practical consequences is that traditionally, it has. From its beginnings in the seventeenth century, modern science has been able to generate striking applications. In general, these applications permit people to further the control they can exercise over their environments. Indeed, technology that has grown out of conceptual advance in science has changed the shape of human life. Thus, electricity, automobiles, television, computers, drugs, food preservatives, synthetic fibers and the like are largely responsible for the tremendous respect and admiration we have for scientific activity.

Perhaps because of the traditional relation between conceptual and technological advance in science, behavior theory has been oriented toward producing important practical applications from the beginning. Conceptual and technological development have been progressing side by side. For B.F. Skinner, the major figure in behavior theory, the true test of the power of theory is the success of the technology. Skinner argues that behavior theory has already passed that test, having produced a wide range of applications, of rapidly growing scope and significance, that other theoretical approaches in psychology cannot match. As we saw in the last chapter, evidence that behavior theory has indeed produced significant and widespread human applications would go a long way toward undercutting the challenge to behavior theory posed by misbehavior, autoshaping, taste aversion and like phenomena. Thus, the status of behavior theory as an important and developing science rests in part upon the status of the technological developments it inspired. Because of this, it is especially relevant to discuss applications of behavior theory, taking stock of their current successes and of their prospects for the future. That is the aim of this chapter. We will see that while it is clear that some very useful and powerful applications have been developed from behavior theory principles, there is some reason to doubt that the success of these applications can be explained in terms of behavior theory alone.

Applications of behavior theory are so diverse, and are growing so rapidly, that we can not attempt to describe and evaluate them all.[1] Instead, we will briefly describe a number of different applications, drawing attention to the behavior theory principles from which they derive. We will then discuss how the success of these applications has been taken as confirmation of the general conception of human nature on which behavior theory depends (see Chapter 1). Finally,

1. See Catania and Brigham, 1978; Kazdin and Wilson, 1978; and Leitenberg, 1976a, for numerous examples of applications of behavior theory.

we will discuss a few of these successful applications critically, identifying features that may be crucial for their success but that appear to be outside the scope of behavior theory.

Behavior Theory and Psychopathology

Though behavior theory principles have been applied in a wide range of settings, including prisons and work places, most of the successful applications of behavior theory have been in two areas. One of these is in the area of education, and the other is in the area of psychopathology. For the most part, behavior theorists have applied their principles to the development of improved educational techniques, and to the development of procedures that will effectively eliminate a wide range of disordered, maladaptive behavior. Since all of us have had experience with traditional educational methods, the contrast between those methods and the ones derived from behavior theory will be clear. However, not all of us have had direct contact with traditional methods of dealing with psychopathology. So before we discuss specific examples, a word should be said about how the general orientation of behavior theory contrasts with other approaches to treating psychopathology.

Traditionally, attempts to treat psychopathology have focused on identifying the source of the problem. If a person feels extremely anxious, or depressed, or is unreasonably afraid of being in enclosed places, the therapist attempts to discover the origin of the problem. Together with the client, the therapist works through events in the client's past hoping to develop insights in the client as to the problem's real causes. Once these insights have occurred, client and therapist together can develop strategies for overcoming the problem.

From this perspective, the particular problem that brings the client to the therapist is often viewed as merely symptomatic of some deeper, less obvious problem. If one could somehow eliminate the symptom without getting at its source, one would expect some other problem to develop in its place. While the client might feel better for a while with the symptom eliminated, such relief would only be temporary. In much the way that aspirin relieves the symptoms of flu, temporarily, without attacking its causes, superficial approaches to psychopathology will only provide temporary relief.

In contrast, the behavior theorist focuses on these so-called symptoms, and relegates presumed underlying causes to the background. The behavior theorist asks how Pavlovian and operant contingencies can be arranged so that the "symptoms" are eliminated. The behavior theorist asks what reinforcement contingencies are currently operative in the environment that are maintaining the symptoms. If they can be identified, they may be eliminated, or perhaps overridden by new contingencies that maintain different, adaptive behavior patterns. The behavior theorist maintains this orientation for a number of reasons. First and foremost, to the behavior theorist, the problems that bring a person to a therapist are not symptoms. To say that something is merely a symptom implies that the real problem lies elsewhere. As we saw in Chapter 2 (p. 38), it is Skinner's view that the internal states that are the focus of traditional psychotherapy are just mediators between environment-behavior relations which are the essence of any human behavior, including pathological behavior. Second, even if there are deep, underlying causes, it is often very difficult to identify them, which may in some cases go back many years into a person's past. Third, there is no reason to believe that all current symptoms are directly traceable to these deep underlying causes. One could imagine that many current symptoms arise indirectly, as a result of earlier symptoms. Thus, a person might, for whatever reason, have had difficulty making friends many years before. This difficulty might have resulted in some mildly pathological behavior, for instance acting extremely loud and obnoxious in social groups. This behavior may have resulted in attention from others—negative attention perhaps, but attention nevertheless. If this attention was reinforcing, it would maintain the behavior. If such a hypothetical story is true, then by changing the contingencies, and eliminating the attention, one should be able to eliminate the behavior. And this should be true no matter what the origin of the pathological behavior might have been.

Finally, the behavior theorist's emphasis on current symptoms reflects a commitment to the explanatory power of behavior theory. According to behavior theory, if a behavior persistently occurs, it must be that the behavior is being reinforced. And even if one identifies the origin of the behavior, if it continues to be reinforced, it will continue to occur. Thus, in the absence of changing currently operative contingencies, developing insights will not be enough to eliminate pathology. That is, insight into causes will not be sufficient. And if one can succeed in identifying and changing currently operative contingencies, developing insight into causes will not be necessary either. If discovering causes is neither sufficient nor necessary for the elimination of pathology, it is hard to see why one should bother looking for them at all.

It is apparent then that the orientation the behavior theorist brings to psychopathology is dramatically different from more traditional orientations. The issue we must turn to now is whether the behavior theorist's orientation works.

Applications of Pavlovian Conditioning Principles

When a stimulus of no particular significance reliably precedes the occurrence of a biologically important stimulus, Pavlovian conditioning occurs. The insignificant or neutral stimulus—the CS—comes to trigger responses that it previously did not. These responses are in some way related to the responses ordinarily triggered by the biologically significant stimulus, or US.

When we discussed Pavlovian conditioning in Chapter 3, we saw how general a phenomenon it was. We saw that it can affect voluntary, goal directed activities as well as reflexes. In addition, Pavlovian conditioning procedures can be used effectively to treat certain forms of maladaptive behavior; they have been used to eliminate fears that have become overpowering and extremely debilitating.[2] They have also been used to treat problems of addiction.

Treating Addiction

Consider behaviors like drinking or cigarette smoking. Can we use Pavlovian conditioning principles to help us understand the act of taking a drink or smoking a cigarette? For a Pavlovian analysis to be relevant, we need to identify the conditioned and unconditioned stimuli. In the case of both drinking and smoking we can identify physiological effects (of alcohol or nicotine) as USs. These physiological effects are presumably pleasurable, since people do voluntarily drink or smoke. What are likely candidates for CSs? The stimuli that most reliably precede the physiological effects of alcohol or nicotine are the tastes of the liquor or the cigarettes. Perhaps then, drinking and

2. See Wolpe and Lazarus, 1969.

smoking are examples of Pavlovian conditioning in which taste is the CS and the physiological effect is the US.

This Pavlovian analysis can provide us with some insight into the acts of drinking and smoking. The physiological effects of either nicotine or alcohol take some time to develop. Appropriate quantities of nicotine or alcohol must first be absorbed into the blood. But if the taste of cigarettes or liquor becomes a CS, then perhaps conditioned effects, resembling the unconditioned ones, are an immediate consequence of smoking or drinking. If so, the taste of liquor or cigarettes would provide an immediate pleasurable experience that mimicked in some ways the physiological effect to come later. An analysis of the Pavlovian contribution to smoking or drinking might look like the diagram in Figure 8–1A.

In the light of this Pavlovian analysis, what is the likely effect of treatment procedures in which a person simply stops ingesting the relevant substance? What effect should this procedure have on the power of the taste as a CS? The answer is none. Simply not presenting a CS does not eliminate the relation between it and the US. As a result, the conditioned responses it triggers are not eliminated. Thus, if the person should happen to take a drink or a smoke after a period of abstinence, the same conditioned responses will occur as occurred before. This kind of procedure is like taking a dog that has been a subject in a Pavlovian salivary conditioning experiment, with tones as CS and food as the US, and giving it a two week vacation from the experiment. When the dog returns to the experiment, and the tone is presented, it will salivate just as much as as it did before the vacation.

As we saw in Chapter 3, there are ways to eliminate Pavlovian conditioned responses. But simply not presenting the CS is not one of them. One effective way to eliminate conditioned responses is through *extinction;* we present CSs, but no USs. Eventually, the CSs stop triggering conditioned responses. In the case of drinking and smoking, this would mean giving the person substances that tasted like cigarettes or liquor, but contained no nicotine or alcohol. An extinction procedure is diagrammed in Figure 8–1B.

While in principle, this procedure should work, there are a few practical problems with it. First, extinction takes time; a number of trials are required before conditioned responding stops. Second, it is not easy to produce substances that taste just like cigarettes or liquor but contain no nicotine or alcohol. Third, if, after treatment, the per-

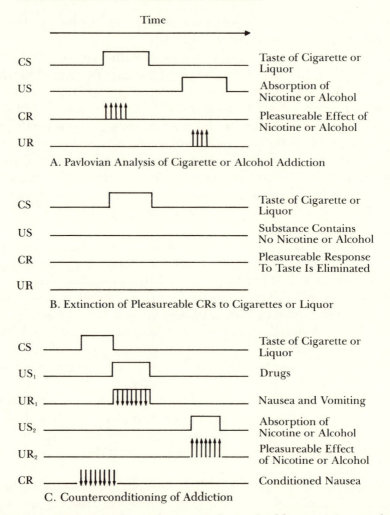

A. Pavlovian Analysis of Cigarette or Alcohol Addiction

B. Extinction of Pleasureable CRs to Cigarettes or Liquor

C. Counterconditioning of Addiction

Figure 8–1. Diagrams of a Pavlovian Analysis of Addiction (A), a Pavlovian Extinction Procedure (B), and a Pavlovian Counterconditioning Procedure (C). *The Pavlovian analysis suggests that pleasureable conditioned responses (upward arrows) develop to the taste of alcohol or cigarettes. Extinction would eliminate these conditioned responses, by breaking the relation between CS (taste) and US (absorption of nicotine or alcohol). Counterconditioning supercedes the pleasurable conditioned responses with aversive ones (downward arrows) by pairing tastes with drug-induced nausea.*

son should happen to redose with either substance, the original taste-US pairing will be reintroduced, and conditioning will quickly redevelop. For practical effectiveness, a procedure more powerful than simple extinction is necessary.

There is such a procedure. It is called *counterconditioning*. In counterconditioning, rather than presenting a CS with no US, we present a CS together with a US that is different from the original one. This new US is more powerful than the old one, and comes to supercede it. The conditioned responses developed to the new US are incompatible with the ones produced by the old US, and the old responses simply stop occurring. Thus, we might pair a tone that had previously been a CS for salivation with a strong electric shock. The new shock US would produce fear responses to the tone, and conditioned salivation would cease.

In the case of alcohol and cigarette smoking, counterconditioning has been done using the taste of alcohol or cigarettes as the CS, and a drug that produces violent nausea and vomiting as a US. This counterconditioning procedure is diagrammed in Figure 8–1C. The expectation is that with repeated pairing of the taste and the drug, ingestion of alcohol or cigarette smoke will induce conditioned nausea which is sufficiently unpleasant that people will abstain from ingesting the CS at all.

In one such case a 63-year-old alcoholic was subjected to about one month of treatment. Twice each day he received an injection of the drug apomorphine (which induces nausea and vomiting) after having had a drink of some alcoholic beverage. An aversion to the taste of alcohol developed, and three years after treatments ended, he had still not taken a drink.[3]

A second case involved a 14-year-old boy who had been smoking a pack of cigarettes or more a day since age seven. Again, the drug apomorphine was paired with the smoking of a cigarette. The boy became nauseous. In this case, it took only one such pairing for the boy to become nauseaus at tasting a cigarette. Two more pairings (spaced a few days apart) eliminated his craving for cigarettes. He even reported feeling nauseated in the presence of the cigarette smoke from other peoples' cigarettes. A year later, he had still not smoked a cigarette.[4]

3. Raymond, 1964.
4. Raymond, 1964.

These two cases suggest that Pavlovian conditioning can be a rapid and dramatically effective technique for eliminating addictions. But research that has followed early reports like the one from which these cases are taken presents a somewhat different picture. It now seems as though Pavlovian conditioning will often produce effects that are only temporary. One can expect the addictive behavior to return at some point after treatment.[5] This is not entirely surprising. As we indicated in discussing a possible extinction procedure, the problem with counterconditioning is that in the person's natural environment, liquor or cigarette tastes will again be paired with their usual physiological effect. So unless the treatment effectively eliminates any tendency to reingest the target substance, we can see how eventually the original conditioned responses will be reestablished. Moreover, if the person continues to inhabit the very same environment in which the addiction arose in the first place, it would be no surprise if whatever influences contributed to the addiction initially reasserted themselves, making readdiction likely. Thus, to make Pavlovian conditioning effects more long-lasting, they must be combined with other techniques for modifying behavior. These other techniques often involve establishing effective access to reinforcers other than the addictive substances. In short, they involve operant conditioning—the development of voluntary behaviors that produce reinforcing, but nondestructive consequences. We turn to some examples of operant conditioning techniques in application now.

Applications of Operant Conditioning Principles

In Chapters 4 and 5 on operant conditioning, we described a number of principles relevant to the control of voluntary behavior. The study of operant conditioning is the study of how the consequences of behavior—reinforcement, punishment, escape or avoidance—control its future occurrence. Many of the principles we described in those chapters have been used in applied settings. We will discuss a few representative examples here.

5. Nathan, 1976.

*Eliminating Disordered Behavior: Punishment, Shaping, and
Satiation*

Our first example of the applied use of operant conditioning principles is the case of a woman who had been in a mental hospital for
some time.[6] The problems that had initially brought her to the hospital
had receded into the background as she developed a number of
behaviors while in the hospital that were extremely pathological. Her
more dramatic symptoms were these: She stole food from other
patients in the dining room; she wore excessive amounts of clothing—
up to six layers at a time; and she hoarded towels, having as many as
25 in her small room on any given day. Her social behavior was
extremely disordered, and prospects for substantial improvement
seemed remote indeed.

The behavior theorist faced with this woman's problems focused
not on identifying how they might have originated, but on what might
be sustaining them, and how they could be eliminated. He discovered
that stealing food had no particularly dramatic consequences. Hospital
attendants might deliver a mild reprimand and return the stolen food,
but nothing more than that. It seemed sensible to arrange things so
that stealing had a more serious effect. Thus, to eliminate stealing, a
punishment procedure was introduced. Whenever the patient was
caught taking food from others, she was immediately removed from
the dining room and missed the remainder of the meal. This technique
rather quickly eliminated the stealing; just as in the case of subjects
in experiments, punishment quickly suppressed the punished behavior
(Chapter 4, pp. 79–85).

Second, to eliminate the patient's peculiar dressing habit, a different technique was used. Since food was clearly an effective reinforcer (removing it worked as a punisher), the therapist decided to
use food to reinforce normal dressing. The problem was that to reinforce a response, and increase its frequency, one must first wait for it
to occur. Since the patient never dressed normally, the reinforcement
procedure might never have a chance to strengthen normal dressing
behavior. To solve this problem, the therapist used a technique that
is often used in animal laboratories—shaping by successive approximation. Recall from Chapter 2 that pigeons are often trained to peck
keys, and rats to press levers, by initially reinforcing responses that

6. Ayllon, 1963.

approximate the desired response. For example, one might begin to train lever pressing by delivering reinforcement whenever the rat made a movement in the direction of the lever. As training proceeds, the criterion for reinforcement is gradually made more stringent until the target response has been established. This shaping technique was applied to the dressing behavior of the patient. She was weighed before each meal, and a contingency was established such that she could enter the dining room only if she was wearing less than 23 pounds of clothing. Though she met the requirement only occasionally at the beginning of the procedure, she came to meet it with increasing frequency as the procedure continued. When she was meeting it regularly, the requirement was made more stringent: Now she could not wear more than 18 pounds of clothing. Next, the requirement was 15 pounds, then 12, and so on, as her dressing behavior was gradually shaped to approach normal dressing habits. The shaping procedure required a great many sessions, but it eventually succeeded.

Third, to treat the towel-hoarding problem, the therapist used a technique we have not discussed. He used a satiation procedure. Common sense will tell you that if a pigeon that is pecking a key for food is given all the food it can eat, it will stop pecking the key. Thus, when a satiation point is reached, the reinforcer stops being reinforcing. To satiate the patient's desire for towels, she was given 25 towels every day until she had over 600 in her room. At this point, she started taking them out faster than they were being brought in. In a short time, the towel hoarding had ceased, and she contented herself with the usual towel supply.

Thus three distinct techniques were used with this patient to eliminate three distinct behaviors. The rationale for choice of technique was only what seemed most likely to control behavior. And the treatment programs had a striking side effect. As a result, no doubt, of having had these bizarre symptoms eliminated, the patient's social behavior improved dramatically. She became an active, functioning member of the hospital population where previously she had been almost entirely isolated. And this improved social behavior was apparently sufficiently positive for the patient that the various treatment programs could be discontinued without any of the symptoms recurring. She even started leaving the hospital for weekend visits with her family, for the first time in nine years. The treatment program had succeeded in eliminating her severely disordered behavior, and started her on a path toward a behavioral repertoire that was socially appropriate.

It should be noted that there was nothing especially startling or unintuitive about the procedures used with this patient. Most of our grandmothers might make us miss a meal if they discovered us stealing food. And the adage that people have to learn to crawl before they can walk, and walk before they can run is testimony to the fact that shaping is not a new invention. Nevertheless, it took the theoretical framework provided by behavior theory before people could apply these rather mundane techniques in systematic and effective fashion in therapeutic settings.

Extinction and Punishment: Eliminating Self-Destruction in Children

There is a type of psychopathology that affects young children that has been extremely resistant to treatment and is extremely painful to observe. These children are labeled *autistic* and they display a variety of symptoms. They are relatively insensitive to environmental stimulation, they show little emotion, they engage in repetitive activities like rocking, twirling, or humming, they engage in dramatic acts of self-mutilation, such as head-banging or wrist biting, they are unresponsive to other people, often avoiding any eye-contact, and they speak little if at all, with most vocalization being parrotlike repetitions of what they have just heard. In addition to these symptoms, they lack most of the abilities of normal children, acting like one or two-year-olds even at the age of 10.[7]

A behavior theorist named O.I. Lovaas has done extensive research with these children, attempting to subject their pathological symptoms to a variety of treatment procedures derived from behavior theory. His procedures have been dramatically successful in treating some behaviors and moderately successful in treating others.[8] We will focus here on procedures designed to eliminate self-mutilation.

Lovaas and his colleagues began by asking not what the underlying origin of self-mutilation might be, but what current conditions might be responsible for maintaining it. What, in short, could be the reinforcer for self-destruction? They came to the hypothesis that what

7. See Lovaas and Newsom, 1976.
8. See Lovaas and Newsom, 1976, for a review.

self-destruction gets the child is attention from its caretakers. They speculated (somewhat paradoxically since these children seem socially unresponsive) that attention from others might be a reinforcer of self-mutilation. They put this speculation to the test by eliminating attention as a consequence of self-mutilation. The procedure was designed to *extinguish* self-mutilation by withholding social reinforcement when self-mutilation occurred. Lovaas' reasoning about what might be sustaining self-mutilation, and the extinction procedure designed to eliminate it, are diagrammed in Figure 8–2A.

In our initial discussion of operant conditioning in Chapter 4, we saw that when reinforcement is discontinued (extinction), the response that had been producing it gradually decreases in frequency. Lovaas obtained similar results in his attempt to extinguish self-mutilation in an eight-year-old boy. In that study, extinction periods of 90 minutes' duration were introduced. During these periods, the boy, who was otherwise required to be restrained, was left free to move about while in social isolation. In the first extinction period, he hit himself 2700 times in 90 minutes! But over a series of these 90-minute periods, the frequency of self-mutilation decreased, until, by the eighth period, no instances of self-mutilation were observed.[9]

Further evidence that social reinforcement (attention from others) maintained self-mutilation was obtained in another study. Here, the therapists intermittently comforted a child during bouts of self-destruction, attempting to encourage him to play with toys. The result of this intermittent social reinforcement was that the boy hit himself 300 times in a 10-minute period. When the intermittent reinforcement was withdrawn, the self-destruction stopped.[10] It is easy to see how well-meaning people, by attempting to provide such a child with warm, social comfort when self-destructive episodes begin, may actually be promoting such behavior rather than eliminating it.

That social reinforcement maintained self-destruction, and that withholding social reinforcement could extinguish it, were important discoveries. But as Figure 8–2 shows, extinction takes time to work, and during that time, these children can do substantial harm to themselves. What is needed is a procedure that suppresses the self-destructive behavior more rapidly. Such a procedure is available.

We saw in Chapter 4 that punishment—the delivery of an aver-

9. Bucher and Lovaas, 1968.
10. Lovaas and Simmons, 1969.

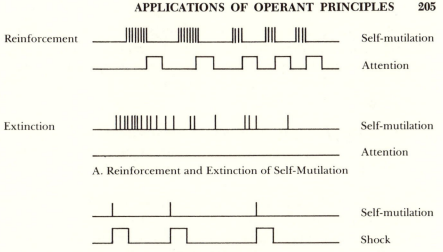

Figure 8–2. Self-Mutilation by Autistic Children and Two Procedures for Eliminating it. *A hypothetical relation between self-mutilation and attention such that attention reinforces self-mutilation is diagrammed in A, along with an extinction procedure in which the relation is broken. In B, self-mutilation is punished with electric shock. As can be seen in the diagram, the effects of punishment are more rapid than the effects of extinction.*

sive stimulus contingent on an operant response—suppresses the target behavior more rapidly than does extinction. This suggests that punishing self-mutilation might be more effective than simply extinguishing it. Such a procedure is diagrammed in Figure 8–2B. If self-destructive behavior is punished by the delivery of a mild electric shock, it is completely suppressed almost immediately. This was dramatically demonstrated in the case of a boy who hit himself up to 300 times per 10-minute period if unrestrained. A single shock to the leg suppressed this self-destruction totally. Over a few days, it returned, but another shock suppressed it again. After four such punishments, the self-destruction seemed to be suppressed permanently.[11] Thus, just as with animals in the laboratory, punishment can be used to accomplish immediately what extinction can accomplish over a protracted period of time.

Simply eliminating self-destructive behavior does not cure autism. Autistic children, as we noted, have a host of different problems. But unless one is able to eliminate self-destruction, working on

11. Lovaas and Simmons, 1969.

these other problems is virtually impossible. Thus, at the very least, the development of these behavior-theoretic applications to manage some aspects of the behavior of autistic children represents a significant contribution to what may eventually become a more complete treatment program.

Extinction of Avoidance Behavior: Treating Phobias

Recall our discussion of avoidance learning in Chapter 4. In typical avoidance experiments, as diagrammed in Figure 8–3A, a response prevents the occurrence of an aversive stimulus. If the response does not occur, the aversive stimulus is presented. When we discussed avoidance learning, we pointed out a puzzling thing about it which has led to a great deal of theorizing about the processes which underlie avoidance learning. Once acquired, an avoidance response typically does not extinguish. On trial after trial, the animal makes the response and prevents the aversive stimulus from being presented as in Figure 8–3B. What makes this puzzling is that the actual consequence of the response is nothing—it is the absence of an event (the aversive stimulus). While we might understand how the absence of an event could be salient in a context in which the event typically occurs (as when, for example, the rat is getting a shock every 30 seconds and a lever press prevents a scheduled shock from being delivered), once the avoidance response has been learned, and the aversive event stops occurring, the animal is no longer in a context in which the event typically occurs. We might expect that after a while, the animal might "forget" why it is responding and stop. Then a few shocks would come and the animal, thus reminded, would resume avoidance responding. But this does not typically occur.

In discussing various accounts of avoidance learning, we mentioned a procedure that does successfully extinguish avoidance responding. We called it response blocking (Chapter 4, p. 89). The procedure is diagrammed in Figure 8–3C. Consider the animal that has been trained to jump over a barrier from one side of a box to the other to avoid a shock that would otherwise be delivered to the dangerous side of the box. Such an animal will jump on trial after trial, never getting a shock. Now suppose we erect a floor-to-ceiling barrier that prevents the animal from jumping, and force it to stay for a prolonged period in the dangerous side of the box, with no shock delivered. The animal will attempt to get to the other side, and show visible distress for a while. Eventually, the distress will stop, as well as

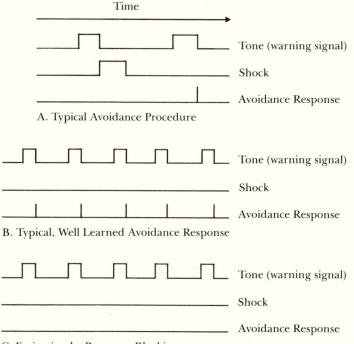

Figure 8–3. A Typical Avoidance Procedure (A), Typical Pattern of Avoidance Responding (B), and a Blocking Procedure (C). *In A, the animal does not respond on the first trial, and gets a shock. It does respond on the second trial, and avoids the shock. In B, an animal is responding on trial after trial, thus never receiving a shock. In C, the response is made impossible (blocked) and the shock is disconnected, thus allowing the animal to learn that avoidance responses are no longer required.*

attempts to flee. At this point, if the floor-to-ceiling barrier is removed, allowing the animal to jump, it will not. Avoidance behavior has been extinguished. This response blocking procedure, which is also known as *flooding,* may work because it forces the animal to remain in a previously dangerous situation long enough to discover that the situation is no longer dangerous.

People engage in avoidance responding all the time, and for the most part, it is appropriate and adaptive. However, there is a class of avoidance behavior that is not adaptive. Indeed, it may be sufficiently maladaptive to interfere with normal functioning in a wide range of situations. Such maladaptive avoidance responses are often called *phobias.* Thus people may have phobias about heights, or about being closed in, or about being in large public areas, or about storms, or about dozens of other things. Such phobias are usually irrational, and the people who have them know they are irrational. Nevertheless, they persist, and phobic people avoid being caught in these fear-producing situations. Thus, we may view phobias as avoidance responses that do not extinguish. And they are reasonably common, observable, in varying degrees of severity, in up to 8 percent of the population.[12]

There are a variety of different approaches to treating phobias, more than one of which involves principles of behavior theory.[13] One of these procedures involves the use of the flooding or response-blocking procedure.[14] In one demonstration of its effectiveness, two men were treated who had an unmanageable fear of urinating in a public bathroom. Before treatment, they could stay in a public bathroom for many minutes without being able to urinate. Usually, they simply avoided these fear-provoking places all together. Treatment involved bringing them to a public bathroom, and requiring them to stay there until they had successfully urinated. Therefore, they could neither escape nor avoid the fear-provoking situation. In the first flooding session, one man took two hours to urinate and the other took half an hour. By the tenth session, both men were able to urinate within a minute of entering the bathroom. A follow-up study of these men nine months later revealed that their fear remained under control and they were able to use public bathrooms without difficulty.[15]

This example of the application of flooding techniques parallels laboratory demonstrations in the following way: Just as the rat or dog avoids the fear-provoking stimulus (the tone in Figure 8–3) before it can discover that the underlying source of the fear (shock) is no longer present, these men avoid staying in public bathrooms long enough to discover that their fears are groundless. When we make it impossible for the dog or rat to avoid aversive stimuli, the animal is forced to learn that none is coming. Similarly, when we make it impossible for the men to avoid the bathroom, they discover that nothing horrible is in the offing. As a result, the avoidance response, and the fear of the bathroom, are extinguished.

12. Agras, Sylvester and Oliveau, 1969.
13. One procedure, known as *systematic desensitization*, involves Pavlovian conditioning principles. See Wolpe and Lazarus, 1969.
14. See Leitenberg, 1976b; and Marks, 1972.
15. Lamontange and Marks, 1973.

Behavior Theory in the University: Personalized
System of Instruction

Up to this point, all of our examples of the application of principles of behavior theory have been taken from attempts to treat psychopathology. Though this area of activity is a significant one, it is not unique. Substantial attention has also been directed at using principles of behavior theory to improve education. One particular example, initially developed by Fred S. Keller in the 1960s, is called the *personalized system of instruction*, or PSI.[16] It is largely directed at university students, and is becoming increasingly popular on a wide variety of college campuses.[17] The central characteristic of the PSI approach is that instruction is individualized and self-paced. Unlike the traditional university format, in which students work through the materials as a group, attending lectures and taking examinations according to a schedule set by the instructor, the PSI method breaks a course down into small, self-contained units. The units might consist of portions of a text, or of text together with supplementary reading materials. They are ordered so that to move to a more advanced unit, the student must first demonstrate mastery of a more elementary one. Quality of work is measured not by how high a score students make on one or two exams throughout the course, but by how many units they successfully complete during the course. When they have done the work required for a given unit, they take an exam. They are given immediate feedback about their performance on the exam, and if they pass, they move on to the next unit, while if they fail, they study more and take another exam on the same material. Thus, the PSI system seems to depend upon the use of progress through the course as a reinforcer, and to capitalize on the principle that immediate reinforcers are much more effective at controlling behavior than are delayed reinforcers. To get a grade of A in the course, a student might have to pass 25 units; to get a B, 20; to get a C, 15; and so on. The student might choose to go through 15 units in the first week of the course, or to do one unit each week, or to work in spurts throughout the semester. This is the sense in which PSI courses are said to be self-paced. Lectures, which are the central part of most university courses, are often a frill, an extra, in PSI courses. Sometimes, one must have mastered a certain number of units, demonstrating proper

16. See, for example, Keller, 1968; 1969.
17. See Lloyd, 1978, for a review.

preparation, to be permitted to attend a lecture. Also, the contents of lectures do not appear on exams. Thus lectures are used as one of several possible reinforcers, contingent upon sufficient progress with the course materials.

This is a skeletal description of PSI courses. Many variants on this basic system have been explored. While most PSI courses use written examinations to test mastery of a unit, some use oral exams—essentially discussion between students and examiners. PSI courses also vary in the size of individual mastery units. And some PSI courses have required students to write papers to demonstrate mastery, rather than taking exams.

What is the evidence for the effectiveness of PSI methods relative to more traditional ones? This is not an easy question to answer. If one tries to compare a PSI class to a traditional class that covers the same subject matter, one faces some problems. Are the students in the two classes of comparable ability; are the teachers of the two classes equally enthusiastic; and are the students equally interested in the subject? One must also worry that the sheer novelty of a PSI class may provide an artificial burst of dedication and enthusiasm to the students engaged in it. Finally, and perhaps most significantly, one must worry about choosing an appropriate measure of what was learned. On the one hand, one wants objectivity, so that short-answer type examinations may be a good measuring tool. But on the other hand, PSI might be better than traditional teaching methods at instilling the knowledge that is required for effective performance on short-answer exams, but worse at instilling the kind of knowledge that makes for excellent performance on more open-ended kinds of evaluations, like research papers.

With these difficulties in mind, the evidence suggests that PSI programs produce slightly better performance on short-answer examinations than do traditional teaching methods. There is also some slight evidence that PSI students retain information longer than do traditionally taught students, and that they do somewhat better than traditionally taught students in more advanced courses in the same discipline.[18] None of these differences are very large, nor are they

18. Lloyd, 1978. What is somewhat clearer is that students like PSI. In one study, in which students shifted back and forth between PSI and traditional methods during a single course, 176 out of 178 students preferred PSI (Lloyd, 1978). While we don't know why students like PSI—it may be easier than traditional methods, students may think they learn more, they may like being able to pace their own work—they do seem to like it.

observed in all studies. Thus, the relative effectiveness of PSI remains very much an open question.

Applications That Combine Pavlovian and Operant Principles

In Chapter 6, we discussed phenomena that involved the joint action of Pavlovianlike and operant conditioning principles. One of these was the phenomenon of conditioned reinforcement, in which, as a result of informative relations between neutral stimuli and reinforcers, the neutral stimuli themselves came to be reinforcers. A particular example of conditioned reinforcement was the demonstration of token reinforcement (pp. 155–159), in which poker chips or some other objects are paired with reinforcers like food. As a result of this pairing, organisms come to make operant responses for the tokens, which they subsequently exchange for the primary reinforcers. Conditioned reinforcement in general, and token reinforcement in particular, have had an extremely prominent place in applications of behavior theory principles. Token reinforcement has been used effectively in both educational and hospital settings; we turn now to examples from each.

Token Reinforcement: Teaching Basic Skills

Most often, when token reinforcement is introduced into the classroom, the primary purpose of the tokens is to maintain appropriate social behavior so that instruction can occur without disruption.[19] The instruction, however, occurs in a traditional manner. But sometimes, the tokens are used as a part of instructional procedures as well. In one particularly dramatic example of the use of tokens in instruction, a token system was established in a pre-school setting, with four-year-old children. Each child had three individualized, five minute training sessions each day. These brief sessions were the only alterations in the children's normal daily routine. One session was devoted to teaching the children to read the alphabet, a second was devoted to teaching them to write the alphabet, and a third was devoted to teaching them numbers and counting. Reinforcers for appropriate behavior were marbles (tokens) that were exchangeable for a variety of back-up reinforcers, primarily consisting of toys and games. This

19. See O'Leary, 1978; O'Leary and Drabman, 1971; O'Leary and O'Leary, 1976; and Staats, 1975, for discussions of the use of token reinforcement in educational settings.

project lasted seven and a half months. The effect of the program was striking. The children progressed from the second to the 24th percentile on a reading readiness test that had been standardized with children two years older. In addition, their scores on standard intelligence tests increased almost 12 points.[20] Note that these gains were made in slightly more than half a year, after only 15 minutes of special instruction per day.

Clearly, the effectiveness of this program depended upon more than just the use of token reinforcement. The children were after all given 15 minutes of special instruction each day. But notice that the instruction itself conformed to behavior theory principles. As in the case of PSI, mentioned above, instruction was individualized, so that each child could move at an appropriate pace, thus obtaining reinforcement at an appreciable frequency. In addition, reinforcement (tokens) was immediate rather than delayed, making it maximally effective. In sum, this example of effective use of token reinforcement in the classroom is really an example of the efficacy of a number of behavior theory principles, only one of which involved the delivery of tokens.

The Token Economy

Tokens as conditioned reinforcers seem an effective way to train basic skills in young children. But it is in a different setting that token reinforcement procedures have had their most extensive tests, and most impressive results. That is in the treatment of severely disordered patients in state mental hospitals.[21]

In many mental hospitals, a ward is set aside for the "chronic schizophrenic" patients. For these long-term residents, treatment has not worked. They do not get better by themselves as other schizophrenic patients sometimes do. After a period of unsuccessful therapy, they are maintained on the ward with little further attempt at treatment. They are fed, cleaned, clothed, and kept alive. Often, these patients seem to have retired from living. They slump against a wall for hours at a time, speaking to no one and listening to no one. They do not respond to meal calls, and do not even feed themselves. They do not dress or wash themselves. They do not use the toilet. The world in which they live seems to extend only to the outer limits of

20. Staats, 1968.
21. The pioneering work in this area was done by Ayllon and Azrin, 1968. See Stahl and Leitenberg, 1976, for a more recent discussion.

their own bodies and they are completely dependent on the nursing staff for sustenance.

In such a bleak situation, it does not seem meaningful to talk of rehabilitation or even therapy, because patients show so little focused responsiveness. Nevertheless the situation is intolerable, demeaning to the patient and extremely taxing on the staff. A practice that could change this situation would be very valuable.

A group of therapists who employed principles of behavior theory in therapy entered a chronic schizophrenic ward in an effort to get patients to attend to some of their own bodily needs. The hospital was too understaffed to provide the kind of constant attention that these patients required. The therapists' task was to get the patients to cooperate with the nurses—to feed themselves, clothe themselves, and use the bathrooms. In this way, some nursing personnel could be freed for service elsewhere in the hospital.

The therapists began by trying to get patients to walk to the dining room unassisted and feed themselves. The current practice was for recalcitrant patients to be spoon-fed on the ward by nurses. To the therapists, this practice looked like a reward for recalcitrance. Suppose a patient was interested in receiving attention and support from a nurse. One way to get such attention was to refuse to eat meals. The consequence of refusing meals was personal attention. To test their hypothesis, the therapists eliminated the supportive activities of the nursing staff. Meals were signaled in the usual way by a gong. Patients who did not come to the dining room did not eat. At the first meal, all the patients who usually failed to enter the dining room stayed where they were, waiting to be coaxed and, finally, fed. When this attention was not forthcoming, they missed the meal. They missed the next one also, and the next one.

At breakfast the following day, again nothing happened, but at lunchtime two patients responded immediately to the gong and walked to the dining room. Once inside, they filled their trays, sat quietly at a table, and ate a little in silence. A third patient wandered in, and a fourth. By the end of a week of this new procedure, meal taking became a normal part of everyone's day.

This small improvement in the patients' behavior had an enormous effect on the operation of the ward in general. The nurses were less rushed and were able to be more supportive and attentive to everyone than they had previously been. For the therapists, however, this was only the beginning. Their plan was to use meal taking as a privilege—a reward for doing other things. They began to implement this plan after the voluntary meal taking had been occurring successfully for two weeks.

Next, a turnstile was installed at the door of the dining room. Tokens were required to pass through the turnstile. At first, the nurses guided the patients through the turnstile. A little later, they handed the patients tokens at the turnstile which the patients themselves deposited. Still later, the patients were required to come to nurses for their tokens. These new demands on the patients were made slowly, but successfully.

The patients were then required to earn their tokens. Each patient was set a few tasks by the nurses and the therapists which, if successfully completed, would produce a token. They centered exclusively on self-maintenance—washing, combing their hair, dressing, going to the bathroom, and the like. The patients performed their tasks readily and, before long, the nurses were almost completely freed from the caretaking functions which had occupied most of their time. The patients looked more alert, clean, and active than anyone could remember.

With control over simple self-maintenance by tokens established, the token program was expanded. The number and range of things for which the tokens could be exchanged increased, including not only food, cigarettes, and the like, but also privacy, choice of mealtime companions, time away from the ward, and so on. In principle, the tokens could be exchanged for any reinforcer, and attempts were made to discover what things were reinforcers for each individual. Each individual could choose which reinforcers he would exchange the tokens for. At the same time, the range of tasks and behaviors for which tokens could be obtained increased—not just self-maintenance, but also jobs connected with ward maintenance, like assisting in the dining room or laundry, or cleaning. Gradually, more complex tasks were introduced, occupying longer spans of time, tasks involving lesser amounts of stereotyped behavior and increased amounts of planning and initiative. Different tasks earned different numbers of tokens, depending upon such factors as the complexity of the task, and different reinforcers required different numbers of tokens. Gradually the program came to simulate an economic system, and finally the patients themselves were given the responsibility for setting the task-reinforcer scale.[22]

22. Ayllon and Azrin, 1968.

The use of tokens as reinforcers in this procedure was indispensable. As we saw in Chapter 4, the control exercised by reinforcers over behavior is strongest when reinforcement immediately follows the relevant behavior, and it weakens as the delay between behavior and reinforcement increases. But primary reinforcers, such as food, cannot be available all the time—and even if they could be their use as reinforcers would break the continuity and rhythm of many tasks. Moreover, their reinforcing power would be absent at times when the person was satiated. Thus, if one utilized only contingencies of primary reinforcement, it would be virtually impossible to maintain desired behaviors over significant periods of time through reinforcement. Tokens do not have this disadvantage. They are small, durable, easy to reproduce, and their effect is not dependent on the person being in a state of deprivation. They make it possible to capitalize on the principle that the power of reinforcement depends upon its immediacy.

The program was a significant, though modest success. It produced and maintained in a group of patients, who initially were apathetic, uncommunicative and largely inactive, a range of behaviors involving self-care, communication and ward maintenance. A minimum of self-dependence and group interaction was established. The success of the program seems readily explained in terms of the principles of behavior theory.

There is also reason to believe that behavior theory principles can explain how patients in the hospital come to be so passive in the first place. The apathetic state so common in mental hospital patients may be produced in the wards themselves, that is, by the immediate environment. Patients are not in this state when they enter the ward, but apparently become this way as a kind of adaptation to living in the ward.[23] Many behavior theorists have attributed this outcome to two factors. First, though only a handful of different types of reinforcers are available within the ward—magazines, television, access to limited recreational facilities—they are all available without regard to the patient's behavior. Their availability does not depend on the occurrence of any behavior; nothing special has to be done to get them; and no matter what one does one cannot get more of them. Second, the one reinforcer that does depend upon the patient's behavior—personal attention from the staff—is maximized by passivity. Not eating or taking care of one's personal hygiene will naturally

23. See Ullman and Krasner, 1975.

attract the staff's attention; one will get fed and groomed by them. According to this hypothesis, passivity is reinforced and ordinarily functional behaviors are not; so the former increases and the latter die out. The program's success is then explained, within behavior theory, in terms of reinforcement being made contingent on functional behaviors rather than passivity. There is little doubt that the tokens really do function as reinforcers. Experimental manipulations on hospital wards have shown that behaviors that produce tokens are established and maintained while other behaviors are not, and that if a behavior stops producing tokens (extinction) its frequency of occurrence rapidly declines and it is then replaced by another behavior that does produce tokens. Also, if the dispensation of tokens is stopped altogether the initial passive state is quickly reestablished.[24] So the careful arrangement of contingencies of reinforcement can establish and maintain desired behaviors, and reduce the occurrence of undesired behaviors.

Evaluating Applications of Behavior Theory

Behavior theorists have an impressive story to tell about how their laboratory-derived principles stand up to the rigors of application. But there is another side to this story. How clear is it that behavior theory principles can indeed provide a complete account of the success of these applications? Can we identify other factors in these applied settings that may be critical to their success, but not amenable to an analysis in terms of behavior theory principles? We believe that, in at least some cases, there are other factors operating that behavior theory is not well-suited to accommodate. Identifying these factors will require a more careful look at a few of our examples.

The central principle around which almost all of behavior theory turns is that significant consequences of activities influence the likelihood that they will be repeated. If the consequences are positive, the likelihood of repetition goes up, while if the consequences are negative, the likelihood of repetition goes down. This principle is of course the law of effect. If one analyzes carefully what goes on in the token economy, or in the PSI method of instruction, one finds little indication that the operation of the law of effect is crucial. This is not

24. Ayllon and Azrin, 1968.

to say that the law of effect does not operate, so much as to say that it may be other aspects of the setting from which token and PSI methods derive their major effectiveness. These settings do not encourage the repetition of previously successful responses as much as they encourage the development of intelligent, flexible and novel goal-oriented activities. If the token economy results in the ability to develop novel solutions to novel problems, rather than the tendency to repeat what has worked in the past, then behavior theory may have little to say to explain the success of the very application it developed.

Another Look at the Token Economy

Let us return to the description of the token economy that so significantly affected the behavior of the patients in the mental hospital ward. In that example, at least four basic principles of behavior theory are illustrated. First, behavior on which reinforcement is made contingent increases in frequency. For example, when patients are required to clean and dress themselves for access to meals, self-maintenance becomes more likely. Second, behavior that has been maintained by reinforcement and whose occurrence then ceases to produce reinforcement decreases in frequency. For example, patients earned the attention of hospital personnel by being passive. When passivity stopped producing attention, passivity stopped. Third, neutral stimuli may become reinforcers after appropriate pairing with already existing reinforcers. Thus, tokens could be used to control behavior by virtue of their association with food. Finally, immediate reinforcement is more effective than delayed reinforcement. Tokens delivered immediately after an appropriate response are more effective than the promise of food at mealtime, later in the day.

Now let us examine some of these exemplified principles more closely. That the tokens became conditioned reinforcers is clear. What is not clear is the mechanism by which they became conditioned reinforcers. Nor is it clear that the therapeutic power of the token economy derived solely, or even principally, from the fact that the tokens became conditioned reinforcers. In Chapter 6 (pp. 150–152), we outlined the conditions that can make a stimulus a conditioned reinforcer. A stimulus becomes a conditioned reinforcer when it reliably and nonredundantly predicts the occurrence or the availability of a primary reinforcer, or when it gives information about the prevailing schedule of reinforcement. Tokens reliably predict the availability of primary reinforcers; they give information about what needs to be done to obtain a primary reinforcer, and they give information about the range of reinforcers that may be obtained with the current number of tokens. But tokens have additional characteristics. They are necessary conditions for obtaining primary reinforcers—something must be done *with* them in order to obtain a primary reinforcer. This feature of tokens must be part of an explanation of why they have reinforcing power even at times when the person is not deprived of the primary reinforcers. They also give information or feedback that certain tasks have been correctly carried out. Perhaps even more important, the token economy requires choice from the patient, and budgeting, planning, organization and the weighing of priorities. The patient must make two decisions: First, which jobs to do to earn tokens, and second, whether to spend them as they are earned. And there is some evidence that choice in itself is a reinforcer. In studies involving school children, subjects worked harder and faster for the opportunity to choose their own reinforcers than they did when this opportunity was not available.[25] None of these remarks, of course, suggest that tokens are not reinforcers, but they raise the question about whether that is all they are. The idea of choice, as well as the tokens, may be crucial to understanding the positive effects of token economies.

Perhaps more significantly, while in the example we described, the use of tokens brought about a wide range of desirable behaviors and eliminated many undesirable behaviors, making ward life more tolerable for the staff and less demeaning for the patients, no one left the ward. In subsequent studies, much more dramatic outcomes have been reported. But in these studies, the procedures used diverged in significant respects from the procedure we just described. We can illustrate the differences by describing one such study, conducted with a similar group of patients.[26]

The first difference in this later study was that, among the primary reinforcers available for which tokens could be exchanged was time outside the hospital. Second, activities engaged in outside the hospital ward were unsupervised, and thus, there were no programmed reinforcements for any specified desired behavior outside the ward. Consequently, such behavior could be quite varied. What the patient did was at his own initiative, and presumably responsive to whatever con-

25. Brigham, 1979. There is even some evidence that choice is reinforcing for pigeons. See Catania and Sagvolden, 1980.
26. Atthowe and Krasner, 1968.

tingencies of reinforcement were present outside the ward, including contingencies involving real money. Third, for a few patients, those who reported regularly and promptly for assignments and who had accumulated a certain number of tokens, immediate reinforcement was discontinued, and replaced by weekly token payments. This required significant planning and budgeting on their part in order to spread their exchange of tokens for primary reinforcers over a whole week. Fourth, wherever possible, increased responsibility was encouraged. Tokens would be given not for engaging in specific behaviors within a supervised context, but rather for successfully completing tasks that required the planning and initiative of the patient, because what was required to carry out the tasks varied from day to day. For example, while running a kitchen involves some routine aspects, the detail and order of the activities involved in the kitchen varies, so that flexibility is required.

The outcome of this study, like the study we described earlier, provided clear evidence for the efficacy of token reinforcement. But unlike the earlier study, a substantial number of patients were discharged from the hospital. The increased discharge rate seems to be attributable to the new features of this program. But these new features have little to do with behavior theory. First, consider the use of passes to leave the ward as reinforcers. That these passes were effective reinforcers raises an important question about how reinforcers are identified. By definition, a reinforcer is an event that makes more frequent those behaviors upon which its occurrence is contingent. Among the events that may be reinforcers are opportunities to engage in certain preferred activities. Behaviors that have a high likelihood of occurrence may be used as reinforcers for behaviors that have a lower likelihood. That is, organisms will do some things for the opportunity to do, other, higher-frequency things.[27] This principle of reinforcement has often been used to discover reinforcers for individual patients. Any behavior that a patient is observed to engage in spontaneously, at a reasonably high frequency, is tried out as a reinforcer.[28]

On this criterion for determining reinforcers, obtaining a pass to spend time outside the ward was not a reinforcer for the patients in the token economy study. Although, before the study, passes were readily available, they were rarely used. In other words, leaving the

27. Premack, 1965.
28. Ayllon and Azrin, 1968.

hospital was not a high-frequency behavior. Nevertheless, after the program was instituted, passes to leave the hospital became reinforcers for many of the patients. That is, many tokens were exchanged for these passes. What this suggests is that an important consequence of a token program can be an increase in the range of reinforcers that can influence a patient's behavior—an important contribution maintaining functional behavior outside the institutional environment. But behavior theory has little to say about how activities can be made into reinforcers.

Second, consider the patient's unsupervised time, and the ward activities that required planning and initiative. One might say that having unsupervised time available, and having the opportunity to use one's initiative are reinforcers. Indeed, this is probably true. But calling these activities reinforcers points out the limits of behavior theory in explaining them. For these activities occur over extended periods of time. They consist of sequences of behavior that presumably possess some internal organization. Behavior theory tells us nothing about their organization, nor does it tell us how to distinguish sequences of behavior that are reinforcers from other sequences of behavior, like tying one's shoes, that are not reinforcers.

Perhaps these organized, flexible activities that earn tokens are not reinforcers. Perhaps they are operants. To discuss this possibility concretely, consider a task like running a kitchen. It involves a number of routine skills, each of which may be shaped using reinforcement in accordance with the principles of behavior theory. The mastery of routine skills alone, however, is clearly insufficient to run a kitchen adequately. One must prepare a menu, order food, check the utensils, plan the order of execution of various sub-tasks, synchronize various sub-tasks so that different parts of the meal are cooked at the appropriate time, and so on. One day's work in the kitchen will be quite different from the next day's. Preparing a meal of roast beef is quite different from preparing a meal of poached fish, and preparing a meal for fifty is quite different from preparing a meal for five—although all preparations will have certain sub-tasks in common, such as turning on ovens, cutting, washing and spicing foods, and so on. The day to day aspects of running a kitchen are quite different.

When a patient earns tokens for successfully running a kitchen, what—if anything—can we say has been reinforced? What is the operant? What becomes more probable as a consequence of having been reinforced? In the study of the token economy, it is clear that the patient is sustained in his activity of running the kitchen by the tokens. That is, he ceases to perform the activity if he no longer earns tokens for it. But sustenance need not be the same thing as reinforcement. Something is a reinforcer only if the probability of behaviors whose occurrence is required for it increases. How can we say that the activity of running the kitchen has been reinforced, if each day's activity is quite different from the previous day's? So too, one might say, can be a rat's pressing a lever—one press with its left front foot, the next with its nose, the next with its right hind foot. In the case of the rat, though, we can readily group these disparate behaviors together, as behaviors with a clearly defined outcome: The lever is depressed. In behavior theory it is quite common to classify behaviors on the basis of their environmental effects. Something is a lever-press if it succeeds in depressing the lever, irrespective of the particular limb and muscular movements involved.

Could we not, in a similar way, classify together the various episodes of running a kitchen in terms of a common outcome—edible food prepared at the right time? It is only when this outcome is realized that tokens are awarded. Thus activities which produce this outcome are reinforced. There is only a superficial plausibility to this suggestion. Having edible food prepared at the right time is not like pressing a lever. The latter can be performed "at will" by any unconstrained rat, without any arrangement of antecedent events—but not the former. A person can't just put edible food on the table at the right time; the right preparation is required. The tokens are playing a role in ensuring that the patient does have edible food on the table at the right time, since the patient stops doing this if the tokens are withdrawn. But it does not thereby follow that reference to the contingency between producing this outcome and gaining the tokens explains the production of the outcome. The process of preparation, including its planned character, is also part of the explanation. But given the flexible character of the processes of preparation, their variation from one day to the next—indeed, their deliberate, planned variations from one day to the next—the principles of behavior theory have little to tell us about them. At a very abstract level, we can say that just as food reinforces whatever activity of the rat produces the outcome of the lever being depressed, so the tokens reinforce whatever activity produces the outcome of edible food being available at the right time.

The problem with this analysis is that it does not explain the variation in the processes of food preparation. And it is just this variation that is essential for the successful running of a kitchen.

It is tempting to adopt the view that while behavior theory can not *presently* explain the planning, flexibility, and intelligent variation that go into the running of a kitchen, it will eventually be able to do so. After all, we must credit behavior theory for the development of the token economy in the first place. If token systems have developed in directions that seem surprising and inexplicable from the perspective of behavior theory, we may view them as posing a challenge for subsequent generations of behavior theorists to meet.

This view is certainly not unreasonable. In the absence of an alternative explanation of the effectiveness of the token economy, it certainly makes sense to give behavior theory the time to develop an explanation. The problem is that there is an alternative to the behavior theory analysis of activities like running a kitchen. This alternative is provided by the language of common sense, the language that, as we saw in Chapter 1, behavior theory is trying to replace.

If we brought the explanatory tools provided by common sense to the token economy, to account for running a kitchen, we might say that the patient has the goal of obtaining tokens, and he does in the kitchen whatever he believes sufficient (and perhaps also necessary) to obtain the tokens. These beliefs correctly will vary in content from day to day, in accordance with the sub-goals of the meal that he is setting out to prepare on a given day and how he plans to reach these subgoals. In cases of flexible, often novel activity, the person does what he does because of what he believes to be the consequences of what he does, but not necessarily because earlier instances of the same pattern of activity had these consequences. Acting in order to ensure certain consequences is not the same as acting because previous instances of similar acts have produced these consequences.

Given this common sense analysis, we might go on to say that goals become reinforcers when the means to achieving the goals become standardized, that is, as intelligent planning is removed from the context of achieving the goals. This point is not a merely semantic one. The possibility exists that when goals are reduced to reinforcers, the role of intelligence (planning, assessing, reasoning, and so on) is eliminated, or at least minimized. This is a suggestion we will elaborate in detail in Chapter 9.

The upshot of this discussion is not, of course, that token economies are unsuccessful. On the contrary their successes are very impressive. But it seems that the more impressive the results, the less the results seem to be attributable to the role of tokens as reinforcers, and so the less the program can be described as an application of the principles of behavior theory.

PSI Revisited

A similar argument can be made in the case of PSI methods. The opportunity for self-pacing seems critically important to the success of PSI. But why? What makes self-pacing a reinforcer? Perhaps self-pacing is a reinforcer because it allows students to budget their time— to plan their work schedule and take the initiative in organizing their activities. But these are just the characteristics of behavior in the token economy about which behavior theory has the least to say.

Also, immediate feedback is crucial to the success of PSI. Since this feedback controls behavior, it, along with progressing to the next unit, are reinforcers. But is it not possible that feedback is important in controlling behavior for reasons having nothing to do with reinforcement? Feedback provides information. It tells someone what he or she is doing properly, and what is being done wrong. Clearly, if a person wants to do something properly, feedback is of great value. And immediate feedback is of especially great value. Rather than persisting on the wrong path for a long time without knowing it, immediate feedback allows students to correct their mistakes quickly, with little or no effort wasted in misdirected activities. Having an educational program with delayed feedback is like having a thermostat with a five minute delay built in between the detection of the temperature of a room, and the signal to turn the air conditioning off. During that five minutes, the air conditioner will continue, wastefully, to cool the air in the room, until the feedback signal turns it off. Thus, significant features of the PSI method may be effective for reasons which have little to do with principles of behavior theory. Indeed, in recent years, a line of argument about the effectiveness of applications of behavior theory principles in general has made precisely this point. Behavior theory methods may work, but not for the reasons behavior theorists claim. Rather, it is argued that applications produce significant changes in a person's cognitive processes, and depend crucially for their success upon these cognitive changes.[29]

29. See Bandura, 1974, for example.

Applications of Behavior Theory: A New Conception of Human Nature

The successful applications of behavior theory we have reviewed are just a handful among many. They are important for two reasons. The first is obvious: To the extent that applications like these continue to develop, they will offer significant opportunities for improving human welfare. The second reason is perhaps less obvious, but more important. Successful applications of behavior theory principles are taken by behavior theorists as evidence for the validity of their underlying conception of human nature. For, as we saw in Chapter 1, behavior theory rests upon a conception of human nature antithetical to our ordinary conception of ourselves. While individual experimental demonstrations, of the sort we reviewed in Chapters 3 through 6, do not depend intimately on this conception of human nature, it is always there in the background. And while one can accept the results of animal research without having to accept the conception of human nature that goes with them, it is not so easy to do the same with successful human applications. Therefore, when we consider applications of behavior theory, we also consider the conception of human nature that goes with them.

What Controls Behavior: Reward and Punishment

Most of behavior theory focuses on attempts to explain our voluntary behavior. What behavior theory tells us is that while voluntary behavior seems to be directed toward its future or anticipated consequences, it is actually under the control of antecedent environmental variables. How can behavior that seems oriented toward the future be explained as being under the control of events in the past? Behavior theory's answer is simple but ingenious. It is that voluntary behavior is not to be explained in terms of its expected consequences, but in terms of the consequences of past occurrences of similar behaviors. Throughout the book, when we have used the formulation that "voluntary behavior" (or, in the language of behavior theory, operant behavior) "is under the control of its consequences," we were really using an abbreviated version of "Operant behavior is under the control of the consequences of past occurrences of similar behaviors." This approach to the relation between behavior and events that follow it dispenses with the apparent "forward looking" character of voluntary behavior. What an organism does is a consequence of its experiences (the consequences of its past behaviors), without needing to posit such forward-looking states as belief, expectancy, or intention. Thus, the rat presses the lever not because it expects that the lever press will produce food, but because in the past lever presses have produced food. What controls voluntary behavior is its past history of association with rewarding or punishing environmental events.

We all acknowledge that some behavior is controlled by rewards and punishments, and that to understand what causes people to act as they do, it is necessary to take rewards and punishments into account. Rewards and punishments are a palpable part of each of our lives. They are bestowed upon us and we use them ourselves to induce people to act in certain ways. Yet, we would argue, there is more to human beings than that. People do many things because of some inner force that guides them. People do things because it is logical or right or moral or humane to do them. People are happy because they have fulfilled their expectations about themselves, and they are depressed because they have not. To understand human nature fully, we must understand these things too. But from the perspective of behavior theory, these other aspects of human nature are myths. All behavior of consequence is controlled by rewards and punishments. Sometimes the controlling environmental contingencies may be obvious, and sometimes they may be subtle, but always they are responsible for what we do.

This view of human nature is fundamentally at odds with the view that underlies ordinary discourse. The latter view presupposes human autonomy, the power of individual agents to control their own actions. We assume this power when we hold people responsible for their actions, when we praise or blame them, reward or punish them for their actions. More generally, any moral discourse presupposes this power. It is in the light of this power that people value freedom, uphold dignity, and affirm human rights. In short, much of the support for our moral, legal, and political institutions presumes that human beings have this power.

These general characteristics of behavior theory suggest that the widespread application of its principles might result in major changes in our social insitutions. If one is not free to act in a particular situation, that is, if there are forces present which demand certain actions, then one cannot be held responsible for engaging in those actions. We accept the principle that transgressions that are committed under duress should not be punished. Acts must be freely chosen before their perpetrators are forced to accept the consequences. But behavior theory rests on the principle that all acts are committed under "duress," in that contingencies of reward and punishment in the environment are responsible for what we do. Acts are never "freely" chosen by the person. They are always determined by rewarding and punishing aspects of the environment, together with the person's past experience of rewards and punishments for similar actions.

Thus, we see that behavior theory is guided by a thesis about human nature that challenges deeply held beliefs which have been a part of our culture and our social institutions for perhaps three thousand years. The leading figure in behavior theory, B.F. Skinner, is well aware of this and he does not hesitate to draw the kind of conclusion we have just sketched. Freedom and dignity, he tells us, are myths, barriers to the kind of implementation of behavioral controls that could contribute to solving the big problems of contemporary humanity—warfare, crime, population explosion, ecological damage, and so on.[30]

Behavior Theory and Everyday Life

Skinner's views about human nature are particularly extreme, and many who call themselves behavior theorists would take exception to much that Skinner has written. But Skinner's critics within behavior theory have not proposed alternative views that are general, like Skinner's, and also consistent with their research. Skinner is the only major figure in behavior theory who has offered a world view. While most behavior theorists seem content to work on particular empirical or theoretical problems within behavior theory, much of Skinner's work has been concerned with specifying the relations between research of this kind and central features of ordinary human experience. Because Skinner's general claims about the nature of people are consistent with key concepts in behavior theory, and because no behavior theorist has offered alternative claims that might challenge Skinner's, Skinner must be taken seriously as the spokesman for his discipline.

30. Skinner, 1971.

And he must be taken seriously for another reason. Although the thesis about human nature on which behavior theory rests is one that many people find repugnant and degrading, behavior theory is becoming an increasingly influential part of our culture. And the reason for its influence is the success of its applications. We have seen that it has yielded a set of empirical principles that is being applied with some success in social settings as diverse as mental hospitals, schools, factories, and prisons. It has provided people with a set of effective tools for working with individuals who, for whatever reason, find it difficult to lead fulfilling lives within society. One may ignore the physicist when he limits his domain to laboratory experiment and abstract theory. But when his domain is extended by the applications of the engineer to automobiles, airplanes, atomic energy, and so on, he can no longer be ignored. Similarly, when behavior theory is extended in application to areas that touch our daily lives, it also cannot be ignored.

Some observers of the applications of behavior theory view it as a threat to human freedom. They see the developing techniques for behavior control and behavior change as future tools for a kind of scientific totalitarianism. Those people who possess the tools will be able to impose their will on society. How does the behavior theorist reply to these concerns?

The central component of any behavior theorist's reply is that behavior control is a fact of life. Though we may not have recognized it, individuals and institutions have always depended upon the use of reward and punishment to manipulate our behavior. We have probably used some principles of behavior theory ourselves to gain control over the behavior of others. Teachers have always induced students to do their work with the promise of reward and the threat of punishment. Churches induce their members to behave in accordance with some moral code with promise of rewards and punishments. Most people work at their jobs for financial rewards. Governments induce people to spend their money in particular ways by introducing tax penalties and incentives. On a more personal level, we control the behavior of our children with promise of reward and, more commonly, threat of punishment. With these principles of behavior control already in operation all around us, the main impact of behavior theory will be to make their use more efficient and effective.

The critic of behavior theory might reply to this argument by stating that because something exists is not a justification for its further existence—not to mention its extension. Perhaps the new awareness of techniques of control inspired by behavior theory should awaken efforts to eliminate it wherever it exists rather than increasing its efficiency. The behavior theorist would disagree. Recall that a central assumption of behavior theory is that an understanding of how rewards and punishments work will provide a *complete* account of human behavior. What this means is that principles of reward are facts of nature. They tell us not that reward *can* work in some situations, but that it is working everywhere. The science of behavior is a description of the way things *are,* and not a blueprint of the way things ought to be. If it is a valid description of the way things are, then one can no more change it or eliminate it than one can change the laws of physics. One cannot eliminate control. One can eliminate an undesirable source of control and replace it with a more desirable one, but the best way to accomplish this is by learning the principles of behavior theory and then applying them.

The critic of behavior theory might reply that showing that the behavior of people *can be* controlled by rewards and punishments is not the same as showing that it ordinarily is so controlled. This was one of the messages of Chapter 7. Recall that in Chapter 7, we provided examples of how behavior that is under pure operant control in some experimental settings is not in others. Perhaps the same argument applies to human behavior. Because it is under pure operant or Pavlovian control in an applied setting does not imply that it is in general. For this reason, the step from claiming that behavior *can be* controlled by reward and punishment to claiming that it *is* controlled by reward and punishment must be taken with great care.

In short, how seriously we take concerns about the consequences of the growing application of principles of behavior theory to everyday life depends in large part upon our judgment about how accurate a picture of human nature behavior theory provides. If we judge the principles of behavior theory to be valid, and if we judge those principles to account for the major part of human action, then the behavior theorist is right. All that the application of behavior theory entails is the *systematic use* of techniques of behavior control that have always been and will always be a central part of human life anyway. If, however, we judge the principles of behavior theory to be invalid, or to be valid for only a limited portion of human life, then the behavior theorist is wrong. The application of behavior theory entails a change in human nature and in the nature of social institutions.

What we are suggesting is that a proper evaluation of the broad social and ethical implications of behavior theory depends upon an evaluation of the validity and generality of its basic principles. In the last chapter of the book, we will present and evaluate possible serious shortcomings of behavior theory that may require a fundamental change in the nature of the theory and its thesis about human nature. In this chapter, we will attempt to make an argument that even in the face of successful applications, principles of behavior theory are inadequate to explain human action.

Chapter 9

Reflections on the Limits of Behavior Theory

BEHAVIOR theory aims to discover a set of principles that can explain the behavior of organisms in all environments. In Chapters 3 through 6, we described many of the important principles that have been developed with the aid of the experimental methods of behavior theory. The experimental evidence certainly indicates that these principles govern at least some behavior in at least some environments. But in Chapter 7, we presented evidence that there may be serious limitations to the scope of behavior theory principles. First, this evidence suggested that in an animal's natural environment, principles may be operative that are not encompassed by behavior theory. Second, it suggested that operant principles may be especially significant only in the special environment of the laboratory, where Pavlovian influences and other influences that are a part of the animal's genetic heritage are prevented from dominating the animal's behavior as they apparently do in its natural environment. According to the argument presented in Chapter 7, operant principles may shed little light on an animal's behavior in its natural environment because operant influence, though real, tends to be dominated or overshadowed by these other influences.

The evidence presented in Chapter 7 makes a persuasive case that behavior theory can not provide a comprehensive account of animal behavior. But as we pointed out in Chapter 8, this argument does not represent a telling challenge to the significance or comprehensiveness of operant principles as applied to human behavior. If human behavior is not ordinarily under operant influence, we would not expect it to be predominantly under Pavlovian or genetically derived influence either.[1] Thus, whether or not operant principles provide a comprehensive explanation of human behavior remains an open question.

It is this question that the present chapter will address. How comprehensive and significant are operant principles in accounting for human behavior? Is the law of effect a significant force in the day to day activities of human beings in a wide variety of contexts? Are there important influences on human behavior that cannot be encompassed either by operant principles or by the human genetic heritage? We will suggest that the answer to this last question is affirmative, while we argue that there are well-defined boundaries to the influence of operant principles. In identifying these boundaries, we will expose serious limitations to the scope of behavior theory, while at the same time we identify a significant and expanding range of contemporary activities that do fall within its scope.

Assessing a Theory's Comprehensiveness

We have seen that behavior theory has formulated numerous principles of increasing power and sophistication. And these principles, in turn, have been applied in many useful ways. As we pointed out in Chapter 2, according to Skinner, the successes of behavior theory are already impressive enough for us to abandon our traditional understanding of human nature and the social practices which grew from it over the centuries. Skinner argues that in their stead we substitute the understanding and social practices suggested by behavior theory. Skinner's claim rests upon his belief in the comprehensiveness of behavior theory. Though it is difficult to assess its comprehensiveness, we must attempt such an assessment if we are to evaluate the theory's alleged, far-reaching implications. We can show that a theory is *not* comprehensive if we can identify well-defined boundaries to the applicability of its principles. But how can we identify such boundaries?

One way we can do so is by experimentation. Suppose one held the theory that all behavior occurs under Pavlovian control, as Pavlov himself may have believed. As tests of this theory, operant conditioning experiments could be viewed as demonstrating the theory's lack

1. See Wilson, 1975, for a different view.

of comprehensiveness. Operant experiments reveal another influence on behavior (the response-reinforcer contingency) that a comprehensive Pavlovian theory would ignore. In similar fashion, experiments on taste aversion learning (Chapter 7) show that there are influences on behavior in addition to Pavlovian and operant contingencies. These experiments lend support to the view that the dominant influence of behavior theory principles is limited to those contexts that depart significantly from the natural habitat of a species. In each of these cases, the boundaries of a theory's application were specified by referring to an important variable that is a part of a more comprehensive theory. Pavlov's theory is bounded by reference to the response-reinforcer contingency, which is a key variable in behavior theory. Behavior theory is bounded by reference to the genetic heritage of the organism, which is a key variable in ethological theory. Still another example can be found in Chapter 5, where the applicability of the matching law is bounded by reference to the variables of demand elasticity and substitutability, key variables in economic theory. In each of these cases, the more comprehensive theory does not deny the relevance of the variables emphasized by the less comprehensive ones. It simply acknowledges that there are more variables operating.

There is a second way to identify boundaries of the application of experimentally-derived principles. In attempting to generalize laboratory principles to the natural environment, perhaps the strongest ground for believing that they play a significant role in nature would be a demonstration that important natural phenomena clearly exemplify these principles (see Chapter 2, p. 43). The demonstration that the motions of the planets clearly exemplified Newton's laws of motion was powerful evidence that Newton's experimentally-derived laws were of great significance in explaining nature. But suppose that all the exemplifications of a set of principles in nature not especially designed as applications of the principles had certain clear characteristics. And suppose that as one encountered situations that were further and further removed from those having these characteristics, it became increasingly difficult to construe the situations as exemplifying the principles. Then there would be strong reason to believe that the comprehensiveness of the principles was bounded by situations having only these characteristics. More concretely, suppose that all natural situations that seemed clearly to exemplify operant principles were characterized by the substitutability of stimuli, responses, and reinforcers. And suppose that as one moved to situations that did not have this character, it became increasingly difficult to identify operant principles at work. If this were the case, one might conclude that the applicability of operant principles was limited to situations that had substitutable elements.

As we saw in Chapters 2 and 7, just because certain principles are reliably demonstrated in the laboratory is no guarantee that they are significant outside it. Experiments are constructed because in the complexity of the natural environment, many influences interact simultaneously to produce a phenomenon. An experiment simplifies by isolating influences so that they can be identified and studied individually. Thus, it can never be inferred from experiments that one has identified all, or even the most significant influences in nature. There is no standing presumption that one may move from experimental success to claims of comprehensiveness in every situation, or that one may move from an experimental demonstration that behavior *can* be controlled by certain influences to the claim that behavior ordinarily *is* controlled by them. Indeed, the phenomenon of auto-shaping (Chapter 7) provides experimental evidence that a given behavior may be under one type of control in one circumstance and a different type in another. Comprehensiveness cannot therefore be assumed. Its plausibility depends on demonstrating that experimentally-derived principles are exemplified in a wide range of natural situations. Thus, no matter how reliably principles can be shown to operate in the laboratory, the question of relevance or significance outside it remains an open one.

Ethology and the Comprehensiveness of Behavior Theory

We have identified two ways to find limits to a theory's comprehensiveness. First, one can identify, with experiments, the boundaries of a given theory's applicability. Second, one can show that principles that seem critically important in the experimental laboratory are not so important in many non-laboratory contexts. These two ways to define boundaries of applicability for a given set of principles will often coincide. We can see this in the ethological challenge to behavior theory. On the one hand, in Chapter 7, we emphasized the *experimental* demonstration of influences acknowledged by ethology but not by behavior theory, and suggested that behavior theory plays a dominant role in those contexts where other, genetically-rooted influences are absent.

But on the other hand, we could view ethology as a theory that denies that operant principles are widely or significantly exemplified at all in the natural environments of animals. Operant principles are exemplified only when Pavlovian and genetically-rooted influences, which dominate in nature, are suppressed. The standard conditioning chamber, in which most research in behavior theory is done, succeeds in suppressing these otherwise dominant influences. Among the features of the procedures typically used in the conditioning chamber that probably contribute to the demonstrable significance of operant principles are these: First, the animal has been severely deprived of food or some other reinforcer. Second, there are few behavioral options available to the animal. Third, the contingencies of reinforcement are externally controlled. Fourth, specific behaviors are reinforced with specific reinforcers, rather than a variety of reinforcers simply being available as a consequence of a whole pattern of activity. And lastly, as discussed in Chapter 7, stimuli, responses, and reinforcers are chosen so as to minimize the chance that any relation between them exists prior to the experiment, and to minimize the chance that any other, nonoperant kind of relation is also introduced during the experiment. Ethology suggests that operant control of animal behavior is only dominant under conditions similar to those prevailing in the conditioning chamber. Thus, it suggests narrow boundaries for the application of operant principles to animal behavior. Under most natural conditions, with the constraints of the conditioning chamber absent, genetically-rooted and Pavlovian influences dominate operant ones.

While the ethological position illustrates both the strategies for challenging behavior theory's comprehensiveness, the argument from ethology does not transfer in a straight-forward way to the case of human behavior. The applicability of operant principles may be narrowly bounded for animal behavior, for reasons suggested by ethology, but still be ubiquitous for human behavior. One of the remarkable, and probably unique, things about human beings is that they make their own environments, not according to a biological program as a bird builds its nest, but according to their desires and plans. People do not, of course, create their environments out of nothing, or without constraints; they do so by modifying the environments into which they are born. But it makes little sense to talk of the "natural" environment of human beings, since that environment changes from generation to generation and in very marked ways from age to age. Unlike animals in their natural environments, we would expect the behavior of humans in their social environments to be quite free from dominant biological and Pavlovian influence. While it would be foolish to deny that there is biological influence upon human behavior, we would expect that normal human behavior will take place in contexts that have suppressed dominant biological and Pavlovian influence. As B.F. Skinner has said: "Civilization has supplied an unlimited number of examples of the suppression of the phylogenetic repertoire of the human species by learned behavior."[2]

We would not expect to find the limits to the scope of operant principles by discovering predominant biological or Pavlovian influences in normal human social activity. Contexts which are artificial for animals may be "natural" for humans; the contexts within which operant principles are dominant may not need to be specially created for humans, but may exist as a routine part of the social environment. Ethology cannot replace behavior theory as a theory of human nature.

Nevertheless, ethology can provide us with a clue about how to define boundaries to the applicability of operant principles to human behavior. Suppose that human behavior is subject to a variety of experiential influences not encompassed by behavior theory. Suppose, too, that for human behavior, operant principles are exemplified only in circumstances with certain features that are not general features of the human environment across cultures, classes and history; and that in many social contexts, other experiential influences are dominant. In that case, there would be good reason to conclude that the circumstances possessing these features constituted the boundary of the application of operant principles. If, in addition, these features resembled those obtaining in the conditioning chamber, we would expect that the principles identified in experiments with animals would generalize to people. But this generality would not indicate that human and animal behavior is ordinarily under the same sort of operant control, but only that operant influence becomes dominant when ordinarily dominant influences are suppressed, influences of genetic and Pavlovian kinds in animals, and other experiential kinds in humans.

Behavior Theory and the Workplace

The clue offered by ethology helps us locate our target. Where in the human environment do we find exemplifications of operant principles? The behavior theorist might cite the applied successes

2. Skinner, 1977, p. 1007.

discussed in Chapter 8. But demonstrations in the laboratory, hospital or classroom only show that contingencies of reinforcement *can* control human behavior, or alternatively that they *do* control human behavior *in certain situations*. Such demonstrations are creations—they occur in situations that are deliberately constructed so that behavior theory principles can be made to operate. We saw in discussing successful applications of behavior theory that what characterizes most of them is the total control the behavior theorist has over all the variables. Under such circumstances, environments can be tailored to maximize the chances that procedures under investigation will be effective. Thus, they cannot be regarded as characteristic human environments. Is there any human context that has not been deliberately constructed in order to apply behavior theory principles, in which these principles can be shown to apply? There is one plausible candidate—the modern factory workplace.

If we systematically observe the factory we will see that factory behavior is, to a reasonable extent, controlled by reinforcement contingencies. But we will also see that the conditions prevailing in the factory are quite similar to those present in the conditioning chamber: Only a single reinforcer (money) is available; there are few alternative means to this reinforcer; the performance of clearly-defined specific tasks is reinforced; the connection between these tasks and the reinforcer is unbiased, that is, different tasks are effectively interchangeable; the schedule of reinforcement is externally imposed and varied by external agents. This suggests that factory work exemplifies principles of behavior theory precisely because the conditions that prevail in the factory are just like those that prevail in the laboratory.

Premodern Work and Modern Work

Consider workers in a clothing manufacturing factory, each performing exactly the same task (e.g. sewing on buttons) over and over again. They perform it simply for pay in the sense that, minor considerations aside, they would just as soon do any other job (e.g. cutting material) if the wages were the same. They work under an explicit contract to pay them either by the hour or by the piece. They are, in effect, in a conditioning chamber performing an operant, on an interval or ratio reinforcement schedule.[3] It is extremely plausible to suggest that their behavior is under the control of the schedule of reinforcement.

3. See Ferster and Skinner, 1957, and Chapter 5 of this book.

The workplace is a pervasive and essential part of modern life, and any theory which could account for behavior there would be a powerful one. Work, after all, occupies the greater part of most people's lives. Indeed, it is reasonable to claim that behavior theory, to the extent that it gives a good model of the dominant occupations of our society, in fact models well most of behavior. In most modern industrial countries, work has had the character we described above for some time.

In contrast, less than 150 years ago, a large proportion of the Russian population were working under very different conditions. They were serfs, and had no legal alternative to the work they did. They were bound to work the land of a lord, in return for protection, and had to turn over a fixed percentage of their yield to the lord. They had no choice of what terms they would work under. The details of their relation to the lord were a part of a longstanding set of political and social practices, now known as feudalism, which was not based on strictly economic considerations, nor could it be changed on the basis of those considerations.

These Russian serfs lived under the last vestiges of feudalism, which had in most respects disappeared from England as an economic system by the eighteenth century, and which never existed in any full sense in North America. But until it was gradually replaced by capitalism, feudalism was the dominant economic arrangement in Europe for several centuries. At least a certain portion of the serf's work was performed to fulfill explicit legal and social obligations. These obligations emphasized stability and equality, rather than material benefits or rewards, in proportion to work done.[4] The serf farmed the land of the lord, and received enough of the harvest to assure subsistence as well as legal and military protection. Though economic benefits may have sometimes been proportional to work, the social arrangements of the time were not designed to encourage making that connection, and there is little reason to suppose that it was the main goal of those arrangements. Thus, while the modern worker strikes a wage bargain with an employer which may be presumed to reflect, in some part, his assessment of where the monetary rewards for work will be greatest, the serf did not, in any clear way, have such a choice.

The factors operating in the choice of work were different in feudal than in modern times; but the nature of the work itself was also different. Serfs, and other premodern workers, engaged in a wide variety

4. Tawny, 1912; Coulton, 1925.

of different activities in the course of a day. Their work required flexibility and decision-making. The rhythm or pace of their work changed from season to season.[5] In contrast, the modern factory worker does the same thing all day, every day, with no flexibility or decision-making required. The work of the modern factory worker is very much analogous to a pigeon pecking a key or a rat pressing a lever in that the behavior is repetitive, and it is an arbitrary means to reinforcement. The pigeon would easily substitute hopping on a foot treadle for pecking, and the factory worker would easily substitute one assembly-line task for another. Also, the rate at which the factory worker performs is governed by the rate and schedule of reinforcement. It is easy to see why the factory seems like such a perfect confirmation of behavior theory principles, and why work which antedated factory work does not.

Transition from Premodern to Modern Work

Over many years, serfs were driven off the land in relatively large numbers and eventually became wage laborers. This change coincided with other changes in work that resulted in the emergence of the factory system. By the end of the eighteenth century in England, many of the descendants of serfs were not only working for wages, but were being paid those wages for operating machines in textile mills or performing some particular operation in the manufacture of some other kind of commodity. The change in work was dramatic. The transition to industrial society "entailed a severe restructuring of working habits, new disciplines, new incentives. . ."[6] Workers now were paid wages, and were legally free to change jobs. Moreover, with increasing mechanization and increasing importance of the division of labor, there was decreasing variety and flexibility in work. But in the early stages of industrialization, despite the dissimilarities to premodern work, the behavior of a worker still did not provide the kind of dramatic evidence for the principles of behavior theory that contemporary work does.

For one thing, employers were not yet establishing all of the conditions of work. At least some workers had autonomy, which they protected by a "moral code." The code included an output quota fixed

5. Rodgers, 1978.
6. Thompson, 1967.

by the workers themselves.[7] Though "workers learned to regard labor as a commodity to be sold in the historically peculiar condition of a free capitalist economy," nevertheless, in the early phases of industrialization, "where they had any choice in the matter [they] still fixed the basic asking price and the quantity and quality of work by non-economic criteria[8]. . . . The worker's labor effort, or standard of output per unit of time, was determined by custom rather than by market calculation."[9]

Thus, the control of work by wage rates was not a part of early industrialization. What makes this point especially important is that so much research in behavior theory has emphasized precisely this relation between rates of responding and rates of reinforcement. Our entire discussion of intermittent reinforcement in Chapter 5 is testimony to the fact that in the laboratory, the rate of operant responding is influenced in an orderly, predictable fashion by manipulation of the magnitude and rate of reinforcement. The evidence that there was a stage of industrialization in which people did not work to maximize reinforcement undercuts the generality of a significant feature of behavior theory. The point here is not that work was uninfluenced by the reinforcement contingency. Clearly, if workers received no pay at all, they would not have worked. Rather, the point is that pay rates did not exert the same kind of control over the workers as reinforcement rates exert over the behavior of laboratory animals.

But the relative insensitivity of work to pay rates was to change. During the nineteenth century, work rates came to be influenced by pay rates in a manner exactly analogous to the results of laboratory studies. And this change was produced in part by something called the scientific management movement.

Scientific Management

The leading figure in the scientific management movement, whose theories were in many ways the culmination of the industrial revolution, was F.W. Taylor. He saw that traditions and customs could interfere with productivity and profit maximization. He was concerned that allowing workers to bring to work either traditional methods or methods they had come to haphazardly, did not result in the most

7. Montgomery, 1976.
8. Hobsbawm, 1964, p. 345.
9. Hobsbawm, 1964, p. 348–349.

efficient work. Scientific management was an attempt to develop principles that could control and manipulate labor with the same efficiency with which industry was coming to control and manipulate machines.

> Owing to the fact that the workmen in all of our trades have been taught the details of their work by observation of those immediately around them, there are many different ways in common use for doing the same thing, perhaps forty, fifty or a hundred ways of doing each act in the trade, and for the same reason there is a great variety in the implements used for each class of work. Now among the various methods and implements used in each element of each trade there is always one method and one implement which is quicker and better than any of the rest. And this one best method and best implement can only be discovered or developed through a scientific study and analysis of all of the methods and implements in use, together with accurate, minute, motion and time study. This involves the gradual substitution of science for rule of thumb throughout the mechanic arts.[10]

How did scientific management produce more efficient ways of utilizing the worker's labor? The central step was to eliminate the laborers' control over the pace and character of their jobs. The way to do the job, in the minutest detail, was to be specified by management. Rather than maintaining traditional work and pay methods whose character was determined by social custom, new units of work and pay were created in the interests of maximizing efficiency. As Taylor observed, "Under our system the workman is told minutely just what he is to do and how he is to do it, and any improvement which he makes upon the orders given him is fatal to success."[11]

To accomplish this "scientific" efficiency engineering the tasks of individual workers were carefully studied and simplified by breaking them into sub-tasks. The means of accomplishing the tasks were investigated until a single, optimally efficient repertoire was delineated. In the course of the different task-efficiency studies, the number of different operations needed to produce a finished product was greatly enlarged. Taylor's notion was that maximum efficiency would be obtained if the number of operations a single worker had to perform were minimized. Workers could then develop great speed and skill

10. Taylor, 1911/1967, pp. 24–25.
11. Taylor, 1911/1967, p. 39.

at this operation, make virtually no mistakes, and come to perform the operation so automatically that lapses of attention or intelligence could have no cost.

These changes obviously did not make work more appealing in itself, but Taylor was convinced that this was not the point. The overwhelming concern of the workers, he argued, was higher wages, and since greater efficiency could produce higher wages, he believed his system would be to the advantage of the workers.

Having analyzed and altered the tasks for which workers received their wages, Taylor next turned to an analysis of wages themselves. The problem was that customary pay rates could be just as inefficient as customary work methods. Therefore, detailed analyses of different pay schedules were undertaken in order to determine which pay schedules would yield the greatest productivity. Day rates (analogous to interval reinforcement schedules), piece rates (ratio schedules), piece rates which differentially reinforced high rates of production (differential reinforcement of high rate schedules), and various complex combinations of these were instituted, studied, evaluated, and altered, to determine the schedule which would maximize worker output and company profit.[12]

Discussing the virtues and drawbacks of different types of pay schedules, L. M. Gilbreth, another important figure in the scientific management movement, made a number of observations similar to those one might find in a contemporary text on behavior theory:

> The principal rewards consist of promotion and pay, pay being a broad word used here to include . . . anything which can be given to the man who does the work to benefit him and increase his desire to continue doing the work. Punishments may be negative, that is, they may simply take the form of no reward . . . to show him that he has not done what is expected of him, and, in theory at least, to lead him to do better.[13]

> Under scientific management, with the ordinary type of worker on manual work, it has been found most satisfactory to pay the reward every day, or at the end of the week, and to announce the score of output as often as every hour.[14]

---

12. See Ferster and Skinner, 1957, for examples of a wide range of simple and complex schedules of reinforcement.

13. Gilbreth, 1914, pp. 274–275.

14. Gilbreth, 1914, p. 282.

Piecework is the opposite of time work, in that under it the man is paid not for the time he spends at the work, but for the amount of work which he accomplishes. Under this system . . . he [the worker] will have great inducements to work.[15]

Thus, we see in scientific management the self-conscious exemplification of what came to be the typical methods of behavior theory: The creation of simple, repeatable behavioral units, the substitutability of one behavioral unit for another, and the manipulation of rates of response by variations in rates and schedules of reinforcement.

The scientific management movement, then, was the culmination of a process which resulted in efficiently organized factories, with workers making a minimum number of different repetitive motions, at high speeds, and under the control of their wage rates and schedules. There is no question but that work had been drastically changed from the time of the serf.

The Significance of the Change in Work

The modern workplace, structured by the scientific managers, exemplifies the principles of behavior theory. In addition, principles of behavior theory have been successfully applied in the workplace to control the worker's productive behavior. The detailed relevance of behavior theory to the workplace would appear to be impressive confirmation of behavior theory. But there are problems with such a conclusion. The situation which is taken to exemplify behavior theory principles is a situation which has been created partly through the application of those same principles (in the version formulated by scientific management). Thus, it is not clear that the phenomena observed in the work situation can provide *independent* support for the generality of behavior theory.

In addition, the success of scientific management may stem from the fact that it discovered or created a situation in which all other potential control over work, apart from monetary reinforcement contingencies, was eliminated, just as experiments and applications in behavior theory may succeed by eliminating all potential influence on behavior from the applied or experimental setting aside from contrived reinforcement contingencies.

15. Gilbreth, 1914, pp. 290–291.

It is tempting to reply to this argument by suggesting that if scientific management had not been based upon an essential feature of human nature, it would have failed. This view might have us believe that contingencies of reinforcement have always controlled human behavior, but that it took time, and scientific study, to discover this fundamental fact. What scientific management represents is just the discovery of this basic fact rather than its creation.

Let us examine what the point of contention is between our argument and this rejoinder. What the rejoinder suggests, quite consistently with the views of behavior theory, is that there is a fundamental, eternal truth about human nature which has only been discovered and systematically explored in the last two centuries. Prior to this time, people operated under an important misconception about what governed their behavior. But the science of behavior, and its precursors, have corrected this misconception, and replaced the speculation of countless observers of human nature in the past. What we are arguing, in contrast, is that the "fundamental" principle of human nature was not overlooked prior to the nineteenth century. Simply, it was not a fundamental principle. It has become one over the last 200 years as a result of economic development. What this means is that the fundamental principle that is exemplified by modern factory work is not that human behavior is controlled by contingencies of reinforcement. Rather, it is that human behavior *can* be controlled by contingencies of reinforcement. Behavior theory does provide an accurate account of much of what people do in the modern world. But the question here is whether its success stems from having *discovered* a fundamental principle which is exemplified in all contexts or a principle which is manifest only in contexts that have been *created* in the last 200 years.[16]

The argument we are making is a complex one, so let us summarize how far we have come. We are attempting to evaluate the prospects for sustaining the claim of behavior theory that the law of effect underlies almost all human behavior, and that operant principles are sufficient, in principle, to reveal the lawfulness of human behavior. We rejected the possibility that competing principles for explaining human behavior might depend upon biological or Pavlovian influences, as they do for explaining the behavior of nonhumans. So our

16. For a fuller version of this argument, see Schwartz, Schuldenfrei and Lacey, 1978.

question became whether there is evidence that operant principles might control all behavior in the normal social environment, or whether there are other kinds of significant experiential influences in that environment. We showed why this question could not be answered strictly on the basis of data from experimental and applied settings. Then we suggested that supporting the claim that control of behavior by operant principles is ubiquitous would require a demonstration that operant principles are exemplified in key social situations. We suggested that there is one such situation—the modern factory workplace. What our suggestion amounts to is that if we were to make systematic and sustained observations of factory work, we would find that the patterns of work conformed reasonably well to operant principles.

The scope of application of operant principles thus penetrates deeply into modern society. But, that scope is still less than total. Observation of precapitalist work would not uncover patterns of work that readily conform with operant principles. In addition, modern work takes place under conditions (money as the dominant reinforcer, interchangeability of tasks, external control of work patterns, etc.), which were not present in premodern work, and in the final stages of the construction of the modern workplace these conditions were consciously imposed and maintained in order that behavior could be controlled by principles virtually identical with operant principles. This insight led to our suggestion that the dominance of operant control in the factory cannot be taken as evidence of dominant operant control in all situations. Rather it is a consequence of prevailing social conditions which suppressed or displaced other influences upon behavior.

Up to this point the argument is suggestive, but less than conclusive. A defender of the comprehensiveness of operant principles has a ready counterargument. There is no denying that there are substantial differences between modern and premodern work. Modern work clearly exemplifies operant principles while premodern work does not. But this does not mean that different principles of behavior are operating. Instead, operant principles may have contributed just as significantly to premodern work as they do to modern work. The difficulty is that under complex, natural conditions, with many variables and reinforcers operating in interaction with each other, it is extremely difficult to identify the operative principles. Moreover, since the period in question is 300 years ago, one cannot even attempt to tease apart operative principles experimentally. Our interpretation is that operant principles that do apply now did not apply 300 years ago. The behavior theorist's interpretation might be that operant principles which apply clearly and unambiguously now applied less clearly, but no less significantly, 300 years ago.[17] How is one to decide between these interpretations?

There is a way that experimental data can be brought to bear on this issue. What we have been suggesting is that operant principles are dominant in the modern factory in part because other influences on behavior have been suppressed. Indeed, the introduction of clear-cut operant contingencies may have contributed to the suppression of these other influences. If it can be demonstrated, in the laboratory, that operant contingencies, in gaining control of behavior, suppress other influences, then our suggestion that this very process occurred historically will gain plausibility. In recent years, a few such laboratory demonstrations have been made.

Turning Play into Work

One such demonstration was a study of nursery school children. The children in the study were given the opportunity to play with felt-tipped drawing pens, an activity that seems to have nearly universal intrinsic appeal to young children. After an observation period, in which the amount of time spent playing with the drawing pens was measured, the children were taken into a special room where they were asked to draw pictures with the pens. They were divided into three groups. Those in the first group were told that they would

17. Another way to challenge our argument is to suggest that the factory is not the best model of operant principles at work, by appealing to material discussed in Chapter 5. In that chapter, we saw how the incorporation of economic principles into the operant laboratory has greatly expanded the scope of behavior theory. It is now possible for behavior theory principles to address matters concerning choice of resource allocation, rather than simply repetitive responses on reinforcement schedules. Indeed, to the extent that these economic principles provide a good account of individual economic decision-making in society, behavior theory may be seen as applicable to the full range of human activity, and not just to factory work. A rejoinder to this view may be found in Polanyi (1944), who made an argument that is quite similar in structure to the present one. Unlike our focus on behavior theory principles, however, Polanyi attempted to show that the very economic principles discussed in Chapter 5 were historically limited in scope and applicability in just the way that behavior theory principles are.

receive "Good Player" awards if they performed the drawing task; those in the second group received the awards after performing the task but were not informed in advance; those in the third group received no award. Subsequently, on return to the regular nursery school setting, with drawing pens available but awards unavailable, those in the first group, unlike the others, played less frequently with the pens than during the initial baseline period. Where prior to the experiment they would play with the pens without the prospect of an award, now they would not. In addition, when the pictures the children made were judged, those of the first group were rated as significantly lower quality, that is, less interesting, creative and complex, and more stereotyped than those of the other two groups.[18]

The authors interpreted their results as showing that imposing a reinforcement contingency upon "intrinsically motivated" activity reduces the subsequent likelihood of the activity and changes its character. We may regard an intrinsically motivated activity as one a person will readily and frequently perform given the opportunity, with no apparent connection with a reinforcer that is distinct from the activity itself. Such activities may themselves be made to function as reinforcers, that is, the frequency of another behavior may be increased if the opportunity to engage in an intrinsically motivated behavior is made contingent upon its occurrence. What this experiment may show is that just by changing the conditions so that reinforcement is made contingent on the activity, the activity is brought under the control of reinforcement where previously it was not.

It should be noted that this study is not an example of the failure of operant principles. On the contrary, the awards seemed to gain control of the behavior. If they had continued to be available for drawing in the classroom, there is little doubt that high rates of drawing would have been maintained. The point of the study is that prior to the introduction of the operant contingency, something else was influencing the drawing, and that other influence was suppressed or superceded by the operant contingency. In like fashion, the introduction of operant contingencies in the factory may have contributed to the suppression or superceding of other influences on work.

This experimental finding, and others like it, are controversial. There is currently dispute both about the reliability of the findings and about how they should be interpreted.[19] But if these results are

18. Lepper, Greene and Nisbett, 1973.
19. See, for example, Feingold and Mahoney, 1975; Lepper and Greene, 1978.

supported by further research, they provide an example of how operant control may be achieved at the expense of other kinds of influence on behavior.

Operant Contingencies and Rule Discovery

The second example to support this assertion is a study of college students who were given a number of problems to solve.[20] The problems involved their interaction with a computer. If they pressed certain keys in the proper order, they would be given an indication that they had succeeded on a given trial. If they pressed the keys in an improper order, they would be given an indication they had failed. Their task was to discover the general rule that determined success or failure.

This task was constructed to be analogous, in some respects, to the tasks faced by a scientist. Just as the scientist seeks some general rule of nature, these students sought general rules of the behavior of the computer. Just as the scientist formulates hypotheses and tests them with experiments, these students had to formulate hypotheses and test them with sequences of key presses. Thus, each trial in the setting the college students faced was like an experiment. Some of the college students (Group A) were brought to the task with no prior experience. The others (Group B) had had a few hours of experience with similar tasks. During that prior experience, the students had earned a monetary reward for each successful trial. Rather than being instructed to discover a general rule, they had been experiencing a situation in which only successful sequences mattered. What they learned to do in that situation was to produce, again and again, a particular sequence of key presses that worked. Though there were many different sequences of presses that would have produced the reward, each student fixed upon one such sequence, and produced it on more than 90% of the trials.

The stereotyped repetition of an effective sequence is quite a sensible strategy if one is interested only in producing reward as often as possible. Once one finds some response pattern that works reliably, it is pointless, even foolish, to deviate from it. Consider, as an analogy, baking bread. If you follow a recipe, and the results are satisfactory, you would certainly be inclined to do precisely the same things, in

20. Schwartz, 1982.

the same order, the next time. Your method need not be the only possible one that would succeed, but since your concern is with finding *a* method that works, rather than *all* methods that work, you would be content to settle on any particular effective method.

But suppose you were interested in discovering the general principles of successful bread baking. Now it would be a mistake to repeat one particular method again and again. Doing that might convince you that one method worked, but it would not help you discover which aspects of that method were essential, and which unimportant. To discover the essentials of bread baking, you would have to vary your methods, keeping track of which methods yielded good results. By varying systematically what you did from time to time, you might eventually figure out what the key to baking good bread was.

The difference between finding a good method for baking bread and finding the essentials of bread baking is the same as the difference between the two types of tasks faced by our college students. Finding a sequence of key presses that produce reward is like finding a good recipe, while discovering a general rule is like discovering the essentials of bread baking. And it is clear that the two types of tasks require different response strategies. Were the college students who had had experience earning rewards and developed a stereotyped sequence of key presses able to abandon their stereotyped sequences and adopt a strategy of systematic variation of sequences when faced with the instructions to discover rules?

The answer is no, at least not entirely. The students in Group B, with previous rewarded experience, were much less effective at discovering rules than the inexperienced students in Group A were. They were less likely to discover the rules at all, and if they did discover them, they required more trials. This was true even in the case of a rule that had been operative during their period of previous training. Thus, even though they had had substantial experience earning rewards by satisfying the rule, they were slow to discover it.

There were a number of different reasons for the relative ineffectiveness of experienced students at discovering rules. They were more likely than inexperienced students to repeat the same sequences on many trials, though nothing new could be learned from such repetitions. They were less likely than inexperienced students to use the results of previously tested, failed hypotheses to shape their choice of new ones. The students in Group A behaved like scientists who choose hypotheses to test not at random, but on the basis of prior research, and then test them with experiments that vary possible key factors systematically. The experienced subjects in Group B behaved like scientists who choose their hypotheses at random, and test them by doing the same experiments repetitively. Obviously, scientists in this latter group are not good scientists. And the pretrained college students were not behaving like good scientists. A history of experience with rewards interfered with the development of effective strategies for uncovering generalizations, strategies that were clearly available to people without this prior experience.

This example, like the first one, is not an example of the failure of operant principles. Rather, operant contingencies clearly succeeded in controlling the behavior of the Group B students during their pretraining. One result of this control was that it altered their method of approach to discovering rules later in the experiment. It seems plausible that the rule discovery strategies of the students without pretraining were under nonoperant influence. And the operant influence introduced by the pretraining changed the nature of these strategies, in this case making them relatively ineffective. Thus, as in the case of factory workers and nursery school children, this experiment may contribute another example of the suppression or superceding of nonoperant influences on behavior by operant contingencies.

Indeed, there was an additional aspect of this study that made this point especially clearly. For some students, the operant contingency (monetary reward for each successful sequence of presses) was present during the rule discovery phase of the study. For others it was not. The presence or absence of this contingency made no difference to the Group A students, without pretraining. Their behavior was not under the control of the contingency. In contrast, for students in Group B with pretraining, the presence of this contingency made a big difference. Their rule discovery was much less effective with the contingency present than with it absent. Thus, it appears that their previous experience had indeed brought behavior under operant control that would not have been otherwise.

If these two examples are important in showing how operant contingencies can suppress other influences on behavior, they are important for another reason as well. They both have implications for the use of operant contingencies in educational settings. We saw in Chapter 8 that operant techniques have been used effectively in classrooms. But suppose that our educational goals include developing the ability to discover general rules, as scientists do, and fostering an interest in learning so that the rewards for acquiring knowledge are an inherent part of the learning process itself. The experiment we just described suggests that operant contingencies are not an effective tool for developing rule discovery. Indeed, they might even interfere with the development of this ability. And the first experiment we described suggests that operant contingencies may take control away from the rewards inherent in an activity, rather than promoting them. Thus, for people who view these educational goals as significant, the lesson of these two experiments may be that operant contingencies can interfere with effective education rather than facilitate it.

Factory Managers versus Factory Workers

We have argued that the effectiveness of operant principles in the factory resulted in part from a set of prevailing conditions, including the operant contingencies themselves, which suppressed other influences. And we have provided two experiments that demonstrate that it is possible to suppress other behavioral influences by operant contingencies. But what are these other influences that are suppressed in the factory and perhaps in the experiments we discussed? How might we account for behavior that is not a clear exemplification of operant principles at work? In addressing this issue, we will attempt to make concrete exactly what has been eliminated in the factory.

Remember the conditions that prevail to a large extent in the factory: Predominance of one reinforcer (money), interchangeability of tasks, repetitiveness of tasks, few and clearly defined means available to obtain the reinforcement, and external control of the patterns of work.[21] There are many work situations in which conditions at least approximate these. That is part of what gives behavior theory its plausibility as a general account of human nature. However, there are also many work situations that do not resemble either the factory or the conditioning chamber, and to which the concepts of behavior theory cannot be easily applied. Nevertheless, we do have a rich set of explanatory concepts that can be used to understand behavior in these situations. It is the set of explanatory concepts from everyday discourse.

21. Clearly, these conditions can be present to varying degrees in the factory. The factory is not, after all, a perfect conditioning chamber. But to the extent that it is not, it is difficult to portray factory work as under operant control.

Consider, for example, the factory manager. We may presume that his predominant goal on the job is the maximization of profit, a goal that behavior theory can easily accommodate. The means to this goal, however, are not so easily explained by behavior theory. They are not well-defined, and they can vary from time to time. The manager must determine the best means, and change the patterns of work in the factory in accordance with his determinations. While what he does is constrained by such external factors as the market, the law, the capabilities of his workers, the flexibility of the machines in the factory, and so on, what he does is not under external control in that he is not performing a routinized activity determined by someone else. He chooses what to do to further his goal in the light of his own assessments and inferences, taking into account the data, thinking and hypotheses of others. He does this according to his own plans and judgments of effective means. And what he does is subject to considerable variation, often including novel actions that are responsive to novel social circumstances. The economic situation does not remain stable; suppliers are unreliable in making deliveries, new machinery becomes available, the union threatens a strike: These are the circumstances that call upon the ingenuity of the manager.

• The task of the factory manager is very much like the task of running a kitchen, which we discussed in Chapter 8. We pointed out there that the concepts of behavior theory played little useful explanatory role. Here too, reinforcement offers little explanatory insight. Amidst the variegated day-to-day activity of the manager can we pinpoint what is being reinforced? All the difficulties of talking about reinforcing the production of an edible meal recur, and more besides. There is no equivalent of an actual meal which is there each day, or even each week or month, to be reinforced. No given number of products as such suffices to this end, for what brings profit varies with the supply and market conditions. So we are pushed to the truism that whatever produces an adequate profit is reinforced. Attempts to use "reinforcement" in explanation fail to account for the detail, sequence, novelty and significant variation in behavior. In contrast, concepts like "goal," "intention," "reason," "plan," and so on, in short, everyday, teleological explanations of the sort we mentioned in Chapter 1, are useful for explaining cases like these. The manager tells us that he is converting his factory from making large to making small cars because he has calculated that the expenditure of conversion will more than be repaid from the greater sales he expects with small cars.

This is thoroughly intelligible, building explictly upon such familiar notions as "calculation" and "expectancy," and implicitly upon "goal"—though this is not a simple extrapolation of the past experience of the manager. It is a new act, a consequence of experience, well-understood, but completely opaque to behavior theory.

One might feel short-changed with this explanation. There is nothing "scientific" about it and it does not rest upon principles discovered experimentally. Moreover, it is thoroughly familiar. One needs no special training or competence to understand it. How can one appeal to such explanations to cast doubt on the comprehensive scope of behavior theory? The answer is: Why not? There is no *a priori* guarantee that human action can be accounted for by behavior theory, or even that it can be explained scientifically, in terms of laws. In addition, a rational explanation like this one is quite useful. It has some predictive implications, concerning, for example, the conditions under which the manager might again convert his factory in the future; and it provides the basis for fruitful interaction with him if, for example, we want to dissuade him from making the conversion. What has happened is that the ease with which we use the explanatory categories of "reason" and "goal" has disguised their powerful explanatory force. Such explanations are so central a part of our daily lives that we have neglected to defend them against "scientific" competitors, in this case, behavior theory.

Discussion of these matters has often been marred by a good deal of conceptual confusion, which sometimes makes it difficult to discern the important distinctions between teleological explanations and the explanations offered by behavior theorists. Like teleological explanations, the explanations of behavior theory attempt to account for behavior by relating it to its consequences. The two kinds of explanation differ, however, in their account of exactly what the relation is. Behavior theorists often assert that their fundamental principle is, "Behavior is under the control of its consequences." This they usually take to be equivalent to "Behavior is under the control of contingencies of reinforcement." Then, any consequence which controls behavior necessarily becomes a reinforcer, from which it seems to follow that any goal of a human action is a reinforcer. With this analysis, our account of the goal-directed character of the manager's activity seems to confirm, rather than undermine, the comprehensive claims of behavior theory.

On the other hand, "Behavior is under the control of contingencies of reinforcement," has a very precise meaning within behavior theory. It is equivalent to, "Behavior occurs because of the contingencies of reinforcement in which earlier instances of the behavior have been involved." But a behavior may occur in order to bring about a certain consequence, without previous instances of the same kind of behavior ever having been reinforced, or even having ever occurred. Also, within behavior theory, something is a reinforcer only if it increases the probability of the behaviors upon which it is contingent. There are goals which a person may act to achieve which do not have this property, and so are not reinforcers. For example, one may marry to attain the goal of loving companionship. But attaining the goal does not mean that marrying will be more probable in the future. Thus behaviors may be performed because they have certain consequences, yet not be under the control of contingencies of reinforcement. For the most part, the variegated behavior of the factory manager and of the good cook is of this kind.[22]

Once we recognize the appropriateness and power of ordinary teleological explanations, we are in a position to see what has been displaced from the modern factory workplace. Factory work is also subject to teleological explanations, but of a rather primitive sort. Conditions have been arranged in such a way that in the factory, for the most part, only one significant goal can be realized and, with few exceptions, this goal (obtaining money—a necessary condition for obtaining food, housing, etc.) cannot be realized by the worker except in this or similar environments. Given the conditions, there is only one way to realize the goal—by performing repeatedly the task set by the externally imposed schedule. The worker repeatedly performs the set task in order to make money. Money has become a reinforcer, and what the worker does in the factory is controlled by contingencies of monetary reinforcement. It is the conditions present in the modern factory workplace, in many applied settings, and in many experimental situations, which convert goals into reinforcers.

Moreover, certain behavioral influences have been removed from the worker under these conditions: He does not do what he does in the light of his own assessments and inferences about how to realize the goals of the workplace or according to his own plans and judgments

22. Chomsky (1959) has noted that the term "reinforcement" has a precise, rigorous meaning within behavior theory, but that this meaning gets replaced by vague analogies to the rigorously defined concept when behavior theorists attempt to analyze and explain behavior in the ordinary, social environment.

of effective means. Choice and planning, and the exercise of human rational capacities which they entail, are removed from the worker in the modern workplace. And it is because the exercise of rational capacities in choice and planning lead to variation and novelty of activity that behavior theory fails to capture the processes which underlie them. It is true that we have not demonstrated experimentally that planning, judgment, and decision-making are a part of human, goal-directed activity. In part that is because the very limited and simplified character of experimental situations tends to convert goals into reinforcers, so that goal-directed behavior which is not also in conformity with a schedule of reinforcement is difficult to display in the laboratory. But these influences are quite clear, and we possess, and use with ease, a conceptual framework within which their action is well explained.

According to this analysis, behavior theory has considerable explanatory scope, and we have defined the limits of this scope with reasonable precision. Its mistake, in effect, is to model ordinary purposive behavior as a more complex version (yet to be articulated in detail) of factory work. Or, put another way, behavior theory models all behavior upon an historical contingency, one of the dominant social contexts of the modern world. It treats a situation that is an extremely common one in which many people spend much of their time, as if it were universal. A contrasting view is that factory work is a limiting, stereotyped instance of purposive action. Because it is limiting, and uncharacteristic of human action, it is inappropriate that factory work provide the model for purposive action in general.

Science as Behavior

Though behavior theory can do a good job of accounting for the behavior of the factory worker, it fails to provide a persuasive account of the behavior of the factory manager. And clearer examples of teleological activity than managing factories exist. One of the clearest, and most significant, is the activity of doing science—of scientific inquiry. The principles developed by the behavior theorist cannot approach giving a satisfactory account of his own behavior as a scientist. The kinds of considerations which make the behavior of individual scientists intelligible are just the sort which made possible our analysis of factory work and its development.

Let us consider the activities of a hypothetical behavior theorist. The ultimate goal of the behavior theorist is to find a set of principles which can provide a comprehensive account of human behavior. This goal is conceded to be far in the future, so that the more immediate goal is to discover some fundamental principles which will be included in the eventual comprehensive account. A rational commitment to behavior theory thus requires a positive assessment of its possibilities. Neither the assessment nor the commitment have previously been reinforced. And if the day-to-day activity of the behavior theorist has been reinforced, the reinforcement does not produce an increased probability of repeating the activity. Scientists do not repeat again and again experiments that have worked (been reinforced) in the past. Nor can we predict the behavior of good scientists. What often distinguishes the good scientist is his or her ability to see the issues somewhat differently than others do, or to find just the right experimental manipulation that has eluded others. In short, the activity of the behavior theorist as scientist requires judgment, planning, expectation, and flexibility—all characteristics for which the concepts of behavior theory are not well-suited.

Suppose the behavior theorist chooses some problem within behavior theory to study, and goes about designing experiments that will address this problem. How does he go about designing the experiments? Obviously, he does not simply repeat the experiments he has just done with another problem, even if they were reinforced (that is, produced important results). Nor does he choose an experimental design at random, hoping that it will bear upon the problem at hand. Instead, he considers the logic of the problem, and considers whether past experiments done by others on similar problems may offer guidance. Then he may construct a number of possible experiments. Next, in attempting to decide which of these possible experiments to perform, he considers the possible outcomes of the various experiments, how they might be interpreted, what further problems they might pose, and so on. Eventually, he settles on the experiment that he anticipates will produce the most unambiguous information about the problem. Notice that the behavior theorist has a goal (solving a research problem). His route to attaining that goal is constrained by external factors (for example, the laboratory equipment at hand). He chooses his route in the light of these constraints, mindful of the ideas and experiments of other researchers. The experiment he eventually does is novel, that is, different in an important way from experiments that he or others have done before. And if the experiment succeeds, we will not be able to say that the success is reinforcing. It will not increase the probability of his doing the same experiment again. Instead, it may influence the behavior theorist to do different experiments in the future, continuing the process of inquiry that characterize science.

We can make more sense of the activity of the behavior theorist with the everyday language of teleology than we can with the language of behavior theory. But even teleology is not enough. Suppose the behavior theorist is interested in some aspect of the process of discrimination, designs a discrimination learning experiment for pigeons, and reports it in a psychology journal. And suppose someone who knows nothing about behavior theory comes upon this report while brousing in the library. This person might understand the report, but nevertheless be very puzzled. Why on earth have pigeons pecked at lit circles? What does that fact have to do with learning? And why pigeons of all creatures? What do they have to do with people? And what is so important about distinguishing red circles from green ones? What does this have to do with learning in school, or on the job? The behavior theorist's report does not address these questions. It presupposes that readers know the answers to them. And indeed, most professional readers will. That is because, of the countless ways one might design an experiment on discrimination learning, training pigeons to peck at red or green keys is more intelligible than most. It is more intelligible because it comes naturally out of the research program that is behavior theory. This research program contains a rich set of assumptions, previous experiments and theories that make such an experiment on discrimination learning not merely intelligible, but perhaps the most sensible of all experiments under the circumstances.

Thus, to make sense of the behavior of the behavior theorist, we must consider it not only as an example of teleological activity, but as an example of an activity that is part of a historical context. When we understand the essentials of behavior theory's research program, we can understand the reasons behind the particular experiments behavior theorists do. Most of these experiments would have made no sense before Pavlov and Thorndike, and would have made little sense immediately after them. It is in the evolution of behavior theory that particular experiments seem just right at a given time. Indeed, as behavior theory develops further, many experiments that seem sensible and appropriate now may seem irrelevant when viewed retro-spectively 20 years from now, unless the people who view them are mindful of the intellectual context in which they were done.

The major point of this chapter is that just as the work of the behavior theorist must be understood historically, in the context of the developing behavior theory research program, so all significant human activity must be understood historically.[23] Behavior theory may tell us why behavior in the factory looks the way it does. But it does not tell us how there came to be factories, or what work was like before them, or how factory organization might have changed the nature of work. By treating the factory as a general model of behavior, behavior theory ignores the social and historical influences that help make factory work intelligible. By ignoring those other influences, behavior theory mistakenly claims to have discovered principles that are comprehensive. This book, to the extent that it has succeeded in making the assumptions, experiments and theoretical claims of behavior theory intelligible, has done so by placing them in the context of a research program that continues to evolve. As a result, the arguments in this book represent a mode of analysis that is different from that of behavior theory—different and perhaps more comprehensive. They permit us to understand behavior theory, see where it is incomplete, and even to see why behavior theorists might mistakenly view their work as more comprehensive than it really is.

The arguments in this chapter suggest severe limitations on the ability of behavior theory to produce a comprehensive account of human behavior. Certain important influences on behavior like the rational processes involved in choice and planning cannot be accommodated within behavior theory. But this incompleteness does not reduce behavior theory to the status of only marginal interest. While the principles of behavior theory are probably not the universal laws of human nature, they do capture significant features of modern life. It is even possible that they are the wave of the future. But the applicability of behavior theory principles depends upon the existence of

23. In recent years, cognitive psychology has been concerned with discovering generalizations about aspects of human nature that we usually describe teleologically. Thus, one could view some of the arguments we have made about human rational activity as support for cognitive psychology as opposed to behavior theory. But cognitive psychology at present ignores the sociohistorical influences on activity at least to the same degree as behavior theory does. Thus, our emphasis on the historical may be as much a criticism of modern cognitive psychology as it is of behavior theory.

certain environmental conditions. Though these conditions are not a general, inevitable part of human society, they are certainly present in large parts of modern society. By creating these conditions more widely, partly through the extended application of behavior theory principles, even more of future human behavior could be brought under the control of these principles. In other words, widespread application of behavior theory principles could make behavior theory become a true description of much of the social world, at the cost, of course, of eliminating from the social world those rational processes we have discussed in this chapter. Just as, given the appropriate conditions, operant principles can wrest control of animal behavior away from the biological and Pavlovian influences dominant in the animal's natural environment, so, given analogous conditions, can they wrest control of human behavior away from the rational influences operative in much significant human behavior.

To see that the application of behavior theory can actually transform the phenomena to which it is applied requires that one look at human behavior from a social and historical perspective. One could not know that the modern factory is not simply an efficient exploitation of fundamental features of human nature without knowing something about what work was like prior to the development of the factory. The sociohistorical view allows one to see just which changes in the workplace made modern factory behavior possible. It also allows one to begin to specify the limits of behavior theory. Furthermore, the sociohistorical perspective shows us that behavior theory is incomplete in two significant respects. First, it is unable to specify the limits of applicability of its own principles. Second, it cannot explain the existence of the very social conditions without which its principles would not apply.

We have suggested in this chapter that behavior theory will never provide a complete account of human nature. Whether or not this suggestion is persuasive, it is worth asking why making this long range assessment matters. One might depend instead upon future research to do the job of determining whether or not it is true; that is, one could continue to go about the business of day to day research activity and leave the issue of comprehensiveness to the future.

But this we cannot do, for the following reason. Behavior theory has made much progress in the laboratory; and indeed, some applications of the theory are of great benefit to people. But application of a theory, as opposed to its experimental investigation, requires some justification. We need to know if it works under the conditions of the application, and if under these conditions, it generates any undesirable side-effects. That it works can be judged by observing if the desired effect is actually produced in an applied setting. But side-effects are another matter. For example, the conditions obtaining in the factory seem to suppress or diminish certain rational processes. This is a side-effect of creating the conditions, and a negative one. But if behavior theory is comprehensive, then there can be no such side-effects. Thus far, behavior theory has not proven itself to be comprehensive, and so underlying all of the research to be carried out in the years to come will be this central question. It is a question not to be put off into the future, for a theory as powerful as behavior theory can produce, through application, widespread societal changes. And such widespread changes can be justified only if behavior theory is comprehensive.

Bibliography

Agras, W.S., Sylvester, D., and Oliveau, D. The epidemiology of common fears and phobias. *Comprehensive Psychiatry*, 1969, *10*, 151–156.

Allison, J., Miller, M., and Wozny, M. Conservation in behavior. *Journal of Experimental Psychology: General*, 1979, *108*, 4–34.

Amsel, A. Frustrative non-reward in partial reinforcement and discrimination learning. *Psychological Review*, 1962, *69*, 306–328.

Amsel, A. Partial reinforcement effects on vigor and persistence. In K.W. Spence and J.T. Spence (eds.), *The Psychology of Learning and Motivation* (Vol. 1). New York: Academic Press, 1967.

Annau, Z., and Kamin, L.J. The conditioned emotional response as a function of the intensity of the US. *Journal of Comparative and Physiological Psychology*, 1961, *54*, 428–432.

Appel, J. Aversive effects of a schedule of positive reinforcement. *Journal of the Experimental Analysis of Behavior*, 1963, *6*, 423–428.

Atthowe, J.M., and Krasner, L. A preliminary report on the application of contingent reinforcement procedures (token economy) in a "chronic" psychiatric ward. *Journal of Abnormal Psychology*, 1968, *73*, 37–43.

Ayllon, T. Intensive treatment of psychotic behavior by stimulus satiation and food reinforcement. *Behavior Research and Therapy*, 1963, *1*, 53–61.

Ayllon, T., and Azrin, N.H. *The Token Economy: A Motivational System for Therapy and Rehabilitation.* New York: Appleton-Century-Crofts, 1968.

Azrin, N.H. Some effects of two intermittent schedules of immediate and non-immediate punishment. *Journal of Psychology*, 1956, *42*, 3–21.

Azrin, N.H., Holz, W.C., and Hake, D.F. Fixed-ratio punishment. *Journal of the Experimental Analysis of Behavior*, 1963, *6*, 141–148.

Azzi, R., Fix, D.S.R., Keller, F.S., and Rocha e Silva, M.I. Exteroceptive control of response under delayed reinforcement. *Journal of the Experimental Analysis of Behavior*, 1964, *7*, 159–162.

Bandura, A. Behavior theory and models of man. *American Psychologist*, 1974, *29*, 859–869.

Barker, L.M., Best, M.R., and Domjan, M. (eds.), *Learning Mechanisms in Food Selection.* Baylor University Press, 1978.

Baum, M. Extinction of avoidance responses through response prevention (flooding). *Psychological Bulletin,* 1970, *74,* 276–284.

Bedford, J., and Anger, D. *Flight as an avoidance response in pigeons.* Paper presented at the Psychonomic Society, St. Louis, 1968.

Bolles, R.C. Species-specific defense reactions and avoidance learning. *Psychological Review,* 1970, *77,* 32–48.

Bower, G.H., McLean, J., and Meachem, J. Value of knowing when reinforcement is due. *Journal of Comparative and Physiological Psychology,* 1966, *62,* 184–192.

Breland, K., and Breland, M. The misbehavior of organisms. *American Psychologist,* 1961, *16,* 681–684.

Brigham, T.A. Some effects of choice on academic performance. In L.C. Perlmuter and A.A. Monty (eds.), *Choice and perceived control.* Hillsdale, New Jersey: Erlbaum, 1979.

Brown, P., and Jenkins, H.M. Autoshaping of the pigeon's keypeck. *Journal of the Experimental Analysis of Behavior,* 1968, *11,* 1–8.

Bucher, R., and Lovaas, O.I. Use of aversive stimulation in behavior modification. In M.R. Jones (ed.), *Miami symposium on the prediction of behavior: Aversive stimulation.* Coral Gables: University of Miami Press, 1968.

Bugelski, B.R. Extinction with and without sub-goal reinforcement. *Journal of Comparative Psychology,* 1938, *26,* 121–134.

Camp, D.S., Raymond, G.A., and Church, R.M. Temporal relationship between response and punishment. *Journal of Experimental Psychology,* 1967, *74,* 114–123.

Catania, A.C. Concurrent performances: A baseline for the study of reinforcement magnitude. *Journal of the Experimental Analysis of Behavior,* 1963, *6,* 299–301.

Catania, A.C. Concurrent operants. In W.K. Honig (ed.), *Operant Behavior: Areas of Research and Application.* New York: Appleton-Century-Crofts, 1966.

Catania, A.C., and Brigham, T.A. (eds.), *Handbook of Applied Behavior Analysis.* New York: Irvington Publishers, 1978.

Catania, A.C., and Reynolds, G.S. A quantitative analysis of the responding maintained by interval schedules of reinforcement. *Journal of the Experimental Analysis of Behavior,* 1968, *11,* 327–383.

Catania, A.C., and Sagvolden, T. Preference for free choice over forced choice in pigeons. *Journal of the Experimental Analysis of Behavior,* 1980, *34,* 77–86.

Chomsky, N. Review of Skinner's *Verbal Behavior. Language,* 1959, *35,* 26–58.

Chung, S.H., and Herrnstein, R.J. Choice and delay of reinforcement. *Journal of the Experimental Analysis of Behavior*, 1967, *10*, 67–74.

Church, R.M. Response suppression. In B.A. Campbell and R.M. Church (eds.), *Punishment and Aversive Behavior*. New York: Appleton-Century-Crofts, 1969.

Collier, G.H., Hirsch, E., and Hamlin, P.H. The ecological determinants of reinforcement in the rat. *Physiology and Behavior*, 1972, *9*, 705–716.

Coulton, G.G. *The medieval village*. Cambridge: Cambridge University Press, 1925.

Cowles, J.T. Food-tokens as incentive for learning by chimpanzees. *Comparative Psychology Monographs*, 1937, *14*, No. 5.

Davenport, D.G., and Olson, R.D. A reinterpretation of extinction in discriminated avoidance. *Psychonomic Science*, 1968, *13*, 5–6.

Deutsch, R. Conditioned hypoglycemia: A mechanism for saccharin-induced sensitivity to insulin in the rat. *Journal of Comparative and Physiological Psychology*, 1974, *86*, 350–358.

de Villiers, P.A. The law of effect and avoidance: A quantitative relation between response rate and shock frequency reduction. *Journal of the Experimental Analysis of Behavior*, 1974, *21*, 223–235.

de Villiers, P.A. Choice in concurrent schedules and a quantitative formulation of the law of effect. In W.K. Honig and J.E.R. Staddon (eds.), *Handbook of Operant Behavior*. Englewood Cliffs, N.J.: Prentice-Hall, 1977.

Dinsmoor, J.A., Flint, G.A., Smith, R.F., and Viemeister, N.F. Differential reinforcing effects of stimuli associated with the presence or absence of a schedule of punishment. In D.P. Hendry (ed.), *Conditioned reinforcement*. Homeward, Ill.: The Dorsey Press, 1969.

Egger, M.D., and Miller, N.E. Secondary reinforcement in rats as a function of information value and reliability of the stimulus. *Journal of Experimental Psychology*, 1962, *64*, 97–104.

Eibl-Eibesfeldt, I. *Ethology: The Biology of Behavior*. New York: Holt, Rinehart and Winston, 1970.

Elsmore, T. Evaluating the strength of heroin maintained behavior. Paper presented at the annual meeting of the Association for Behavior Analysis, 1979.

Estes, W.K. An experimental study of punishment. *Psychological Monographs*, 1944, *57*, 3 (Whole No. 263).

Estes, W.K., and Skinner, B.F. Some quantitative properties of anxiety. *Journal of Experimental Psychology*, 1941, *29*, 390–400.

Fantino, E. Conditioned reinforcement, choice, and information. In W.K. Honig and J.E.R. Staddon, (eds.), *Handbook of Operant Behavior*. Englewood Cliffs, New Jersey: Prentice-Hall, 1977, pp. 313–339.

Feingold, B.D., and Mahoney, M.J. Reinforcement effects on intrinsic interest: Undermining the overjustification hypothesis. *Behavior Therapy*, 1975, *6*, 367–377.

Felton, M., and Lyon, D.O. The post-reinforcement pause. *Journal of the Experimental Analysis of Behavior,* 1966, *9,* 131–134.

Ferster, C.B., and Skinner, B.F. *Schedules of reinforcement.* New York: Appleton-Century-Crofts, 1957.

Gamzu, E., and Williams, D.R. Classical conditioning of a complex skeletal act. *Science,* 1971, *171,* 923–925.

Gamzu, E., and Williams, D.R. Associative factors underlying the pigeon's key pecking in autoshaping procedures. *Journal of the Experimental Analysis of Behavior,* 1973, *19,* 225–232.

Garcia, J., Kimmeldorf, D.J., and Hunt, E.L. The use of ionizing radiation as a motivating stimulus. *Psychological Review,* 1961, *68,* 383–385.

Garcia, J., and Koelling, R.A. The relation of cue to consequence in avoidance learning. *Psychonomic Science,* 1966, *4,* 123–124.

Gilbreth, L.M. *The Psychology of Management.* New York: Sturgis and Walton, 1914.

Gonzalez, R.C., Gentry, G.V., and Bitterman, M.E. Relational discrimination of intermediate size in the chimpanzee. *Journal of Comparative and Physiological Psychology,* 1954, *47,* 385–388.

Hammond, L.J. The effect of contingency upon the appetitive conditioning of free-operant behavior. *Journal of the Experimental Analysis of Behavior,* 1980, *34,* 297–304.

Hearst, E., and Jenkins, H.M. *Sign Tracking: The Stimulus-Reinforcer Relation and Directed Action.* Austin, Texas: Psychonomic Society, 1974.

Hendry, D.P. (ed.), *Conditioned Reinforcement.* Homeward, Ill.: The Dorsey Press, 1969.

Herman, R.L., and Azrin, N.H. Punishment by noise in an alternative response situation. *Journal of the Experimental Analysis of Behavior,* 1964, *7,* 185–188.

Herrnstein, R.J. Method and theory in the study of avoidance. *Psychological Review,* 1969, *76,* 49–69.

Herrnstein, R.J. On the law of effect. *Journal of the Experimental Analysis of Behavior,* 1970, *13,* 243–266.

Herrnstein, R.J. Nature as nurture: Behaviorism and the instinct doctrine. *Behaviorism,* 1974, *1,* 23–52.

Herrnstein, R.J. Acquisition, generalization and discrimination reversal of a natural concept. *Journal of Experimental Psychology: Animal Behavior Processes,* 1979, *5,* 116–129.

Herrnstein, R.J., Loveland, D.H., and Cable, C. Natural concepts in pigeons. *Journal of Experimental Psychology: Animal Behavior Processes,* 1976, *2,* 285–311.

Hinde, R.A. *Animal Behavior: A Synthesis of Ethology and Comparative Psychology.* New York: McGraw-Hill, 1970.

Hinde, R.A. and Hinde, J.S. (eds.), *Constraints on Learning.* New York: Academic Press, 1973.

Hineline, P.N., and Rachlin, H. Escape and avoidance of shock by pigeons pecking a key. *Journal of the Experimental Analysis of Behavior*, 1969, *12*, 533–538.

Hobsbawm, E.J. *Laboring Men: Studies in the History of Labor*. London: Weiderfelt and Nicolson, 1964.

Hursh, S.R. The economics of daily consumption controlling food- and water-reinforced responding. *Journal of the Experimental Analysis of Behavior*, 1978, *29*, 475–491.

Hursh, S.R. Economic concepts for the analysis of behavior. *Journal of the Experimental Analysis of Behavior*, 1980, *34*, 219–238.

Hursh, S.R., and Natelson, B.J. Electrical brain stimulation and food reinforcement dissociated by demand elasticity. *Physiology and Behavior*, 1981, *18*, in press.

Jenkins, H.M., and Harrison, R.H. Effects of discrimination training on auditory generalization. *Journal of Experimental Psychology*, 1960, 59, 246–253.

Jenkins, H.M., and Harrison, R.H. Generalization gradients of inhibition following auditory discrimination learning. *Journal of the Experimental Analysis of Behavior*, 1962, 5, 435–441.

Jenkins, H.M., and Moore, B.R. The form of the autoshaped response with food or water reinforcers. *Journal of the Experimental Analysis of Behavior*, 1973, *20*, 163–181.

Kamin, L.J. Effects of termination of the CS and avoidance of the US on avoidance learning. *Journal of Comparative and Physiological Psychology*, 1956, *49*, 420–424.

Kamin, L.J. Predictability, surprise, attention and conditioning. In B.A. Campbell and R.M. Church (eds.), *Punishment and Aversive Behavior*. New York: Appleton-Century-Crofts, 1969.

Kamin, L.J., Brimer, C.J., and Black, A.H. Conditioned suppression as a monitor of fear of the CS in the course of avoidance training. *Journal of Comparative and Physiological Psychology*, 1963, *56*, 497–501.

Kazdin, A.E., and Wilson, G.T. *Evaluation of Behavior Therapy: Issues, Evidence and Research Strategies*. Cambridge: Ballinger, 1978.

Keil, F.C. Constraints on knowledge and cognitive development. *Psychological Review*, 1981, *88*, 197–227.

Kelleher, R.T. A multiple schedule of conditioned reinforcement with chimpanzees. *Psychological Reports*, 1957, *3*, 485–491.

Keller, F.S. Goodbye teacher . . . *Journal of Applied Behavior Analysis*, 1968, *1*, 79–89.

Keller, F.S. A programmed system of instruction. *Educational Technology Monographs*, 1969, *2*, 1–27.

Kendler, H.H., and D'Amato, M.F. A comparison of reversal shifts and nonreversal shifts in human concept formation. *Journal of Experimental Psychology*, 1955, *49*, 165–174.

Kendler, H.H., and Kendler, T.S. Vertical and horizontal processes in problem solving. *Psychological Review*, 1962, *69*, 1–16.

Lacey, H.M. Skinner on the prediction and control of behavior. *Theory and Decision*, 1979, *10*, 353–385.

Lamontagne, Y., and Marks, I.M. Psychogenic urinary retention: Treatment by prolonged exposure. *Behavior Therapy*, 1973, *4*, 581–585.

Lawrence, D.H. Acquired distinctiveness of cues, I: Transfer between discriminations on the basis of familiarity with the stimulus. *Journal of Experimental Psychology*, 1949, *39*, 770–784.

Lawrence, D.H. Acquired distinctiveness of cues, II: Selective association in a constant stimulus situation. *Journal of Experimental Psychology*, 1950, *40*, 185–188.

Lawrence, D.H., and DeRivera, J. Evidence for relational transposition. *Journal of Comparative and Physiological Psychology*, 1954, 47, 465–471.

Lea, S.E.G. The psychology and economics of demand. *Psychological Bulletin*, 1978, *85*, 441–466.

Leitenberg, H. (ed.), *Handbook of Behavior Modification and Behavior Therapy*. Englewood Cliffs, New Jersey: Prentice-Hall, 1976(a).

Leitenberg, H. Behavioral approaches to the treatment of neuroses. In H. Leitenberg (ed.), *Handbook of Behavior Modification and Behavior Therapy*. Englewood Cliffs, New Jersey: Prentice-Hall, 1976(b).

Lepper, M.R., Greene, D., and Nisbett, R.E. Undermining children's intrinsic interest with extrinsic rewards: A test of the "overjustification" hypothesis. *Journal of Personality and Social Psychology*, 1973, *28*, 129–137.

Lepper, M.R., and Greene, D. (eds.), *The Hidden Costs of Reward*. Hillsdale, New Jersey: Erlbaum, 1978.

Lloyd, K.E. Behavior analysis and technology in higher education. In A.C. Catania and T.A. Brigham (eds.), *Handbook of Applied Behavior Analysis*. New York: Irvington, 1978.

Locke, J. *An Essay Concerning Human Understanding*, 1690.

Locurto, C.M., Gibbon, J. and Terrace, H.S. (eds.), *Autoshaping and Conditioning Theory*. New York: Academic Press, 1980.

Lorenz, K. The companion in the bird's world. *Auk*, 1937, *54*, 245–273.

Lovaas, O.I., and Newsom, C.D. Behavior modification with psychotic children. In H. Leitenberg (ed.), *Handbook of Behavior Modification and Behavior Therapy*. Englewood Cliffs, New Jersey: Prentice-Hall, 1976.

Lovaas, O.I., and Simmons, J.Q. Manipulation of self-destruction in three retarded children. *Journal of Applied Behavior Analysis*, 1969, *2*, 49–53.

Lovejoy, E. *Attention in Discrimination Learning*. San Francisco: Holden-Day, 1968.

Mackintosh, N.J. *The Psychology of Animal Learning*. New York: Academic Press, 1974.

Mackintosh, N.J. A theory of attention. *Psychological Review*, 1975, *82*, 276–298.

Mackintosh, N.J. Stimulus control: Attentional factors. In W.K. Honig and J.E.R. Staddon (eds.), *Handbook of Operant Behavior*. Englewood Cliffs, N.J.: Prentice-Hall, 1977.

Mackintosh, N.J., and Little, L. Intradimensional and extradimensional shift learning by pigeons. *Psychonomic Science*, 1969, *14*, 5–6.

MacPhail, E.M. Avoidance responding in pigeons. *Journal of the Experimental Analysis of Behavior*, 1968, *11*, 625–632.

Maier, S.F. Failure to escape traumatic shock: Incompatible skeletal motor responses or learned helplessness? *Learning and Motivation*, 1970, *1*, 157–170.

Maier, S.F., and Seligman, M.E.P. Learned helplessness: Theory and evidence. *Journal of Experimental Psychology: General*, 1976, *105*, 3–46.

Marks, I.M. Perspectives on flooding. *Seminars in Psychiatry*, 1972, *4*, 129–138.

Marler, P. A comparative approach to vocal learning: Song development in white-crowned sparrows. *Journal of Comparative and Physiological Psychology*, 1970, *71*, 1–25.

McAllister, W.R., and McAllister, D.E. Post conditioning delay and intensity of shock as factors in the measurement of acquired fear. *Journal of Experimental Psychology*, 1962, *64*, 110–116.

Miller, N.E. Studies of fear as an acquirable drive. *Journal of Experimental Psychology*, 1948, *38*, 89–101.

Montgomery, D. Worker's control of machine production in the 19th century. *Labor History*, 1976, *4*, 487–509.

Morse, W.H. Intermittent reinforcement. In W.K. Honig (ed.), *Operant Behavior: Areas of Research and Application*. New York: Appleton-Century-Crofts, 1966.

Mowrer, O.H. On the dual nature of learning—A reinterpretation of "conditioning" and "problem solving." *Harvard Educational Review*, 1947, *17*, 102–148.

Nathan, P.E. Alcoholism. In H. Leitenberg (ed.), *Handbook of Behavior Modification and Behavior Therapy*. Englewood Cliffs, New Jersey: Prentice-Hall, 1976.

Newman, F.L., and Baron, M.R. Stimulus generalization along the dimension of angularity. *Journal of Comparative and Physiological Psychology*, 1965, *60*, 59–63.

Obrist, P.A., Sutterer, J.R., and Howard, J.L. Preparatory cardiac changes: A psychobiological approach. In A.H. Black and W.F. Prokasy (eds.), *Classical conditioning II*. New York: Appleton-Century-Crofts, 1972.

O'Leary, K.D. The operant and social psychology of token systems. In A.C. Catania and T.A. Brigham (eds.), *Handbook of Applied Behavior Analysis*. New York: Irvington, 1978.

O'Leary, K.D., and Drabman, R. Token reinforcement programs in the classroom: A review. *Psychological Bulletin*, 1971, *75*, 379–398.

O'Leary, K.D., and O'Leary, S.G. Behavior modification in the school. In H. Leitenberg (ed.), *Handbook of Behavior Modification and Behavior Therapy*. Englewood Cliffs, New Jersey: Prentice-Hall, 1976.

Pavlov, I. *Conditioned Reflexes*. Oxford: Oxford University Press, 1927.

Peterson, G.B., Ackil, J., Frommer, G.P., and Hearst, E. Conditioned approach and contact behavior toward signals for food or brain-stimulation reinforcement. *Science*, 1972, *177*, 1009–1011.

Polanyi, K. *The Great Transformation*. New York: Rinehart, 1944.

Popper, K.R. *The Logic of Scientific Discovery*. London: Huchinson, 1959.

Premack, D. Reinforcement theory. In D. Levine (ed.), *Nebraska Symposium on Motivation*. Lincoln: University of Nebraska Press, 1965.

Rachlin, H. Self control. *Behaviorism*, 1979, *2*, 94–107.

Rachlin, H., and Green, L. Commitment, choice and self-control. *Journal of the Experimental Analysis of Behavior*, 1972, *17*, 15–22.

Rachlin, H., Green, L., Kagel, J.H., and Battalio, R.C. Economic demand theory and psychological studies of choice. In G. Bower (ed.), *The Psychology of Learning and Motivation* (Vol. 10). New York: Academic Press, 1976, pp. 129–154.

Raymond, M.J. The treatment of addiction by aversion conditioning with apomorphine. *Behavior Research and Therapy*, 1964, *1*, 287–291.

Rescorla, R.A. Pavlovian conditioning and its proper control procedures. *Psychological Review*, 1967, *74*, 71–80.

Rescorla, R.A. *Pavlovian Second-Order Conditioning*. Hillsdale, New Jersey: Erlbaum, 1980.

Rescorla, R.A. and Solomon, R.L. Two-process learning theory: Relations between Pavlovian conditioning and instrumental learning. *Psychological Review*, 1967, *74*, 151–182.

Revusky, S.H., and Bedarf, E.W. Association of illness with prior ingestion of novel foods. *Science*, 1967, *155*, 219–220.

Revusky, S.H., and Garcia, J. Learned associations over long delays. In G.H. Bower and J.T. Spence (eds.), *The Psychology of Learning and Motivation: IV*. New York: Academic Press, 1970.

Richter, C.P. Experimentally produced behavior reactions to food poisoning in wild and domesticated rats. *Annals of the New York Academy of Sciences*, 1953, *56*, 225–239.

Rodgers, D.T. *The Work Ethic in Industrial America, 1850–1920*. Chicago: University of Chicago Press, 1978.

Rozin, P., and Kalat, J.W. Specific hungers and poison avoidance as adaptive specializations of learning. *Psychological Review*, 1971, *78*, 459–486.

Rudolph, R.L., and Van Houten, R. Auditory stimulus control in pigeons: Jenkins and Harrison (1960) revisited. *Journal of the Experimental Analysis of Behavior*, 1977, *27*, 327–330.

Rzoska, J. Bait shyness, a study in rat behavior. *British Journal of Animal Behavior*, 1953, *1*, 128–135.

Schick, K. Operants. *Journal of the Experimental Analysis of Behavior*, 1971, *15*, 413–423.

Schneiderman, N., Fuentes, I., and Gormezano, I. Acquisition and extinction of the classically conditioned eyelid response in the albino rabbit. *Science*, 1962, *136*, 650–652.

Schwartz, B. Maintenance of keypecking in pigeons by a food avoidance but not a shock avoidance contingency. *Animal Learning and Behavior*, 1973, *1*, 164–166.

Schwartz, B. On going back to nature: A review of Seligman and Hager's *Biological Boundaries of Learning. Journal of the Experimental Analysis of Behavior*, 1974, *21*, 183–198.

Schwartz, B. Reinforcement induced behavioral sterotypy: How not to teach people to discover rules. *Journal of Experimental Psychology: General*, 1982, *111*, in press.

Schwartz, B., and Gamzu, E. Pavlovian control of operant behavior. In W.K. Honig and J.E.R. Staddon (eds.), *Handbook of Operant Behavior*. Englewood Cliffs, N.J.: Prentice-Hall, 1977.

Schwartz, B., Schuldenfrei, R., and Lacey, H. Operant psychology as factory psychology. *Behaviorism*, 1978, *6*, 229–254.

Schwartz, B., and Williams, D.R. The role of the response-reinforcer contingency in negative automaintenance. *Journal of the Experimental Analysis of Behavior*, 1972, *17*, 351–357.

Seligman, M.E.P. Chronic fear produced by unpredictable shock. *Journal of Comparative and Physiological Psychology*, 1968, *66*, 402–411.

Seligman, M.E.P. Control group and conditioning: A comment on operationism. *Psychological Review*, 1969, *76*, 484–491.

Seligman, M.E.P. *Helplessness*. San Francisco: W.H. Freeman, 1975.

Seligman, M.E.P., and Hager, J.L. (eds.), *Biological Boundaries of Learning*. New York: Appleton-Century-Crofts, 1972.

Seligman, M.E.P., and Johnston, J.C. A cognitive theory of avoidance learning. In F.J. McGuigan and D.B. Lumsden (eds.), *Contemporary Approaches to Conditioning and Learning*. Washington, D.C.: Winston-Wiley, 1973.

Shepp, B.E., and Eimas, P.D. Intradimensional and extradimensional shifts in the rat. *Journal of Comparative and Physiological Psychology*, 1964, *57*, 357–361.

Shepp, B.E., and Schrier, A.M. Consecutive intradimensional and extradimensional shifts in monkeys. *Journal of Comparative and Physiological Psychology*, 1969, *67*, 199–203.

Shettleworth, S. Constraints on learning. In D.S. Lehrman, R.A. Hinde, and E. Shaw (eds.), *Advances in the Study of Behavior: Vol. 4*. New York: Academic Press, 1972.

Siegel, S. Conditioning of insulin-induced glycemia. *Journal of Comparative and Physiological Psychology*, 1972, 78, 233–241.

Siegel, S. Evidence from rats that morphine tolerance is a learned response. *Journal of Comparative and Physiological Psychology*, 1975, 89, 498–506.

Siegel, S. Morphine tolerance acquisition as an associative process. *Journal of Experimental Psychology: Animal Behavior Processes*, 1977, 3, 1–13.

Siegel, S., Hinson, R.E., and Krank, M.D. The role of predrug signals in morphine analgesic tolerance: Support for a Pavlovian conditioning model of tolerance. *Journal of Experimental Psychology: Animal Behavior Processes*, 1978, 4, 188–196.

Skinner, B.F. Drive and reflex strength. *Journal of General Psychology*, 1932, 6, 32–48.

Skinner, B.F. The generic nature of the concepts of stimulus and response. *Journal of General Psychology*, 1935, 12, 40–65.

Skinner, B.F. *Behavior of Organisms*. New York: Appleton-Century-Crofts, 1938.

Skinner, B.F. Are theories of learning necessary? *Psychological Review*, 1950, 57, 193–216.

Skinner, B.F. *Science and human behavior*. New York: MacMillan, 1953.

Skinner, B.F. The phylogeny and ontogeny of behavior. *Science*, 1966, 153, 1205–1213.

Skinner, B.F. *Beyond Freedom and Dignity*. New York: Alfred A. Knopf, 1971.

Skinner, B.F. Herrnstein and the evolution of behaviorism. *American Psychologist*, 1977, 32, 1006–1012.

Solomon, R.L., and Wynne, L.C. Traumatic avoidance learning: Acquisition in normal dogs. *Psychological Monographs*, 1953, 67, Whole No. 354.

Solomon, R.L., and Wynne, L.C. Traumatic avoidance learning: The principles of anxiety conservation and partial irreversibility. *Psychological Review*, 1954, 61, 353–385.

Staats, A.W. *Language, Learning and Cognition*. New York: Holt, Rinehart and Winston, 1968.

Staats, A.W. *Social Behaviorism*. Homewood, Ill.: The Dorsey Press, 1975.

Staddon, J.E.R. Operant behavior as adaptation to constraint. *Journal of Experimental Psychology: General*, 1979, 108, 48–67.

Staddon, J.E.R., and Simmelhag, V.L. The "superstition" experiment:

A reexamination of its implications for the principles of adaptive behavior. *Psychological Review*, 1971, *78*, 3–43.

Stahl, J.R., and Leitenberg, H. Behavioral treatment of the chronic mental hospital patient. In H. Leitenberg (ed.), *Handbook of Behavior Modification and Behavior Therapy*. Englewood Cliffs, New Jersey: Prentice-Hall, 1976.

Stiers, M., and Silberberg, A. Autoshaping and automaintenance of lever contact responses in rats. *Journal of the Experimental Analysis of Behavior*, 1974, *22*, 497–506.

Sutherland, N.S. The learning of discrimination by animals. *Endeavour*, 1964, *23*, 69–78.

Sutherland, N.S., and Mackintosh, N.J. *Mechanisms of Animal Discrimination Learning*. New York: Academic Press, 1971.

Tawney, R.H. *The Agrarian Problem in the Sixteenth Century*. New York: Longmans, Green and Co., 1912.

Taylor, F.W. *Principles of Scientific Management*. New York: W.W. Norton, 1967 (originally published in 1911).

Thomas, D.R., Mariner, R.W., and Sherry, G. Role of pre-experimental experience in the development of stimulus control. *Journal of Experimental Psychology*, 1969, *79*, 375–376.

Thompson, E.P. Time, work discipline and industrial capitalism. *Past and Present*, 1967, *38*, 56–97.

Thorndike, E.L. Animal intelligence: An experimental study of the associative processes in animals. *Psychological Monographs*, 1898, *2*, Whole No. 8.

Tinbergen, N. *The Study of Instinct*. Oxford: Clarendon Press, 1951.

Trabasso, T.R., and Bower, G.H. *Attention in Learning: Theory and Research*. New York: Wiley, 1968.

Ullmann, L.P., and Krasner, L. *A Psychological Approach to Abnormal Behavior*. Englewood Cliffs, New Jersey: Prentice-Hall, 1975.

von-Frisch, K. *The Dance Language and Orientation of Bees*. Cambridge, Mass.: Belknap Press, 1967.

Williams, D.R., and Williams, H. Automaintenance in the pigeon: Sustained pecking despite contingent non-reinforcement. *Journal of the Experimental Analysis of Behavior*, 1969, *12*, 511–520.

Wilson, E.O. *Sociobiology*. Cambridge: Belknap, 1975.

Wolfe, J.B. Effectiveness of token-rewards for chimpanzees. *Comparative Psychology Monographs*, 1936, *12*, No. 60.

Wolff, J.L. Concept-shift and discrimination-reversal learning in humans. *Psychological Bulletin*, 1967, *68*, 369–408.

Wolpe, J., and Lazarus, A.A. *The Practice of Behavior Therapy*. New York: Pergamon, 1969.

Wyckoff, L.B. The role of observing responses in discrimination learning, Part 1. *Psychological Review,* 1952, *59,* 431–442.

Zeaman, D., and House, B.J. The role of attention in retardate discrimination learning. In N.R. Ellis (ed.), *Handbook of Mental Deficiency: Psychological Theory and Research.* New York: McGraw-Hill, 1963.

Name Index

Subject Index

addiction, 196–200
  counterconditioning treatments for, 199, 200
  extinction as treatment for, 197–99
  Pavlovian analysis of, 198
  Pavlovian conditioning treatments for, 196–200
  physiological effects of, 197, 200
  stimuli in, 196–97
anxiety, 57–60
appetitive responses, 45, 89
attention, 140–43
  in discrimination, 140–43, 159
  in transfer of training, 140–42
autism, 203–6
autoshaping, 163–65
  behavior theory and, 171
  information conveyed in, 163
  negative operant contingencies and, 165
  as Pavlovian conditioning, 163–65
avoidance, 63, 85–90, 190
  development of, 86–87
  escape and, 85–87
  experiments in, 85–89
  extinction in, 89, 206–7, 208
  flooding in, 207
  intuitive explanations of, 87, 89
  Pavlovian conditioning in, 87, 88, 89, 90
  phobias as, 207–8
  response blocking in, 89, 206–7
  two-factor theory of, 87–90

behavior theory:
  addiction treated with, 196–200
  animal behavior as focus of, 36–37
  associative bias in, 185, 186–87
  assumptions of, 11–14, 35–44, 67, 174

autism treatments based on, 203–6
autoshaping and, 171
avoidance theory in, 87–90
behavior-outcome pairs in, 66–68
belongingness bias in, 183–84
causal laws in, 12–13, 14, 66
choice behavior studied in, 105, 112
common understandings vs., 15–16, 173–74, 222, 225–26
comprehensiveness of, 190–91, 228, 231–33, 243–45, 254, 257
critics of, 227–28
as cultural influence, 227
deduction in, 78–79
as descriptive, 228, 258
dominant influences suppressed in, 234
economic concepts in, 93, 112–23
in education, 209–12, 223
environmental conditions necessary for, 257–58
environmental events emphasized by, 13, 14–15, 38–39, 41–42
ethical implications of, 227–29
ethology vs., 188–89, 233–35
evaluation of applications in, 216–17, 223, 227–28
in everyday life, 226–27
evolution of, 256–57
experimentally-derived generalizations in, 43–44, 232–33
experiments in, 20, 37–38, 67, 173
generalization in, 64–65, 76–79, 174
genetically determined behavior and, 172–73, 174–75, 191, 232
goals of, 40–44, 79, 160, 183, 255
historical factors neglected by, 257
in historical terms, 243–45, 254, 257–58
and human autonomy, 225

A brief introduction to animal learning

Behaviorism, Science, and Human Nature

Barry Schwartz and Hugh Lacey
Both of Swarthmore College

This innovative text is an unusually clear and succinct introduction to animal learning—its principles, methods, applications, and limitations. It provides the untrained student with the basics of Pavlovian and operant conditioning. But the authors go well beyond this: Weaving everyday examples and analogies into their presentation, Professors Schwartz and Lacey focus on the major discoveries and essential studies that have marked changes in the field. In addition, the authors bring a critical perspective to these findings, showing the student where they do and do not hold up. Unlike other introductory texts in learning, *Behaviorism, Science, and Human Nature* contains a full chapter on human applications and another on the limitations of the field. In sum, this contemporary text offers the student of learning a complete picture depicting where behaviorism fits in psychology, science, and the real world. It is ideal for instructors who include animal learning as part of their undergraduate course in learning, general psychology, behavior modification, or psychology of education.

The Authors

BARRY SCHWARTZ is an associate professor and chairman of the psychology department at Swarthmore College, where he teaches one of the most popular courses in the department: psychology of learning. He is also adjunct associate professor of psychology at the University of Pennsylvania and recipient of the James McKenn Cattell Award for distinguished research. He received a B.A. from New York University and a Ph.D. from the University of Pennsylvania. He is the author of the major undergraduate textbook in animal learning: *Psychology of Learning and Behavior* (Norton).

HUGH LACEY is a professor and chairman of the philosophy department at Swarthmore College. He received his Ph.D. from Indiana University. He has taught at the University of Sydney and the University of São Paulo and has held Fulbright and National Science Foundation fellowships. He and Professor Schwartz regularly teach a course on behaviorism.

Norton
W • W • NORTON & COMPANY   NEW YORK • LONDON

...ncan. Reprinted by permission.

ISBN 0-393-95197